Storybridge to Second Language Literacy

*The Theory, Research,
and Practice of Teaching English
with Children's Literature*

Storybridge to Second Language Literacy

The Theory, Research, and Practice of Teaching English with Children's Literature

Irma-Kaarina Ghosn
Lebanese American University

INFORMATION AGE PUBLISHING, INC.
Charlotte, NC • www.infoagepub.com

COLORADO MOUNTAIN COLLEGE
Timberline Library
Leadville, CO 80461

Library of Congress Cataloging-in-Publication Data

Ghosn, Irma-Kaarina.
 Storybridge to second language literacy : the theory, research, and practice of teaching English with children's literature / Irma-Kaarina Ghosn, Lebanese American University.
    pages cm.
 ISBN 978-1-62396-277-7 (pbk.) – ISBN 978-1-62396-278-4 (hardcover) – ISBN 978-1-62396-279-1 (ebook) 1. Children's literature–Study and teaching (Elementary) 2. English language–Study and teaching–Foreign speakers. 3. Children–Books and reading. 4. Second language acquisition–Study and teaching. I. Title.
 PN1008.8.G56 2013
 372.47–dc23

                                            2013008454

Copyright © 2013 Information Age Publishing Inc.

All rights reserved. No part of this publication may be reproduced, stored in a retrieval system, or transmitted, in any form or by any means, electronic, mechanical, photocopying, microfilming, recording or otherwise, without written permission from the publisher.

Printed in the United States of America

*Dedicated to all the teachers and children
from whom I have learned so much over the years.*

Contents

Acknowledgments xiii
Preface xv
Introduction xxiii

PART **I**

The Case: Theoretical Foundations
for Literature-Based Instruction   1

1 **Significance of Literature for Children** 3
   "Homo Narrans" 3
   Children's Literature Defined 4
   Literature and the Developing Child 6
      Awareness of Self and the World 6
      Fantasy and Imagination 8
      Moral Judgment 8
      Catharsis of Negative Emotions 9
      Emotional Intelligence and Empathy 9
   Literature as Instructional Material 10

2 **Coursebook Language versus Language of Stories** 13
   Coursebook Language 13
      Emergence of Language versus Exposure to Language 14
      The Need for Past Tense Verbs 15

    Coursebook Language versus Real Life Language............................ 16
    Simplified Texts and Comprehension 17
    Rich Language of Stories 17

3 Literature as Appropriate Content and Context 23
    Coursebook Content 23
        Assumed Shared Reality.. 24
        Discourse Around Unfamiliar Topics... 25
    The "Communicative" Approach as the Problem 28
    Storybook Content and Approach.. 29
    Literature and Culture Learning 31

4 Literature Link to School Subjects **33**
    Language and School Subjects... 33
    Story and Mathematics... 34
    Story and Science.. 38
    Story and Social Studies 40

5 Interest, Memory, and Language Learning: Exploring the Connections... **43**
    Motivation and Interest 43
    Emotions and Learning 46
    Memory.. 47
        Meaningful Materials and Rehearsal... 49
        Connectionist Theory 50

PART II

Expert Testimony: Research in Support of Literature-Based Instruction   53

6 Talking like Texts or Talking about Texts? 55
    Stories Captivate and Motivate 55
    Classroom Interactions... 59
        Discourse Around Stories.. 60
        Discourse Around Communicative Language Practice..................... 63

  Teacher Questions and Classroom Discourse 65
   Classifying Teacher Questions 66
   Teacher Questions and Student Output 66
   Teacher Feedback and Student Initiations 69
   Teacher Validation of Student Contributions 69

7 Literature and Second Language Reading Development 73
  Reading Instruction in Young Learner Materials 73
  Improving Reading Skills with Literature 75
   Small-Scale Studies 75
   Large-Scale "Book Floods" 76
   Retrospective Studies 79
   Outcomes of Strategy Instruction 80

8 Vocabulary from Stories 85
  Vocabulary Challenge 85
  What It Means to Know a Word 86
  Vocabulary Learning 87
  Learning Words from Stories 89

9 Learning Grammar from Stories 93
  Experimental Research 95
  Retrospective Studies 96

10 Writing from Reading 99
  Writing Instruction for Young Learners 99
  Instructional Texts as Models for Children's Writing 101
  Writing in Story-Based Programs 102
   Retrospective Studies 102
   Experimental Studies 103

11 Literature and School Subjects: Emerging Evidence 109
  Literature and Mathematics Learning 109
   Experimental Studies 109
   Non-Experimental Studies 111
  Literature and Science Learning 113
  Literature and Social Studies Learning 114

PART **III**

Eyewitness Accounts: One Story, Different Paths   119

- 12 **Preparing for the Story Journey** 121
  - Teachers and Their Classes 121
    - *English as a First Foreign Language (EFL1)* 123
    - *English as a Second Foreign Language (EFL2)* 123
  - Getting Ready for the Story 123
    - *Jasmine's Third-Grade EFL2 Class* 124
    - *Zinnia's First-Grade EFL1 Class* 126
    - *In Rose's Second-Grade EFL2* 128
    - *In Iris' Third-Grade EFL2 Class* 129
    - *In Dahlia's Fourth-Grade EFL2 Class* 131

- 13 **The Story Experience** 133
  - In the Story World 133
    - *In Zinnia's First-Grade EFL1 Class* 134
    - *In Jasmine's Third-Grade EFL2 Class* 134
    - *Marigold's First-Grade EFL2 Class* 135
    - *In Rose's Second-Grade EFL2* 136
    - *In Dahlia's Fourth-Grade EFL2 Class* 137
    - *In Iris' Third-Grade EFL2 Class* 138
    - *In Violet's Sixth-Grade EFL1 Class* 138
  - Reflecting on the Story Experience 139
    - *Readers' Aesthetic Responses* 139
    - *Oral Reading* 144

- 14 **Revisiting the Story World** 147
  - Storymapping 147
  - Choral Reading 148
  - Language Experience Stories 149
    - *LEA Story in Dahlia's Fourth-Grade EFL2 Class* 150
    - *LEA Story in a Pre-Service Teacher Education Class* ... 151
  - Summarizing 152
  - Comparing Stories 152

    Script Writing 154
    Rating Scales 155
    Plot Profiles 156
    News Reports 158
    Examining Author's Craft 158

15 Linking the Story to Subject Matter 161
    Mathematics 161
    Science 163
    Social Studies 165
    Creating New Stories 166

PART IV
Closing Summations   169

**16 Summary in Defense of Authentic Children's Literature
    in Primary School ELT 171**
    Language, Content and Approach 171
    Value and Motivational Power of Stories 172
    Research Evidence 173
        Discourse Evidence 173
        Skills Evidence 173
        Potential for English-Medium Instruction 173
    Characteristics of Literature-Based Approaches 174
        Focus on Literacy 174
        Role of the Mother Tongue 174

17 Selecting Books for Language Teaching 179
    Literary and Aesthetic Merit 179
        Enduring Value 180
        Developmental Appropriateness 180
        Themes 180
        Plot 181
        Illustrations 181
    Language 181

  School Subject Focus 184
   Mathematics Focus 184
   Science Focus 185
   Social Studies Focus 186

References **189**
  Children's Books Cited 213

Subject Index **215**

Author Index **221**

Children's Book Index **229**

Acknowledgments

Classroom data presented in Part III were collected over a number of years between 1995 and 2010. I wish to extend my sincere gratitude to all the teachers who have welcomed me into their classrooms, some graciously accepting also the presence of a video camera or a tape recorder. Appreciation is due also to children who have allowed me to sit in on their literature discussions, and to those who contributed reading comprehension and writing data for some of the empirical studies described. Without the cooperation of the teachers and children, the full scope of this book would not have been possible. All names of teachers and students are pseudonyms. I have chosen plant names for the teachers to reflect the rich and multicolored field of instructional philosophies and classroom practices they represent.

I wish to thank professors Gertrude Tinker Sachs and Tony Mahon for permissions to quote from their classroom transcripts, and professor Tricia Hunsader for permission to use her figure on mathematics tradebooks. I also thank my student, Magida El–Khoury, for helping collect some of the classroom data.

Last but not least, I want to thank my husband, Ghassan, for his tireless proofreading of my many drafts. Any mistakes left will be due to my not noticing all his comments.

Preface

Background

Storybridge to Second Language and Literacy has evolved from my 30 years of teaching, teacher training, and several years of research. When I began teaching English in a small rural school in Lebanon in the early 1980s, I used an English language course based on a structured syllabus, with controlled vocabulary and brief narrative reading selections. Students were not very motivated by the simplistic narratives, which they deemed "boring." When searching for materials to supplement the textbook, I found *I Can Read* books by World's Work. The series, intended for native English-speaking children who were beginning independent readers, included several titles by well-known children's authors, among them Arnold Lobel, Else Holmelund Minarik, Syd Hoff, and Russel Hoban. When I introduced the books to my primary school students, their response was overwhelmingly positive. Students' enthusiasm for English improved, as did their reading achievement, which was very important, because children had to study some of the school subjects in English. Since that initial experience, I have been a firm believer in authentic literature as a medium for primary school second language teaching.

Story-based language instruction is not a new idea by any means. Literature has been a staple in first language reading programs for decades, and has found its way to many second language classrooms as well. Story-based instruction rests on a solid theoretical foundation, and, at the time of this writing, my view is not only shared by scores of English language teachers, but is also supported by research evidence of nearly 30 years.

Although a number of books exist that discuss how to teach English to young learners (e.g., Gordon, 2007; Pinter, 2006; Cameron, 2001; Vale & Feunteun, 1995; Brumfit, Moon, & Tongue, 1995) or how to use story-telling (Paran & Watts, 2003; Taylor, 2000; Wright, 1995) and reading aloud (Smallwood, 1991), none of the current titles cover the theoretical and empirical foundations *and* how teachers actually implement story-based instruction in their classrooms. This book fills that gap by bringing the three perspectives together in one volume. This triangulation enhances the validity of the argument.

Aim and Target Audience

The aim of this book is not to promote literature-based instruction as a new *method* but rather to show that storybooks are a valid *medium* for teaching young learners, a medium that is adaptable to diverse approaches, as will become evident from the classroom vignettes. The book is for pre-service teachers of TESOL/TEFL and in-service teachers of young English language learners who wish to gain a deeper understanding of their practice or to refresh their teaching. It will also be useful for anyone developing instructional materials for young learner classrooms.

"Positionality"

I borrow the term *positionality* from Graham Crookes. Because, as he notes, the nature of knowledge is now viewed by many as "local, personal, and interested (i.e., not *dis*interested)" (Crookes, 2003, p. 3), it is important for the author to make explicit his or her position rather than presuppose shared, common interests and understandings with the reader.

Personal Bias

I was raised in southern Finland and, as an avid reader since age four, was a weekly visitor to the local public library, always borrowing the full allowed load of books. In addition to works of Finnish authors, I read British and American children's classics in translation. I have also taught children's literature classes to pre-service and in-service teachers, and I write books for children. So, I am clearly biased in favor of storybooks. Yet, my argument in favor of story-based instruction does not rest solely on personal bias or experience but is supported by sound theory, 30 years of empirical research and classroom observations.

During the hundreds of hours of in-service teacher development workshops I have conducted in the Middle East, I have become aware of the difficulties with which many teachers struggle, and my personal experience and discussions with English language teachers over the years have convinced me that in many teaching and learning contexts, the internationally marketed global coursebook is not the best option, and that well-chosen children's books are often more appropriate.

Social Intent of Second/Foreign Language Instruction

As one of the founding members of TESOLers for Social Responsibility, a special interest section of TESOL, I believe that all education is socially grounded, having its roots in some social intent. Second language education is no different in this regard, and when selecting language teaching materials, I believe we must examine the social purposes they intend to serve. I take the position of those language teaching professionals who believe that teachers of English—the *lingua franca* of today's global world—have a collective responsibility to consider the extent to which their materials and approaches promote cultural awareness, empathy, and tolerance for diversity of opinions, beliefs, values, and ways of life. The content of language teaching materials functions as part of the hidden curriculum; materials reflect what is perceived important and worth talking, reading and writing about, as well as what is valued and what is discarded as unimportant.

While educational aims expressed in many English Language Teaching (ELT) curricula today include references to developing cultural awareness and appreciation for diversity, these stated aims are not significantly reflected in the internationally marketed textbooks for young learners. Many global young learner courses are laden with trivial content that fails to address the social purposes of education in the increasingly global world, while, at the same time, often minimizing opportunities for meaningful learner engagement and cognitive development. What is trivial in terms of language teaching materials is not without controversy, of course. I agree with Brian Tomlinson who argues that language teaching materials ought to be humanizing, taking into account learners' "experience of life, their interests and enthusiasms, their views, attitudes and feelings and, above all, their capacity to make meaningful connections in their minds" (Tomlinson, 2003, p. 162). As Tomlinson points out, "not many coursebooks encourage [learners] to do this" (ibid). In the case of primary school learners, language teaching materials would take into account also the holistic development of the young learner, who is still developing, not only linguistically but also cognitively and psycho-socially.

Structure of the Book

The book is divided into four sections following the Introduction which reviews the rapid spread of English language teaching to ever younger learners, and discusses concerns regarding the increasing demand for English-medium instruction in contexts where English is neither the mainstream community language nor the learners' mother tongue.

Part I presents *The Case* laying the theoretical foundations for story-based second language instruction. Chapter one discusses the appeal of stories and their significance for children and defines children's literature. Chapter two compares the typical textbook language with the rich language found in children's literature, while Chapter three takes a critical look at the content and culturally situated contexts of language practice common in the global textbooks. Chapter four explores the potential of literature to enhance academic literacy and subject matter learning where English serves as the instructional language. Chapter five closes *The Case* by proposing a connection between memory and story-based language learning, particularly as regards learning of vocabulary and grammar.

Part II presents *Expert Testimony*, reviewing 30 years of research in favor of story-based instruction. Research cited in Chapters six through 11 unequivocally points to the positive influence of story-based, reading-focused instruction on young second language learners' language development. Motivation, classroom interactions, reading, vocabulary and grammar learning, writing and emerging links between literature and academic subject matter are given a chapter each. In Part III, *Eye Witness Testimony*, we visit several classrooms to observe how different teachers guide their students through stories, often using distinctly different approaches and teaching styles. From the classroom vignettes in Chapters 12–15, a practical model for literature-based instruction emerges that is adaptable to diverse teaching and learning contexts. Part IV presents a brief *Closing Summation* in Chapter 16, summarizing the defense for literature-based instruction and outlining the main characteristics of successful literature-based approaches. Chapter 17 defines the criteria for selecting quality literature and offers also guidance on selecting titles with mathematics, science, and social studies focus.

Context of Classroom Vignettes

With some exceptions drawn from international research, the classroom vignettes come from primary school classrooms in Lebanon. Although the context may at first seem limited in terms of usefulness to a wider readership, the diversity of existing primary school English language programs in the country reflect the range of school-based English language programs worldwide. (There are no language school programs for children in the country.)

The new national curriculum introduced in 1998 mandates that all students must learn *two* foreign languages in addition to Arabic, the official language and mother tongue of the majority of the population. The first foreign language (FFL) is typically introduced in grade one (age 6–6.5) or kindergarten (age 4–6) and serves as the mandatory instructional language in the core curriculum subjects from grade seven (age 12). Although the second foreign language (SFL) is officially introduced in grade seven, many schools now introduce it earlier. The great majority of private English-as-the-first-foreign-language (EFFL) schools begin also science and mathematics instruction in English from the onset of schooling, and an increasing number of private English-as-the-second-foreign-language (ESFL) schools introduce English as a subject in the primary school, beginning with 1 or 2 hours a week. State schools, which enroll less than half of the total student population, teach English or French as a subject 6 to 7 hours a week in the primary grades.

Primary school (K–6) English language programs fall into the following four categories.

1. English language enrichment programs in ESFL schools, where children learn English as a subject between ages seven and eleven. They typically have one or two English lessons a week and study academic subjects either in Arabic, French, or Armenian.
2. Programs where children study English as the first foreign language 6–7 hours a week and other subjects in Arabic.
3. EFFL programs where children learn English 6–8 hours a week and study also mathematics and science in English from age six or seven.
4. Total English-immersion programs, where all subjects (except Arabic language) are taught in English from pre-kindergarten. These are found in elite international schools, where student population is often multilingual and multicultural, and where many teachers are native English speakers.

The classroom vignettes in Chapter 13 demonstrate the range of approaches available to teachers using literature for language teaching. Excluded from the classroom examples are schools in the fourth group, as they do not represent typical EFL or ESL programs.

I have chosen to open each chapter with a quote from Lewis Carroll's classics *Alice's Adventures in Wonderland* (1865/Bodley Head, 1974) and *Through the Looking Glass* (1872/Bodley Head, 1974), because Alice's experiences so well reflect what I have come to believe about second language teaching and language teacher training: it is a journey through a wonderland of surprises, a wonderland that can sometimes be confusing, even frustrating. Along my journey, I have encountered rushing rabbits, haughty "you-really-don't-know-much" caterpillars, and "off-with-their-heads" Red Queens. But most of the time, the journey has been wondrous and pleasurable, filled with magic and discovery.

Transcription Conventions

The following transcription conventions are used in all transcripts, with the exception of some quoted from other sources:

T	teacher
S	a student
Ss	a group of students
(( ))	mother tongue or other language utterance
[ ]	observer comment
underline	emphasis
italics	denotes someone reading from a text
xxx | | xxx	interrupted or overlapping utterances

In the transcripts, some of the procedural and disciplinary exchanges have been omitted.

About the Author

Irma-Kaarina Ghosn holds a PhD in Applied Linguistics from the University of Leicester School of Education in the United Kingdom and an MEd in Psychology and Social Foundations of Education from the University of Virginia in the United States. She is Associate Professor and Director of the Institute for Peace and Justice Education at the Lebanese American University, where she has been a full-time faculty member since 1991. Prior to her appointment at LAU, she was a classroom teacher in Northern Virginia for six years and in Lebanon before that.

Dr. Ghosn has conducted over 800 hours of teacher development workshops attended by hundreds of primary school teachers. She has presented papers and workshops in international conferences and published journal articles and book chapters on children's language learning, instructional materials, and classroom practices. In 1998, she received the *Mary Finocchiaro Award for Excellence in the Development of Pedagogical Materials* from TESOL for her *Caring Kids: Social Responsibility through Literature.* She has also developed primary school ELT textbooks and teacher training materials for the Lebanese Ministry of Education and for UNRWA schools in Lebanon. She is an author of 12 children's books in English and one in Arabic in collaboration with her husband, Ghassan. Her website (www.caringkidsbooks.com) features some free stories and resources for teachers, as well as articles, workshop slides and links to other relevant sites.

Introduction

> *"Where do you come from?" said the Red Queen. "And where are you going?"*
> —Lewis Carroll, *Through the Looking Glass* (1872/1974, p. 147).

Spread of English Language Teaching in Primary Schools

The practice of teaching English in the primary school has been rapidly gaining popularity throughout the world. In many countries, where English is neither the mother tongue of young learners nor the mainstream community language, children must also study some or all of the school subjects in English.

Former British Colonies

In India, there is considerable disagreement about the appropriate onset of English language instruction. Since 2000, government schools have been teaching English from grade three, but many private schools, which are not bound by the national curriculum, are teaching English from grade one (Mohanraj, 2006). In Hong Kong, English still plays a prominent role in the government, commerce, and higher education but functions as a foreign language for the great majority of the population, whose primary medium of communication is Cantonese. English language instruction in Hong Kong begins officially in grade one, but is often introduced in the preschool (Tinker Sachs & Mahon, 2006). In Sri Lanka, there are two official languages, Sinhala and Tamil, with English considered not only as the link-language between the two language communities but also a sign of high status (Hayes, 2006). Since the 1970s, English, a foreign language to the majority of Sri Lankans, has been introduced in grade three, but a decision was made in the 1990s to introduce it in grade one (Wijesinha, 2007).

Europe

In European Union member states, English is the most widely taught foreign language in primary schools, with the exception of Belgium and Luxemburg (Eurydice, 2008). Europe has witnessed radical changes in foreign language starting age, and in 13 out of the 27 European Union member states foreign language instruction is now mandatory at age seven or below, with only four countries still retaining the traditional starting age of 10 or 11 (Enever, 2011). The 2011 national curriculum in Sweden sets English as one of the three core subjects from grade one (Enever, 2011), and in Bulgaria, teaching foreign languages beginning at grade one is "the first priority" (Berova & Dachkova, 2003, p. 103), with overwhelming majority choosing English. In Austria, where there are several language communities and three official languages, children begin learning their first foreign language at age six, with English being by far the most popular choice (Jantscher & Landsiedler, 2003). In Croatia, foreign language is obligatory in state primary schools and is experimentally taught in grade one (ages six and seven), with English the most popular of the four options (Stokic & Mihaljevic Djigunovic, 2003).

In Italy, foreign language instruction in the third year of school was officially introduced in the 1980s, with English now being compulsory, and, since 2003, English has been introduced to 5.5- to 6-year-olds in the first year of school (Lopriore, 2006). In Spain, where there are five regional official languages in addition to Spanish, English language has been mandated in year three. However, most of the autonomous communities begin teaching English in first or second grade, along with Spanish and the regional official language (Pinilla-Padilla, 2006).

In Germany, English has been introduced as a compulsory subject to 10 and 11-year-olds, but Kubanek-German (2003) reports on a trend to lower the starting age, with foreign language instruction beginning at age eight in grade three in "most cases" (ibid, p. 61). Similarly, children in Romania begin foreign language learning in grade three (ages eight and nine), but schools, which have local autonomy, may offer foreign language instruction earlier (Ralea, 2003). Grade three is also the starting year for foreign language instruction in Estonia, with two thirds of students choosing English as their first foreign language (Order, 2003). According to the Hungarian National Curriculum, foreign language instruction begins in grade five, but due to heavy pressure from parents, schools often introduce foreign language instruction in grades one to three (Nikolov, 2003). In France, where resistance to early EFL has been considerable, English became mandatory in grade three in 2002, with the aim of eventually lowering the onset of English language instruction to kindergarten (Dolitsky, 2006). Children begin learning English as a subject in grade four in Greece (Kourtis-Kazoullis & Skourtou, 2004) and Czech Republic (Faklova, 2003).

Eastern Mediterranean and Middle East

After Cyprus gained independence in 1960, English language instruction was (re)introduced into the curriculum in 1965, with fifth graders (ages nine and ten) learning English two lesson periods per week. In 1992, the onset of English instruction was lowered to grade four (ages eight and nine) (Ioannou-Georgiou, n.d.). Since then, a pilot project has been initiated to teach English language in grades one to three in two 40-min lesson periods a week (Hadjikyriacou et al., n.d.). In Turkish state schools, English language instruction begins in grade four, but in private schools earlier (Kirgöz, 2006).

In Lebanon, where children must learn two foreign languages in addition to their mother tongue, English is taught as the first foreign language from kindergarten (ages four and five) in over 40% of the schools (Ministry of Education and Higher Education [MEHE], 2006). While French has traditionally been the dominant foreign language, English is steadily gaining ground in the country. In Jordanian primary schools children study English from grade one (Al-Shaboul, Asassfeh, Al-Tamimi, & Alshboul, 2010) as they do also in Egypt (McCloskey, New Levine, Thornton, & El Naggar, 2006), Syria, Oman, and Bahrain (Bacha, Ghosn, & McNeil, 2008). Morocco and Israel are introducing English at ages nine and ten (Christian, Pufahl, & Rhodes, 2005).

East Asia

The same early English trend is noted in East Asia. In Korea, EFL was introduced to the primary school curriculum, beginning grade three in 1995 (Guan-Lea Lee & Myers, 2010). English classes are offered also to toddlers, and even prenatal English education is available (Lee, 2009). In China, English is mandatory in grade three but recommended in grade one, if possible (Zehang, 2006), and some Chinese schools are experimenting with English in kindergarten (Qing, 1993). Third grade is the first year of EFL also in Taiwan (Lo, 2006) and Vietnam, where some schools experiment with EFL in grade one (Sinh, 2006). In Thailand, English is compulsory in grade one (Pufahl, Rhodes, & Christian, 2000). While Japan is experimenting with primary school English language instruction, it is not yet compulsory (Butler, 2004).

Latin America

In Latin America, English instruction typically starts in secondary school. One exception is Mexico, where Coahuila, the largest state, introduced an experimental primary school EFL program in 1995 in one hundred schools, and by 2006, the program had five hundred schools (Flores, 2006). In Brazil, some municipalities have introduced English in grade four of primary school, with the aim to lower the starting age further (Gimenez, 2009). In Argentina, with a history of direct contact with English-speaking communities, English is playing an increasingly important role, and the Federal Law of Education enacted in 1996 made foreign language instruction mandatory in year four (age nine). Out of the 23 provinces, 14 have opted to teach English, some teach English and French or English and Portuguese, and some offer schools the option to choose between English, Portuguese and in some cases French (Maersk Nilesen, 2003).

Increased Demand for English-Medium Instruction

Not only is ELT spreading to ever younger learners, but English-medium instruction (EMI) is also gradually gaining ground in several countries where English is a foreign language for the majority of learners. While in some of these countries English-medium instruction is optional, in others it is the mandatory vehicular language in the general curriculum. In many international schools around the world, as in many European schools within the European Union, English is the *lingua franca*. Recently, *Content and Language Integrated Learning* (CLIL) has been introduced in some European Union countries, but typically on an experimental basis and mainly in the middle grades. In CLIL, knowledge of the language becomes the means of learning content (Darn, 2007), and students are expected to become English proficient academically within five to seven years. In Valencia, Spain, the plan is eventually to introduce trilingual education at the onset of schooling (age three) using CLIL (Pinilla-Padilla, 2006).

In the Arab Middle East, the demand for western-style education has been increasing, and many private elementary and secondary schools now use English as the instructional language. In Kuwait, Egypt, and the United Arab Emirates, the number of English-medium schools is steadily rising, partly to accommodate children of the expatriate labor force, but also to cater to the demands of the affluent local population.

In Zambia, the initial literacy instruction happens through English (Gregory, 1996), whereas in many other countries the vernacular language serves as the instructional language only in the first few years of school, after which it is replaced by English. Ghana, Nigeria, Botswana, and Brunei Darussalam are some examples. In Malaysia, where English was made the second official language in 1996, English-medium instruction of science and mathematics was (re)introduced in the primary and secondary schools in 2003 (Tsui, 2005). The practice is spreading exponentially, with some Asian countries introducing EMI now as early as in preschool (Marsh, 2005). The practice of EMI is likely to spread in so far as it is perceived by educational policy makers to help position the nation more favorably on the global market.

Some Concerns

The spread of ELT and EMI and their anticipated reach to ever-younger learners raises some concerns about the viability and success of the practice. When children feel unsuccessful, they are likely to become demotivated, and when teachers feel that they are unable to engage their students, they are likely to become stressed and, consequently, less enthusiastic in their teaching. Thus, an unfortunate cycle of failure can be set in motion.

Teacher Qualifications

Teacher qualifications are one of the key problems identified in countries experimenting with early ELT as there is a shortage of qualified teachers trained or experienced in teaching English to young learners. This is true, for example in Bulgaria, Italy, Hungary, and Estonia (e.g., Nikolov & Curtain, 2003). In addition to the inadequate preparation for primary school language teaching—which is significantly different from teaching older learners—large numbers of teachers do not possess adequate skills in English themselves (e.g., Dolitsky, 2006). Where EMI or CLIL has been introduced, other problems have surfaced. First, there is a lack of adequate training of teachers in teaching content through a foreign language. For example, despite the long history of English-medium instruction in Lebanon, there is no formal preparation for subject matter teachers in how to teach their subject through English. Many subject matter teachers are reluctant to take on foreign language teaching responsibility, while language teachers do not receive training in how to reinforce subject matter within the context of the English language class.

Research in the English-speaking countries has shown that acquiring the level of mastery in the instructional language that would assure success in academic subjects is far from simple. Large numbers of language minority students are not achieving the academic standards of their age-peers, despite years of ESL, sheltered English, and mainstream instruction (e.g., Thomas & Collier, 1997; Collier, 1995; Hamayan & Perlman, 1990; Bullock report, 1975; Swann report, 1985). Depending on their home and school context, some learners may achieve proficiency within three years while others may take up to ten years to acquire native-like proficiency in English.

If children have difficulty acquiring sufficient language proficiency for academic success while immersed in an English-speaking school environment in core-English countries, then what about children who must study school subjects *in* English where English is not the mainstream community language? Referring to English learners in core-English countries, Genesee (1994) contends that students' academic success and, ultimately their economic survival and well-being later in life, hinges on their English language proficiency. English language competence has nearly, if not precisely, the same implications for children in countries where English is a foreign language but serves as the vehicular language and a prerequisite for access to secondary and tertiary education. David Marsh, a prominent English language teaching expert, goes as far as to claim that "Where English has been imposed as the language of instruction the result has often been failure...confusion, despair and high drop-out rates" (Marsh, 2005, p. 3). High drop-out rates are a reality also in Lebanon, where, in the absence of enforced mandatory schooling, ten percent of children drop out before finishing grade five (age ten). The drop-out numbers increase steadily after that, as Ministry of Education and Higher Education 2007 statistics show.

Language Teaching Texts

In light of the above, the question about language teaching texts emerges. As Cameron (1994) notes, materials development needs to consider, amongst other things, what is known about children's cognitive development, what constitutes real, up-to-date information for the learners, and what is known about how native speakers actually use the language in real life. I would add that children's psycho–social needs must be taken into account also, since language learning does not happen in isolation from the overall development of the child but is "intimately linked with, constrained by and a contributor to cognitive and social development" (Genesee, 1994, p. 4). Where English serves as the instructional language, the language teaching materials must develop not only children's communicative English skills but also their academic language proficiency.

Although many young learner coursebook publishers now offer supplementary materials, such as posters, DVDs and other audiovisuals, publishers have been "slow to respond" (Enever, 2011, p. 29) to the unique needs of young learners and their teachers. As Enever (2011) notes, this is likely due to "high costs, the uncertainties of the market and the well-established tradition of coursebooks for older learners" (p. 29). Because the coursebook is not necessarily the best option for young learner classes, many teachers spend time preparing instructional materials, such as posters, vocabulary cards and manipulatives (Enever, 2011). In Croatian primary school language programs stories are "a significant part of the syllabus... [and] are extremely useful in developing both children's communicative and linguistic competence" (Stokic & Mihaljevic Djigunovic, 2003, p. 41).

In summary, we are witnessing a rapid spread of English language teaching to ever younger children. The demand for English-medium instruction is also increasing in some countries where English is not the national or mainstream language. These two phenomena, taken together with the less than satisfactory achievement of large numbers of immigrant children on both sides of the Atlantic, raise questions about the language teaching materials and approaches in serving the needs of young learners in general, and learners who need to learn school subjects in English, in particular. In Chapters one to five, I will build a case in favor of literature- or story-based instruction, whether children are learning English only as a subject or study also school subjects in English.

For more on the spread of teaching English to young learners, see *Young learner English language policy and implementation: International perspectives* by Janet Enever, Jane Moon, & Uma Raman (2009), and *Key data on teaching languages at school in Europe, 2008 edition* by Eurydice Network.

THINK ABOUT IT

1. At what age is English language instruction introduced in your context? Has anything changed in the past 20–30 years as regards learner age and weekly hours? If so, what might have contributed to the change?

2. Are there any national data about student achievement?
3. If English is not taught at the primary school level, are there any plans to lower the onset of ELT?

PART I

The Case

Theoretical Foundations for Literature-Based Instruction

There are several good theoretical reasons for using children's literature as a medium for teaching English to young learners. As was shown in the Introduction, English language instruction is introduced now to ever younger children, and materials developers are trying to keep up with the demand for materials. At least one international publisher is already offering coursebooks for children as young as three years of age. However, rather than produce traditional, structurally organized coursebooks for the youngest learner groups, it would be wiser to use carefully selected children's literature as the foundation for the young learner syllabus.

The first part of this book presents the theoretical foundations for story-based instruction. Chapter 1 discusses the significance of story narrative for humans in general and defines the term 'literature' as it is used in the context of this book. The chapter then outlines the developmental benefits of literature to children. Finally, it discusses literature as instructional material. Chapter 2 compares the language of typical coursebooks with the rich language in children's literature, showing the superior quality of the latter. Chapter 3 compares coursebook and storybook content, concluding that storybooks provide socially more appropriate content and context for learning. Chapter 4 identifies links literature offers to school subjects such as math, science and social studies. Finally, Chapter 5 explores the connections between interest, memory and language learning.

1

Significance of Literature for Children

> "The time has come," the Walrus said, "to talk of many things:
> Of shoes—and ships—and sealing wax—Of cabbages—and kings..."
> —Lewis Carroll, *Through the Looking Glass* (1872/1974, p. 169)

"Homo Narrans"

"Once upon a time there lived a king and queen who had three very beautiful daughters" (Apuleius, 1951, p. 96) wrote Lucius Apuleius at the beginning of *Cupido and Psyche* in the 2nd century Rome. By then the human story tradition had been well established. The Mesopotamian hero epic of *Gilgamesh* can be traced to the third millennium B.C.E., Homer's *Iliad* and *Odyssey* to 800 B.C.E. and Indian *Mahabharata* and *Ramayana* to the 4th and 5th centuries B.C.E. (the former possibly traceable to the 8th century). Clearly, story is as old as human existence. Across time, stories have recorded our history and our dreams. They have helped us explain the mysterious phenomena of nature in the absence of scientific knowledge, and moved us to laughter and tears, at times providing an escape from the mundane. Plato in his *Republic* defined stories as soul-shaping forces for children, thus cautioning us to supervise the storytellers and to "select their stories whenever they are fine and beautiful" and to "persuade nurses and mothers to tell their children the ones we have selected, since they will shape their children's souls with stories" (Plato, ca. 377/1992, pp. 60–61). And German poet Friedrich Schiller is quoted as having said, "Deeper meanings reside in the fairy tales told to me in my childhood than in any truth that is taught in life" (www.goodreads.com/quotes/show/6563).

Contemporary philosopher Alasdair MacIntyre characterizes us humans as "homo narrans" (MacIntyre, 1981, p. 216), story-telling animals, who experience life as "a series of narratives, conflicts, and characters, with beginnings, middles and ends" (Dégh, 1994, p. 245). MacIntyre further notes that "There is no way to give us an understanding of any society, including our own, except through the stock of stories which constitute its initial dramatic resources" (MacIntyre, 1981, p. 211). Because stories give us our memories and our history, they are essential for us. As Aidan Chambers (1985) puts it:

> In every language, in every part of the world, story is the fundamental grammar of all thought and communication. By telling ourselves what happened, to whom, and why we not only discover ourselves and the world, but we change and create ourselves and the world too. (p. 59)

Livo and Riertz (1986) see story as

> ...a universal mirror that shows us the "truth" about ourselves—who and why we are. When we look into this mirror, we see daily routine and mundane circumstances transformed into something profound. "Story" takes the ordinary...revealing the significance of the trivial. (p.4)

Children's Literature Defined

The word *literature* is used in many different contexts; researchers write literature reviews and read scientific literature, college students study English literature, and so on. Similarly, *a story* is used in a number of ways: "You are late. What's your story?" "Want to hear the story of my life?" "Do you know the story about Snow White?" Therefore, a discussion of what literature and story mean in the context of this book is in order. One of the definitions of literature in the Merriam Webster's Collegiate Dictionary (1994, p. 680) is "writings in prose or verse; especially writings having *excellence of form or expression* and expressing *ideas of permanent or universal interests*" (italics mine). In discussing teaching of literature in the context of teacher education, Hermes (2009, p. 26) asks, "Should [learners] read literature, and if so, what kind of literature, originals or simplified texts?" Quoting

Day and Bamford (1998), she uses the term *language learner literature* to describe adaptations of literary texts used in language instruction. While such texts may fit within the broader definition of literature, they are unlikely to fit within the dictionary definition above. In this book, I adopt definitions used by children's literature experts. I will also use *children's literature* and *storybooks* interchangeably, but within the framework of the definitions offered by the experts below.

A foremost expert of children's literature, Zena Sutherland, whose *Children & Books* is in its 9th edition at the time of this writing, defines children's literature as consisting of "books that are not only read and enjoyed [by children], but also that have been written for children and that meet *high literary and artistic standards*" (Sutherland, 1997, p. 6; italics mine). Another expert, Frances Goforth, the author of *Literature & the Learner*, elaborates on this notion, defining children's literature as fiction and nonfiction that "*authentically and imaginatively* express the thoughts, emotions, experiences, and information about the *human condition, offer insights* and/or *intellectual stimulation*, relate to the *experiences, developmental levels*, and *literary preferences* of the intended audience" (Goforth, 1998, p. 3; italics mine). Yet another criterion is offered by C.S. Lewis, the author of the classic *Chronicles of Narnia*. He goes as far to say "a children's story which is enjoyed only by children is a bad children's story" (Lewis, 1963, p. 460). Chapter 15 provides guidelines for selecting literature.

Story in the context of this book is not just any piece of narrative text that has some characters and some action, but refers to stories written by professional children's authors, not for didactic purposes but rather for children to enjoy. They meet the above-cited criteria of quality literature. Stories come in individual titles known as *trade books* (or *real books* in the United Kingdom) or compiled into reading anthologies for first language reading instruction. Nursery rhymes, contemporary realistic fiction, classic folk- and fairytales and other fantasy, fables, poetry, myths and epics, biographies, humor, historical fiction, and high quality informational books are all within the realm of children's literature. When carefully chosen, titles in any genre can have a place in the second language classroom as long as the content is age-appropriate.

Most simplified, controlled-vocabulary stories and graded readers do not qualify as literature, because titles in this genre rarely have any literary or aesthetic merit, although some exceptions can be found. One good example is *The Rabbit and the Turnip,* in Addison-Wesley's now out-of-print *Amazing English* course (1996). This and some of the other titles in the series have delightful storylines and employ just the right amount of repetitive refrains for young learners to pick up and help confirm their predictions.

Although written with language learners in mind, they also meet the above discussed expert definitions of children's literature as regards themes and developmental appropriateness. Regrettably, the series went out of print in the wake of the publisher mergers in the 1990s.

Stories that have been abridged and simplified from classic adult literature appear in many primary and middle school language teaching courses, and also as separate titles in supplementary reading collections. These do not qualify as literature as defined in this book. In fact, I strongly object to this practice, particularly in the context of primary school language teaching. First, the content and themes in adult literature are meant for adults, whose understanding of the world and the human condition differs considerably from that of children. This does not contribute to motivation, but may actually bore young children. Second, the abridged and simplified work has lost its original literary value; what of the original plot line and literary elements can be left when works of Charles Dickens, Herman Melville and the Brontë sisters are watered down to 500 or 1000 words drawn from a controlled vocabulary list?

When young language learners have been fed these simplified versions in their language classes, they are unlikely to read the original works later in life. Whenever I mention some of the great classics of English literature to students in my university classes, many claim that they have read several. However, discussion usually reveals that they have read these works in abridged, simplified versions in their middle or high school English classes. Consequently, they really have no concept of the literary merit of these works. Many are not even aware that books identified as great masterpieces of English literature had been simplified and abridged, leaving many students with the impression of English as "so easy" and "simple."

Literature and the Developing Child

In all societies across time, literature has functioned to provide what Gordon Wells views as "a cultural interpretation of those aspects of human experience that are of fundamental and abiding concern" (Wells, 1986, p. 195). Wells points out that because such fundamental concerns are not unique to the adult world but exist also in the world of children; stories are of great importance to children.

Awareness of Self and the World

Bruno Bettelheim speaks about children's pressing concerns about their identity, how they should behave and how to deal with life's problems:

"He wonders who or what projects him into adversity, and what can prevent this from happening to him" (Bettelheim, 1989, p. 47), and whether there is "hope for him, though he may have done wrong? Why has all this happened to him? What will it mean to his future?" (ibid).

While Bettelheim argues that classic fairy tales, in particular, help children process these difficult questions, all good children's literature, both fantasy and realistic fiction, contribute to children's psycho-social development. Stories open up worlds within which children can explore different roles, or, in the words of children's literature professor Kay Vandergrift, "try life on for size" (Vandergrift, 1990, p. 160). As psychologist Jerome Bruner puts it, stories provide a "map of possible roles and possible worlds in which action, thought, and self-definition are possible (or desirable)" (Bruner, 1986, p. 66). Because the story world has no boundaries, within it, each child can explore and process the pressing questions that puzzle them at a given time (Laulajainen, 1998, cited in Luoto & Luoto 2001). This explains the powerful appeal of stories, and it is no wonder young children are such eager listeners of narrative and also create narratives of their own to share with others. Through stories, children's literacy emerges, as they construct meanings from the words and pictures.

Stories enable young children to make sense of their world and help adolescents expand their understanding of life and human condition (Appleyard, 1990). Indeed, stories avail to children vicarious experiences with a much wider range of human relationships and emotions than what is possible through their own life experience. Achievement, love, jealousy, conquering of fear and overcoming adversity, hunger, poverty and human suffering—even death and dying—can all be experienced through stories. Through good quality age-appropriate stories, children can deepen their understanding of the range of these emotions. Story narratives enhance their understanding of human character and present them with models for their own interactions.

From stories children can derive not only pleasure, new information, and new insights, but also learn about the values and mores of their society as well as those of others. Stories open whole new worlds for children and provide connections between their own immediate world and the wider world. International literature presents children with mirrors, windows, and doors: mirrors that enable them to reflect on their own experiences; windows that provide glimpses of other worlds; and doors that enable vicarious travel to other places and times (Botelho & Rudman, 2009).

Furthermore, story discussions provide teachers and caregivers a medium through which they can cultivate children's ability to listen to others and to accept viewpoints different of their own.

Fantasy and Imagination

Fantasy, whether of the classic or contemporary kind, stimulates imagination when it makes "the impossible seem possible, and sheds light on the hidden realities of the human mind and the heart" (Goforth, 1998, p. 131). Young children are not only eager audiences for fantasy but are also known to invent and tell such stories themselves. Imagination is important for us, because without imagination we cannot envision a better or more peaceful world or anticipate problems yet to be encountered. An early study by Biblow (cited in Bettelheim, 1989) shows that children who have extensive experience with fantasy, such as the type found in classic fairy tales, for example, demonstrate more thought, creativity, and structure in their play than those with limited fantasy experience. Moreover, when children's play features aggression, "high fantasy" children tend to express it verbally, while "low fantasy" children use physical aggression. Children with rich fantasy exposure also seem to be able to deal better with aggressive fantasy in movies than children who have more limited experience with fairytale-type fantasy. Tolkien's *The Hobbit* from 1938, Milne's *Winnie-the-Pooh* books from the 1920s, and Lewis' *Chronicles of Narnia* from the 1950s are still in print, and the more recent *Harry Potter* series by Rowling that are selling in the millions, all attest to the powerful draw fantasy has on young readers.

Moral Judgment

Stories have also the potential to contribute to children's moral judgment. Studies conducted by Lawrence Kohlberg and his colleagues (Colby & Kohlberg, 1987) show that experience with sophisticated moral dilemmas is associated with the development of higher moral reasoning in children and youth. Although these studies do not pertain to literature, both fantasy and realistic fiction present problems at different levels of moral complexity for young readers to explore. Stories provide a context within which children can measure their own values against those of the characters and re-evaluate their attitudes about themselves and others (Goforth, 1998). For example, in *The Hundred Dresses* by Eleanor Estes (1973), one of the characters faces a dilemma of whether to follow her bullying friend or do what her conscience tells her. In *The Hundred Penny Box* by Sharon Bell Mathis (1975), a young boy tries to understand his mother's behavior he perceives as wrong.

By working through moral dilemmas encountered in such stories, children can develop their moral reasoning. While the ability to demonstrate high level of moral reasoning does not always predict moral conduct, especially in young children, older children and adolescents at higher levels of moral reasoning level demonstrate moral conduct more often than those on lower levels (Colby & Kohlberg, 1987; Rest, Thoma, & Edwards, 1997). There are numerous stories that invite the reader to grapple with decisions about right and wrong.

Catharsis of Negative Emotions

Young children often experience negative, even hostile emotions that, at times, can reach great intensity. Sibling rivalry, jealousy, and struggle against parental authority are typical sources of angry emotions. The classic folk tales have been argued to enable children to overcome anxious and angry emotions, thus contributing to healthy psycho–social development (e.g., Bettelheim, 1989). Although violence in the classic tales such as those collected by Jacob and Wilhelm Grimm, has frequently been criticized—and purged entirely from many children's editions—psychoanalysts view it as constructive. Fairy tale violence is argued to provide a safe outlet for the potentially destructive emotions by enabling the reader to project these emotions to evil story characters. In contrast, if allowed to go unresolved, hostile emotions may result in inner conflict and a sense of guilt too difficult for a young child to overcome. The perception of being a "bad" person, in turn, may lead to a low self-image and, consequently, poor peer relationships, hostility, and aggression. One explanation for the enduring appeal of the Grimm stories may well be found in the existential anxieties and dilemmas, which they present at a level accessible to children at different stages of development. For more on the psychoanalytic view of the classic fairytales, read Bettelheim's *The Uses of Enchantment* (1989).

Emotional Intelligence and Empathy

In his popular *Emotional Intelligence*, Goleman argues that "fundamental ethical stances in life stem from underlying emotional capacities" (Goleman, 1995, p. xii), and four measurable areas of emotional intelligence (EI) have been identified by Mayer, Caruso, and Salovey (1999) as follows. Emotional perception is the ability to identify emotions, while emotional understanding refers to how much an individual knows about emotions. Through stories, children can vicariously experience the whole spectrum of human emotions, both those found in their own life and those they have yet to experience or are unlikely to experience. An example is William Steig's *Sylvester and the Magic Pebble*, where Sylvester the donkey is turned into a rock in a meadow. The story enables children to gain insight into how one can remain stoic and patient in an intolerable situation, or what it means for parents to lose a child.

Emotional facilitation of thought is the ability to think about one's feelings or state of mind and relate them to emotions, which can well be nurtured during story discussions. Judith Viorst's *Alexander and the Terrible, Horrible, No Good, Very Bad Day* and the other Alexander books invite children to talk about Alexander's state of mind and help them develop the ability to relate feelings to emotions, not only of Alexander's, but their own as well.

Emotional management is the ability to choose appropriate responses to emotions. Quality story narratives model ways of expressing one's emotions and alternative ways of responding to different emotions of others (for ideas on how to use stories to foster emotional intelligence, see Ghosn (2001a).

Empathy, which Goleman (1995) includes in his EI theory, has been empirically linked to tolerance, with studies showing that individuals high in empathy exhibit more tolerant behaviors than those who score low in empathy scales (e.g., Underwood & Briggs, 1980; Sheehan, Lennon, & McDevitt, 1989). Citing evidence from neuroscience, Goleman contends repeated emotional experiences shape the brain circuits of the developing child. From this follows that empathic arousal can become a life-long skill through repeated experience. I have argued elsewhere (Ghosn, 2001a) that stories can provide vicarious experiences, which, if frequent and intense enough, might also help shape brain circuits for empathy, thus leading the reader to identify and empathize with ever-widening circles of people. Pinsent (1997) of Roehampton Institute argues that lack of stories in a child's life, in fact, *hinders* the development of empathy. Discussions about stories also nurture children's role-taking ability, which Hoffman (1984) identifies as the highest mode of empathic arousal. High quality realistic fiction for children always invites exploration of emotions at some level. This is true also of some contemporary fantasy.

Literature as Instructional Material

Instructional materials, as an integral part of the learning environment, shape the learners' perception about the subject, learning and themselves as learners. Bruno Bettelheim stresses the significance that reading material, for example, has for the developing child. He argues that if reading material is "so shallow in substance that little of significance can be gained," reading becomes devalued because "what one has learned to read adds nothing of importance to one's life" (Bettelheim, 1989, p. 4). If we substitute *language* for reading, it is easy to see the significance of his notion to foreign language learning: If language learning material is so shallow in substance that little significance can be gained, language learning becomes devalued since what one has learned to talk or read about adds nothing of importance to one's life. In order for children to expend their full effort on learning a new language, they must perceive that they are gaining something from the endeavor, whether pleasure, information, new understandings, or skills of some value. This is particularly important where children learn English as a subject but do not need it for their daily communication. Good children's literature deals with themes and topics of immediate interest and concern to children, thus offering a natural medium for primary school language teaching.

Regarding language learning, the affective filter hypothesis (Krashen, 1981) suggests that learning is either facilitated or hindered depending on the learner's level of anxiety, among other factors. The higher the anxiety level, the less input can filter in. Needless to say, there are many factors beyond the teacher's control that can influence learner anxiety, but the learning environment and lesson content undoubtedly contribute to engaging the young learner. Amusing illustrated storybooks, or stories with universal themes of interest to children are likely to create an anxiety-free environment, lower the affective filter and get children involved in the lesson.

Neuroscience research resonates with the affective filter hypothesis, showing that learning is as much an affective process as a cognitive one, with some putting affect ahead of cognition when it comes to learning, as we will see in Chapter five.

To summarize, we humans have a deep-rooted need for stories, and children are no different in this regard. The narrative of stories plays an important role in the cognitive development of children, and quality literature will enhance their language development. The universal appeal of a good story guarantees learner motivation, while the value of stories as a socializing agent is a value added aspect of literature-based language instruction in primary school. In a second language class, literature offers rich opportunities to foster children's critical and creative thinking while enhancing their language learning. Pleasurable experiences with literature develop children's love of reading, enhance their language development and promote literacy. As Galda and Cullinan (1991) note, the more young language learners read, the more they grow in their reading and writing ability.

EXPLORING IT

1. Think back to your own childhood. What storybooks did you read? Did you have a favorite story that you wanted to hear or read over and over again? Why do you think it captivated you?
2. Examine your instructional texts in light of the above. Are there any universal themes that might contribute to children's psychosocial or emotional development?

2

Coursebook Language versus Language of Stories

> 'Twas brillig, and the slithy toves Did gyre and gimble in the wabe...
> —Lewis Carroll, *Through the Looking Glass* (1872/1974, p. 198)

Coursebook Language

English language teaching syllabuses have traditionally been based on the observed sequence in which learners' linguistic features emerge, the assumption being that acquisition of syntactic features is a necessary precursor for conventional use of language (Larsen-Freeman & Long, 1991). This notion has, for years, influenced the content and organization of language teaching coursebooks, which tend to be structure- and skills-based, with mastery of simpler structures expected before more complex forms are introduced. Activities typically consist of dialogues, role-play, and "conversations," within which formulaic chunks of language are presented in the observed sequence and practiced. This is still the case, although more recently textbook authors have attempted to dress the skills-based syllabus in the guise of simplified stories, songs, and activities. Yet, research clearly tells us that young children's second language acquisition differs from that of adolescents and adults, being a developmental process, resistant to influence from drill and practice, which most coursebooks still offer.

As a matter of fact, the approach in typical young learner courses also goes contrary to how the brain learns, and it would behoove materials developers to look into recent brain research about learning. It tells us that "the brain systems interact together as a whole brain with the external world" (Elman, Bates, Johnson, Karmiloff-Smith et al., 1996, p. 340). Basis of learning resides in the interconnectedness of neurons (nerve cells) in the brain and in the strengthening, weakening, and formation of synapses. As learning occurs, connections are formed both among adjacent neurons and neurons elsewhere in the brain that are related to the given concept or experiential domain. This neural activity does not flow only from simple to complex, as "higher order brain centers that process complex, abstract information can activate and interact with lower order centers, as well as vice versa" (Genesee, 2000, para. 14). Thus, teaching unidirectionally from simple to complex does not match with how the brain learns.

Emergence of Language versus Exposure to Language

Although ample evidence from both L1 and L2 acquisition studies show that linguistic structures do *emerge* in fairly predictable patterns of sequence, it does not automatically follow that, in order for acquisition or learning to happen, *exposure* to structures should mirror the observed sequence, or that exposure to more complex forms would negatively influence learning; possibly quite the contrary. Consider, for a moment, the consequences, if parents and caregivers refrained from exposing infants in their care to any language structures beyond the infant's current level of mastery. It is easy to see the absurdity of such a notion; where would the process begin and how long would it take for children to acquire any meaningful language and to begin developing communicative competence? In other words, a distinction needs to be made between *exposure to input* on one hand, and observed or *expected output* on the other. The structured courses follow the sequence in which language learners are observed to begin to produce given grammatical structures, failing to consider that learners in naturalistic settings normally have exposure to by far richer and non-sequenced language than what they are able and ready to produce.

The Need for Past Tense Verbs

In a language teachers' conference a few years ago, when I criticized the absence of past tense verbs in young learner courses, a well-known coursebook editor (whom I shall refrain from naming here) argued "One cannot expose learners to a past tense form of a verb before they have learned it in the present tense." Yet there is no evidence to suggest that children would not comprehend the meaning of a past tense verb if presented in a clear, meaningful context, even when they have not yet learned its present tense form. A case in point is the verb *ate* in Eric Carle's *The Very Hungry Caterpillar*. The past tense form appears several times in the story, and many teachers of young learners have observed children effortlessly pick up the word even when they are not yet familiar with its present tense form. In natural daily discourse, some verbs actually appear more often in their past tense form than in their present tense form (although that is not the case with "eat"). For example, a brief search of the British National Corpus (http://www.natcorp.ox.ac.uk) in July 2012 yielded 195,306 instances of *said* but only 67,135 of *say*; in other words, in natural daily discourse, the past tense form of say is much more common than the present tense form. This is true also about "sit," "ask," and "find," for example.

Since the primary mode of children's discourse is narrative (Meek, 1995), past tense verb forms are important to them, and story narratives can facilitate the acquisition of past tense verb forms children need in their own communication. The absence of past tense in language teaching materials denies children access to language that would allow them to construct their own narratives in the new language, and enable them to "create their own personal history and identity" (Escott, 1995, p. 20) in the new language.

The absence of the past tense results also in unnatural and stiff language that often resembles more a sports commentary than natural language, as David Crystal (1987) has aptly pointed out. Interestingly, Lightbown and Spada (2006) have observed that in some French immersion programs, even history concepts are being taught in the present tense, which must be rather awkward, to say the least. Although many of the more recent young learner courses include short story scripts, they still appear in the present tense. The following very typical excerpt is from level three of a 2004 edition of a series advertised by the publisher as being based on "classic storylines":

> Jack is hiding behind the stove. The mean giant smells a boy. Then he sees a hat. "Aha! Whose hat is this?" asks the giant. The woman is afraid. "I don't know," she says." (Eisele, Yang Eisele, York Hanlon, & Hanlon, 2004, p. 87)

Crystal's note of sports commentary does, indeed, come to mind when reading the text. Although one can see how children might well enjoy pantomiming the scene in a total physical response (TPR) fashion, the passage would certainly sound more natural if presented in the narrative, as in the following excerpt from a tradebook version of the same story:

> "Fee, fie, fo, fum! I smell the blood of an Englishman!" The outside door crashed open. "Quick!" hissed the woman in a panic. She opened the cold oven and Jack jumped inside. (Poole, 1997, n.p.)

The past tense verbs *crashed, hissed, opened,* and *jumped* present the regular *-ed* ending in an immediately meaningful context, while the opening *fee, fie, fo, fum* would offer an amusing opportunity to practice vowel sounds.

Coursebook Language versus Real Life Language

Corpus analyses cited by Fox (1998) support Crystal's above claim, showing that the language in many coursebooks does, indeed, differ from the language used by native speakers in real life situations. Take a common airport scene, which is often presented along the following lines:

> **Passenger:** "Here is my ticket."
> **Clerk:** "Thank you. Do you have any luggage?"
> **Passenger:** "Here is my suitcase."

Hardly the dialogue most readers have experienced when checking in at an airline counter. The following is probably more likely:

> **Passenger:** [gives the clerk his ticket and passport] "Morning."
> **Clerk:** "Good morning. How are you today?"
> **Passenger:** "Fine, thanks."
> **Clerk:** "Boston?"
> **Passenger:** "Yes."
> **Clerk:** "Any luggage."
> **Passenger:** [places his suitcase on the scale] "Just this and my carry-on."

It is easy to see that some teachers (and parents) might object to such "real-life" language in the coursebook. In workshops I have often heard teachers argue that children must learn to speak and respond to questions in complete sentences. Recently, I encountered also a young mother, who reminded her three-year-old to speak in "full sentences, please." She explained: "We are working on full sentences now, and using polite language." Yet, language in real life often consists of fragments and single word utterances. If we do not expose learners to any real life usage of language, they may find it difficult to understand native speakers in face-to-face communication. Furthermore, the limited vocabularies—drawn from lists of frequently used words—short formulaic sentences, and controlled syntax of the typical coursebook offer limited opportunities for learners to deepen their awareness of the new language (Hill & Reid Thoma, 1988), or to acquire new vocabulary.

Simplified Texts and Comprehension

The simplified language not only limits learners' access to natural language but poses also a problem regarding learners' reading comprehension. Yano, Long, and Ross (1994), who investigated the reading comprehension of nearly 500 Japanese English language learners, came to the conclusion that simplification may actually *limit* language learning by not presenting items that learners need to learn, and because the choppy, unnatural discourse does not aid comprehension. Their study suggests that, although literal comprehension is improved by linguistic simplification, it does not improve overall comprehension, quite the contrary. In their study, they found that elaborated versions of text, which included paraphrasing and provision of definitions, and which were longer and more complex than the unmodified version, resulted in better inferential comprehension, despite that the simplified versions were several grade levels below the elaborated versions.

When investigating the relative effects of simplification and elaboration on 430 Korean secondary school students' English reading comprehension, Oh (2001) came to the same conclusion: elaborated versions of texts improve overall comprehension, even when they are at a higher difficulty level than the simplified versions. Although simplification may be helpful in getting the main idea of the text or in obtaining detailed information, it apparently does not enable the reader to develop important inferential reading skills. Blau's (1981) study in Puerto Rico confirms that simplification poses a problem also for younger L2 readers. She concludes that "choppy, unnatural sentences are difficult to read" and that "readers do indeed seem to benefit from the information regarding relationships that is revealed by complex sentences" (p. 525).

Rich Language of Stories

In contrast to the simplified discourse of coursebooks, good children's literature often contains the kind of elaboration that can improve young learners' comprehension. For example, in *Velveteen Rabbit* (Williams, 1985), a toy rabbit is left "out until long after dusk" (n.p.). While the word "dusk" is likely to be unfamiliar to young learners, the next sentence elaborates by explaining that someone had to look for the rabbit with a candle, and that the boy could not sleep unless he had his rabbit. Thus, it becomes clear that dusk has something to do with evening. Illustrations further help clarify the meaning.

Aidan Chambers (1985), an award-winning author, points out stories can provide a link between languages and enable learners to move beyond word and sentence-level awareness of language to a more overall awareness associated with differences in discourse sequence, the ways words link, and the understanding of inferences. In other words, stories can teach language learners something about "*how* language means" and not only "*what* it means" (Carter & McRae, 2002, p. 10). Stories present language in a variety of registers within clearly defined, meaningful contexts of discourse. Because stories come in so many different themes, motifs, and examples of diverse real life situations, by listening to and reading stories, children become familiar with a wide range of language patterns, vocabulary words, idioms, and metaphors. In stories, children can also encounter words used in interesting and unusual ways, words that "tumble and scramble and fall, engaged with meanings" (Butzow & Butzow, 2000, p, 14). Therefore, literature can promote awareness of language use (i.e., the knowledge of how to use language rules for communication). It may also help learners internalize the language by providing them with access to a much more extensive experience of contextualized linguistic items than what is offered in the primary school language coursebooks.

Let us take an example from Nick Butterworth's delightful *One Snowy Night*, in which a cold and hungry fox enters the park keeper Percy's little cottage, where several other animals are already sheltering.

> "Can I come in, too?" [the fox] asked.
>
> "Well, if you promise to behave"...
>
> "I promise," said the fox, and he squeezed into the bed next to all the other animals.
>
> Bump! Oops! The squirrel fell out. "Who did that?" asked the squirrel crossly. (Butterworth, 1989, n.p.)

In a meaningful context, the text offers expressions directly relevant to young children. One can see the immediate usefulness of *Can I come too? If you promise*, and *Who did that?* to children. It is not difficult to imagine how children will be captivated by the storyline, eagerly acting it out over and over again, each repetition reinforcing the chunks of language. With their narrative structure and good use of contextualized verbs, stories can facilitate young learners' communicative efforts. As Margaret Meek aptly points out, "stories teach children the verb tenses of the past and the future when they are intensely preoccupied with the present" (Meek, 1995, p. 6). This is how Alexander uses the future tense to express his emotions about the family's imminent move in *Alexander Who's Not (Do you hear me? I mean it!) Going to Move*: "I'll never have a best friend like Paul again. I'll never have a great sitter like Rachel again. I'll never have my soccer team or my car pool again" (Viorst, 1995, n.p.). Again, one can see how the context and the repetition of *I'll never have... again* will help children understand and appropriate the language for their own use.

Some of the best young learner lessons I have observed have involved *big books*, the over-sized illustrated easel books with oversize print. The following example is from *The Rabbit and the Turnip* (Addison-Wesley, 1989) mentioned in the Preface. Little Rabbit finds two turnips, and after gobbling one up, he thinks about his friend:

> "Little Donkey is probably hungry, too. I'll take this turnip to him." Little Donkey was not at home. Little Rabbit left the turnip on his doorstep. Little Donkey came home.... He was very surprised to see the turnip. "How kind of someone to give me this turnip." (Addison-Wesley, 1987, p. 7)

Most of the phrases are repeated over and over again as surprised friends pass the turnip around. At the end, the turnip finds its way back to the little rabbit. Although the story is intended for language teaching, the text is not simplified in the same way as in the typical young learner coursebooks or graded readers. Despite being repetitious and constructed primarily of simple sentences, the language sounds natural, and present, past and future verb tenses appear as they would be used in real life. It is easy to see the value some of the repetitious words and phrases will have for young learners. The plot involves the topic of thinking of others and sharing, which is very appropriate for young learners, and will help hold their interest while affording a meaningful learning experience. The language teaching power of the story is in the repetition of key phrases in a clearly meaningful context.

The Doorbell Rang by Pat Hutchins is another example showing how an authentic and captivating story line can be realized even with relatively simple and repetitious, yet not contrived, language:

> "I've made some cookies for tea," said Ma.
>
> "Good," said Victoria and Sam. "We're starving."

> "Share them between yourselves," said Ma....
>
> "No one makes cookies like Grandma,"... the doorbell rang.
>
> It was Tom and Hannah from next door.... (Hutchins, 1986, n.p.)

The story continues with the doorbell ringing every time the children are about to taste the cookies. More children arrive at each ring, and finally, the crowd of children is down to one cookie each, when the doorbell rings again. In comes Grandma—with a tray full of cookies that only Grandma can bake! The story begs children to participate in the anticipated refrain, and I have seen young language learners (as well as teachers-in-training) groan with disappointment at each subsequent doorbell ring and chime in with the refrain.

Yet another example of a truly delightful story with a simple, but captivating, repetitious refrain is Esphyr Slobodkina's classic, *Caps for Sale*, a tale about a cap peddler and some mischievous monkeys. The peddler falls asleep under a tree and wakes up to find his caps confiscated by a troop of monkeys in the tree.

> "You monkeys, you," he said, shaking his finger at them.
>
> "You give me back my caps."
>
> But the monkeys only shook their fingers back at him and said, "Tsz, tsz, tsz." (Slobodkina, 1940/1987, n.p.)

The peddler gets progressively more furious, shaking his fist, and stomping his feet with the monkeys imitating his every move. In desperation, he throws his own cap to the ground... and you can guess what happens next. Children rarely tire of this story, asking it to be read over and over as they begin gradually to join in. No wonder that the story is still in print, 70 years after its original publication. Patterned and predictable books like these not only offer young learners immediate access to a satisfying story experience but will also help develop children's language and widen their background knowledge.

In summary, language teaching texts are characterized by limited vocabulary and carefully controlled syntax, rendering the texts artificial and not reflecting language in actual use. The input to learners is limited, and the controlled simple-to-complex presentation is not aligned with how the brain learns. In contrast, children's literature features connected discourse and rich, natural language within immediately clear context, providing young language learners with real life models of language use.

EXPLORING IT

1. Read some simplified graded readers (or story narratives in ESL/EFL coursebooks) intended for primary school children. What can you tell about the vocabulary and sentence structures in them? How does the language influence the mood of the story, your reading experience and your enjoyment of the story?
2. Now, read some original children's titles written for the same, or slightly younger, age group. How does the language influence the mood of the story, your reading experience and your enjoyment of the story? Did this experience differ from the experience of reading the simplified titles? If so, how?

3

Literature as Appropriate Content and Context

> "Have you seen the Mock Turtle yet?"
> "No," said Alice. "I don't even know what a Mock Turtle is."
> —Lewis Carroll, *Alice's Adventures in Wonderland* (1865/1974, p. 88)

Coursebook Content

Content of young learner courses centers around the familiar; self, family, peers, daily routines, and free-time activities. Yet, young children are active and curious explorers of their environment. They are fascinated by dinosaurs, space, and many other topics. Mem Fox, award-winning children's author knows that little children are "Bright as buttons and.... Their critical faculties are highly developed, much more so than most adults realize. In fact, they are altogether smarter than most adults give them credit for" (Fox, n.d., para. 38). She also points out that "Young children have large, active brains, and writing for them is enormously difficult" (ibid, para. 14).

Children bring to the language classroom their own socio-cultural schemata, which might be very different from those in the minds of the coursebook authors. It is, therefore, not surprising second language learners often have limited background knowledge about the topics in their language learning texts, which hinders their comprehension (Droop & Verhoeven, 1998; García, 1991). Globally marketed young learner courses are typically set in North American or British school context, reflecting classroom realities in these countries, which is, of course, very useful to learners within the target language culture, but may not be quite so meaningful to young learners elsewhere in the world. Classroom routines, apparently presupposed by coursebook authors to be universal, may differ considerably from those observed in North American and British classrooms. Thus, the content and language of activities associated with them may not serve their intended aims.

Assumed Shared Reality

Although many young learner courses today feature games, simplified stories, and subject matter content, some persistent assumptions are evident. The following song extract illustrates this: "For breakfast I like milk and fruit, an egg with toast and jam. Or, maybe, I'll have some cereal, or bread with tomato and ham" (Herrera & Pinkley, 2005, p. 74). These seemingly familiar breakfast foods—to someone living in a western cultural context—may be meaningless where the text and young learners inhabit a different world, as Gregory's (1996) example of the five-year-old Tony in his first year of school in Britain so well illustrates. Gregory observed Cantonese Tony and his British teacher as they were reading Hargreaves' *Mr. Men* book. Tony is eager to learn the labels for the various items on the pages:

Tony: What's that?
   T: It's a glass... Oh no, it's a jar of marmalade.
Tony: Jar marmalade?
   T: Yes... to put on your bread... you know, in the morning. (Gregory, 1996, p. 2)

Readers accustomed to spreading marmalade on their breakfast toast might see nothing amiss in the scenario. Yet, young Tony is clearly confused. Most likely, his breakfast experiences did not include toast and marmalade. In this case, the label "marmalade," gave Tony very little information that he could relate to or vocabulary that he might find meaningful or useful. Let's examine another extract:

I work hard in school all day, so after school it's time to play. I go and get my ball and bat, and my favorite baseball hat. I meet my friends at five o'clock sharp, and then play baseball 'til it's dark. I go back home and watch TV... (Herrera & Pinkley, 20056, p. 8)

Playing with friends is a significant part of children's lives, of course, and learning to talk about such topics enables immigrant children to communicate with their native-speaker peers. For children learning English outside core-English countries such content may not always be meaningful, and may even be de-motivating, particularly if they are expected to activate the coursebook language in their own discourse practice. It is quite presumptuous of textbook authors to think that cereal, toast, jam and ham, or baseball are relevant to all young English language learners, or that all primary school children can play outside until it is dark. Diets vary widely across cultures, extreme heat or cold poses obstacles to outdoor play in some parts of the world, and in many big cities there may be few safe parks for children. While children can memorize texts like the above, talking about such unfamiliar concepts is likely to be rather meaningless.

The above extracts, which represent fairly typical content in young learner courses, reflect the assumption that the end users of the book share the primarily Western, Anglo-Saxon socio-cultural reality of the authors, which is often not the case at all. An examination of several internationally marketed young learner courses reveals frequent instances of this shared-reality assumption. One fourth-grade teacher expressed to me her frustration about food preparation activities in her coursebook. "I had no idea about tacos, or taco salad. The [supermarket] did not even know. Just like peanut butter they didn't have. So I had to skip the lessons with taco salad and peanut butter and jelly sandwiches."

Discourse Around Unfamiliar Topics

The following episode from a 4th grade class shows what can happen in the classroom when language practice activities involve culturally unfamiliar content or content that is not relevant to learners. Children are working on an "ask and answer" activity in their coursebook, where two children, Rick and Lisa, are talking about pocket money:

"My dad gives me pocket money. He gives me three pounds every week. I buy books, comics, and sweets. Sometimes, I save my money and buy a computer game."

"My mum gives me pocket money. She also gives me three pounds every week." (Holt, 2005, p. 34)

The book instructs learners to ask and answer questions, such as *Do your parents give you pocket money? How much do they give you? Do you save it? Do you spend it? What do you buy?* The author's assumption is clearly that all learners get pocket money and spend it on items such as those listed. What if children using the book do not get pocket money or do not yet have English words for the things they actually would buy, if they had? This is what happened in the classroom (italics denote students reading from the book):

S1: *Do your parents give you pocket money?*
S2: *My dad gives me pocket money.*
S1: How much do they|
 T: |He said his dad gives him
S1: How much he|
 T: |How much <u>does</u> he
S1: *How much* does he *give you?*
S2: *He gives me three pounds.*
 T: Don't read what Rick's dad gives him! Say how much <u>your</u> dad gives <u>you</u>.
S2: ((I don't get pocket money)) [in a quiet voice, blushing, looking down ads some students giggle].
 T: Oh, OK. Pretend that he gives you, say, three thousand Lebanese pounds [3000 Lebanese pounds is equivalent to two U.S. dollars]
S2: He give me three thousand pounds.
 T: Good. Now, Ramzi, you continue and ask him what he does with the money.
S3: What you buy?
 T: What <u>do</u> you buy?
S3: What do you buy?
S2: I buy, I buy *books, comics, and sweets.*
S4: [laughing] ((All that with three thousand!))

From the ensuing dialog it quickly becomes obvious that not all children in this class get pocket money and if they do, they do not necessarily spend it on the items mentioned in the text, and thus do not have an idea what they might cost. The teacher makes a decision to revise the task:

 T: OK, grade four. Maybe not everyone gets pocket money. Let's change the questions, OK. [writes questions on the board] Do Rick's and Lisa's parents give them pocket money? How much do they give them? What do they buy? Do they save it? Now, you ask these questions. Samia, you begin, please. You can choose to ask about Rick or Lisa.

Children then continued the dialogue practice, reading the questions from the board and picking the answers from the book. But the exercise was just that—an exercise without any personal meaning to the learners. The emotions evident in the classroom did not reflect engagement but boredom and disengagement.

Here is another classroom episode to further illustrate the point. A group of fifth-grade students are expected to exchange information about their free time activities and then tell others about their partner's activities. The question they are expected to ask is, *What do you do in your free time?* Twelve illustrated response suggestions are given for students to select from: read; listen to music; garden; care for pets; paint; play soccer; play music; cook; bowl; play video games; collect coins; watch TV. How this language practice was realized in the classroom is hardly what the authors of the course had intended (italics denote student reading from the book):

T: Now you ask her [to S1, pointing to S2] about her activities.
S1: *What do you do in your free time?*
T: Now you answer him [to S2, pointing to S1]:
S2: *I watch TV.*
T: Next. Now you tell us about her activities
S1: She watch|
T: |She?
S1: She watches TV.
T: Now you [points to the next pair of students]
S3: *What do you do in your free time?*
S4: *I play video games.*
T: Now you tell us about his activities
S3: He play the Nintendo
T: He play?
T: He play? He play? Or he play<u>z</u>?
S3: *He plays videogames*
T: OK. Next. (Ghosn, 2003a, p. 294)

Students continued in this manner through the list. Notice how the teacher focuses on form, leaving the student's original "Nintendo" contribution invalidated, and how the student then returns to the safety of the text. The teacher is concerned about the students getting the forms correctly, "...making sure that they don't learn it wrong," as she put it in an interview after the observation. As Lynne Cameron notes, "the course book dialogue is a rather strange invention" (Cameron, 2001, p. 68), particularly in the ways it often plays out in the real world of the classroom. When students have limited vocabulary of their own, they must rely on the vocabulary provided by the book. In Chapter six we will see how very different discourse is generated around stories, even when the content is culturally unfamiliar.

If and when language practice is restricted to mere decoding of questions and answers from the book, it does not provide the anticipated shortcut to communication that Hatch (1978) has suggested practice of formulaic language chunks might do. Moreover, such a diet of controlled practice does not prepare students for learning school subjects in English, which requires complex language use and ability to express one's understanding of concepts through language.

Contextual support provided through pictures cannot be automatically assumed to facilitate language learning either. According to Leung "even seemingly simple support material assumes a degree of shared cultural or linguistic commonality which may or may not be there" (Leung, 1996, p.29). Drawings of baseball gloves and bats, bowling balls, and action figurines, for example, would have limited value for children who lack experiences with such items.

The "Communicative" Approach as the Problem

The problem is not the culture-specific *content*, which has the potential of serving as a valuable source of culture learning. Rather, it is the combination of the content *and* the approach that appears to be at the root of the problem. First, when children try to take on unfamiliar roles and exchange ideas about unfamiliar topics, they may well find themselves in a similar predicament as the children in the above classroom episodes. Unable to relate to the content, children are restricted to the coursebook language even when it is not personally relevant to them. This results in de-motivating drill-like pseudo-communication as opposed to personally meaningful discourse most likely envisioned by the coursebook authors.

Second, the global coursebooks present plenty of potentially highly motivating pair work and small-group work which the teacher is expected to observe and provide guidance as necessary. However, interpersonal communication patterns are governed by cultural beliefs and values about relationships, authority, knowledge, and the world. In hierarchical societies, for example, conformity to predetermined role behaviors is expected; in the classroom, the teacher is the authority and directs the discourse, while the student role is to comply with the teacher's requests (Lustig & Koester, 2006). Teacher, with the help of the coursebook, is to provide learners with knowledge, while learners are expected to demonstrate their learning to the teacher. The observer role associated with pair- and small-group work is not necessarily comfortable—or even acceptable—to many teachers. Over the years, the topic has received wide attention in discussions about communicative language teaching. This is what one Japanese English language teacher had to say:

> If I do group work or open-ended communicative activities, the students and other colleagues will feel that I'm not really teaching them. They will feel that I didn't have anything really planned for the lesson and that I'm just filling time. (Richards & Lockhart, 1994, p. 108)

This teacher's sentiments resonate with those of many Middle Eastern teachers I have interviewed. A Lebanese fourth grade teacher, who initially embraced the communicative approach promoted in the ESL course she was using, decided to shift to a more controlled teacher-fronted approach, because:

> When I first started teaching at [the school], I tried to follow the teacher's book and I think students liked it... but anyway, the coordinator told me to stop doing it because some parents were complaining. They said my class was out of control and that I wasn't teaching the children anything, and that they were just talking to each other and playing games. So, now I don't do that anymore. (Ghosn, 2004, p. 114)

Storybook Content and Approach

The body of English language children's literature is extremely rich, and themes and topics presented in quality stories are of relevance to children of all ages and backgrounds. I want to stress the word *quality*, as not all books written for children are *quality literature* the way it is defined by experts. Friendship, hopes, aspirations, achievement, fears, courage, and other issues of concern to children, even when situated in culturally unfamiliar context, provide opportunities for meaningful discourse. There is a critical difference between how cultural content of stories and culture-specific content in language exercises can be approached. Language exercises require children to engage in artificial discourse about unfamiliar content and concepts, using new and unfamiliar language. In contrast, when talking about new and unfamiliar concepts encountered in a story, they can remain in their own *persona* and use their own inter-language. This enables their own narrative to develop and makes possible a genuine idea and information exchange between teacher and children, and between children. The following episode recorded in a third-grade class of a Lebanese teacher, illustrates this. Most of the eight-year-olds in the class have been studying English since age four or five. Children have read Judith Viorst's (1972) popular *Alexander and the Terrible, Horrible, No Good, Very Bad Day* and are discussing it.

> T: Why did Alexander think it was such a bad day?
> S1: Miss, because, Miss, his mother not put ((sweets)) for him!
> S2: Miss, what it mean "cupcake"?
> T: Uh, cupcake, cupcakes are little cakes ((cake)) baked in a paper cup. See, here [pointing to a picture].
> S3: Miss! Miss! What "jelly roll"? is the same jello?
> T: Jelly roll, no, it's a little bit like... it's also a little cake but with kind of jam inside. It's not jello.
> S3: Miss, like a donut?
> T: Yeah, something like a donut, yes. OK. Now if you were in Alexander's place, how would you feel?
> S1: If me, if I am Alexander I will be very sad when I see all my friends eat cookies.
> T: Uhuh, so you would be sad if you had no cookies for dessert.
> S2: Miss! Me, me! Me angry because my mother she did not put any cookies. (Ghosn, 2004, p. 118)

The teacher follows children's lead and makes use of their mother tongue contributions, which enables the discourse to flow.

Role playing story events provides further language practice of a different nature from that offered by coursebook dialogues. When acting out stories, children take on roles of story characters, with whose situations and emotions they have already become familiar while reading, listening to and talking about the story. That is quite different from practicing the new language while trying to take on a role of someone whose ways and ideas are unfamiliar.

Contrary to the skills-based, communicatively oriented approach featured in young learner courses, story-based instruction is culturally much more flexible in that it allows for local cultural expectations and classroom norms to be maintained when necessary. Although a story has a fixed content, the way teachers approach it can vary significantly. Classroom vignettes from different teachers' classrooms in Chapter 13 illustrate the adaptability of a story-based approach to different teaching styles.

Literature and Culture Learning

"Elementary school foreign language programs have the potential for preparing citizens to be functionally bicultural as well as bilingual" contends Pesola (1991, p. 331), suggesting that a story about one character's experience and emotions can deepen the understanding of the target culture. Because literature is culturally situated, stories set in English-speaking countries will give children a glimpse of the life experiences of children in the target language culture, enabling development of empathy toward them. Through literature they can also acquire knowledge about the customs of the culture and can explore and raise questions about content that they find interesting, confusing, or unusual. For example, in one fifth-grade class, where children were reading about Tom Sawyer's fence painting episode, a girl asked, "Why did his aunt make him paint the fence? Didn't she love him?" The teacher explained that in America children often do chores, such as washing dishes, taking out garbage, and yard work, and that at the time the story was written, it was not uncommon for children to help paint a fence, for example. This interested the class, because in Lebanon, middle and upper class children, in particular, rarely engage in such chores, first because children are expected to dedicate much of their free time to schoolwork, and, second, because their families have hired household and gardening help.

When Wenli Tsou (2005) set out to teach explicit culture lessons to young English language learners in Taiwan, she discovered that "Students in the [experimental group exposed to culture lessons] became more motivated, participative and cooperative" (p. 50) than their control peers. Interviews with children revealed that the experimental group children found English interesting and enjoyed learning about cultural differences, whereas children in the control group did not share their views.

Judith Viorst's *Alexander and the Terrible, Horrible, No Good, Very Bad Day, Alexander Who's Not (Do You Hear Me? I Mean It!) Going to Move,* and *Alexander, Who Used to Be Rich Last Sunday* are excellent examples of literature that illustrates daily life of children in the United States. They resonate with Chastain's (1988) recommendation that culture instruction should feature topics related to behavior in the family, personal needs and concerns and the like. Reading about Alexander's experiences, children learn not only about American foods and snacks, carpooling, and other cultural concepts, but also about concerns of an average child not unlike themselves. Emotional experiences, such as sibling rivalry, friendships and disappointments, mirror those of children elsewhere, making them immediately relevant to young learners, regardless of their cultural background.

In summary, literature-based instruction allows children to maintain their own identity as they work with the story content, rather than being forced into role-playing unfamiliar situations using new language. They can explore unfamiliar cultural concepts safely in their own persona and gain insight into life experiences of children in the target language country while their own narrative skills develop. I want to emphasize that the aim of the book is not to propose literature-based instruction as a new method, but literature as a *medium* that enables teachers to select the methods and pedagogical approaches that are most appropriate in their particular cultural context and that suit their personal teaching style.

EXPLORING IT

1. Examine the coursebook you are currently using. How familiar or unfamiliar is the content to your particular students. How is the content presented? Are there selections to read, discuss, and answer questions about, or are there dialogues within which to practice chunks of language? What might that imply about motivation?
2. Talk to your students about the content and topics of the coursebook. What do they think? Do they find the content interesting? Find out some of their reasons.
3. If you are using a locally authored course, compare the content and tasks it presents with those in a global coursebook published in the United Stated or the United Kingdom.

4

Literature Link to School Subjects

"Reeling and Writhing, of course, to begin with," the Mock Turtle replied;
"and then the different branches of Arithmetic—
Ambition, Distraction, Uglification, and Derision."
—Lewis Carroll, *Alice's Adventures in Wonderland* (1865/1974, p. 91)

Language and School Subjects

Developing second language competence that will enable children to deal with school subjects has proven to be a complex and time consuming phenomenon. Jim Cummins calls such competency Cognitive Academic Language Proficiency (CALP), which enables students to examine and interpret information, formulate and express arguments, and use higher order thinking skills. Cummins stresses that CALP is "socially grounded and could only develop within the matrix of human interaction" (Cummins, 1984, p. 4) and suggests that its development takes five to seven years, even in total immersion programs. Longitudinal research by Virginia Collier and her colleagues (Collier, 1995; Thomas & Collier, 1997) of over 700,000 English language learners in the United States shows that it can take even up to ten years, depending on the age and first language literacy levels of students upon arrival to the country.

Kieran Egan (1979), a prominent educationalist and educational philosopher, also suggests that fictional stories can help clarify the concepts of almost any curriculum area and cautions us not to underestimate their potential. His argument is supported by many cognitive scientists, who believe information is learned and retained better when it is presented within a story (Bruner, 1987; Graesser, Hauft-Smith, Cohen, & Pyles, 1980; Mishra, 2003). Stories are characterized by their narrative structure, and speech and language clinicians view children's narrative abilities as important for later academic achievement (e.g., Dickinson & McCabe, 1991; Hemphill, Picardi, &Tager-Flusberg, 1991). Feagans (1982) and Fazio, Naremore, and Connell (1996) findings indicate narrative abilities to be, in fact, predictors for school achievement. Thus, development of narrative will be important for young second language learners who must access school subjects in English. Where children learn English only as a subject, exposure to stories featuring subject matter concepts can foster children's cognitive development, thus supporting also their language learning.

When managing academic discourse, students need general language functions such as the ability to ask questions and understand written text, including written instructions for academic tasks (Uhl Chamot & O'Mally, 1994). In addition, learners must also master the linguistic skills that will enable them to demonstrate to teachers their cognitive abilities to classify, compare, sequence, evaluate, hypothesize, infer, predict, and generalize (Gibbons, 1995; Solomon & Rhodes, 1995). Clearly, such skills are demanding for young language learners to acquire, and it is, therefore, not surprising that it takes such a long time. Table 4.1 shows how literature-based instruction can activate these language functions at different levels of thinking skills.

Story and Mathematics

Contrary to popular belief, development of mathematical ability is closely related to command of mathematical language, which differs from everyday language in many significant ways. The *Principles and standards for school mathematics* of the National Council of Teachers of Mathematics [NCTM] (2000) in the United States stresses the importance of communication in mathematics, cautioning that limited language proficiency can be a serious obstacle for mathematics learning, because understanding and being able to manipulate many aspects of mathematics learning implies a considerable level of language proficiency.

TABLE 4.1 Literature to Activate Academic Language Functions

Language Functions	Sample Story Tasks
Seek information	• Answer factual questions from the teacher and peers. • Write questions about a story for peers to answer.
Inform	• Describe setting and characters. • Identify main characters or key events.
Compare	• Compare "Mufaro's Beautiful Daughters" with "Talking Eggs." • Explain how "Harry and the Terrible Whatzit" is similar to "There's a Nightmare in my Cupboard."
Order	• Arrange jumbled story events in order. • Tell what Mrs Haktak put into the pot first. What did she put in next?
Classify	• Group stories into trickster tales and fables. • Explain why "Stone Soup" is a trickster tale and "The Tortoise and the Hare" is not.
Analyze	• How does Harry change during the story? • Fill in the plot profile for "Harry and the Terrible Whatzit."
Infer	• Who do you think is at the door? What makes you think that? • What do you think will happen next?
Justify/ Persuade	• Do you think it was right or wrong for the soldiers to trick the villagers with the stone soup? Why?
Solve problem	• What else could Doctor De Soto and his wife have done about the fox? • How did Strega Nona's magic pot work?
Synthesize	• Write a new Cinderella story by changing the setting, the magic help, and the lost object. • Summarize "The Story of Ferdinand." • How could you avoid the problem Alexander had with his money?
Evaluate	• What do you think about Harry's decision to go to the cellar? Justify. • Would it be more important for Ferdinand to behave like the other bulls or to do what he likes? Justify.

Source: Adapted from Uhl Chamot, A. & O'Malley, J. M. (1994). The CALLA Handbook (p. 42). Reading, MA: Addison-Wesley Publishing Company.

The use of children's literature in mathematics education has been promoted by curriculum reformers in the United States for years, and the NCTM journal, *Teaching Children Mathematics*, regularly features a section on literature. There are a number of reasons for this. First, as Welchman-

Tischler (1992) notes in *How to use children's literature to teach mathematics*: "Children must find mathematical experiences interesting if they are to achieve their mathematical potential, and using literature as a springboard is one way to capture their interest" (p. 1). Second, stories allow children to explore and test their mathematical concepts in a non-threatening context and help them understand the value of mathematical thinking in everyday life (Whitin & Gary, 1994). This is particularly important for young learners who are trying to make sense of mathematics in a language that is not their mother tongue.

Carefully selected stories can foster "mathematical communication skills which is a prerequisite to formal abstract thinking" (Lewis, Long, & Mackay, 1993, p. 470). They give an insightful example from Lewis Carroll's *Alice's Adventures in Wonderland*. Upon meeting the Caterpillar, Alice demonstrates her inability to grasp the fact that change in shape does not mean change in her characteristic properties: "'I can't explain myself, I'm afraid, sir,' says Alice, 'because I'm not myself, you see'" (Carroll, 1974, p. 42). One can equate poor Alice's sentiments to those experienced by young second language learners, who must try to make sense of new concepts while also trying to communicate their understanding in a language that is not their own. Whitin and Gary (1994) provide a number of classroom examples to illustrate how stories can be used to set problem-solving tasks that help children develop their ability to communicate mathematical ideas. In the second language classroom, story-context can lower the affective filter for both language and mathematics learning.

Friedman (1997) proposes that children's literature can be used also to teach children what she calls *math morals*, or general mathematical statements. For instance, the moral that "incomplete information can be inaccurate" is succinctly illustrated in the classic folktale about the blind men and the elephant; because each man felt only one part of the elephant, they formed a completely erroneous perception about what the elephant was really like. "Exponential growth is very rapid" is yet another math moral identified by Friedman (1997) and brilliantly illustrated in *Anno's Magic Seeds* (Anno, 1995). In the story, Jack gets two magic seeds from a wizard, and the seeds first grow by ones, but soon with ever-increasing speed. Another example of the same concept, but with more complex language, is *The King's Chessboard* (Birch, 1988), one of many variations of the classic story about the multiplying grain of rice. *The Doorbell Rang* (Hutchins, 1986) communicates the math moral that "the division of a set of objects equally to more subsets results in fewer objects in each subset." The story presents an excellent context for teaching the language and symbols of division. *A Remainder of One* (Pinczes, 1995) is another delightful division story in which a poor bug soldier finds himself always left out of the parade, "a remainder of one."

The NCTM advocates problem solving as the central focus of mathematics curriculum. The Council has also stressed the role of communication in development of mathematical understanding, as communication enables students to

> construct links between their informal, intuitive notions and the abstract language and symbolism of mathematics; it also plays a key role in helping children make important connections among physical, pictorial, graphic, symbolic, verbal, and mental representations of mathematical ideas. (NCTM 1989, p. 26)

Rathmell suggests that some mathematical problems can be taken from children's literature, and children can be provided with opportunities to talk about their ideas and explain their thoughts. This gets children away from the common notion that mathematics involves only computation and numbers, moving them towards the more comprehensive view of mathematics as "a way of thinking about problem solutions, which may or may not involve numbers" just as "solutions to life's problems that call for mathematical solution may or not involve numbers" (Rathmell, 1994, p. 292).

Leitze (1997) reports having successfully connected mathematical problem solving and literature in primary school by using stories as a spring-board for mathematics lessons. The problems may require a variety of problem-solving strategies, such as looking for patterns, making an organized list, working backward, or making a table, and students must decide upon the most appropriate strategy themselves.

Stories can also expose children to language structures common in mathematics word problems. The following type of structures can appear as early as in grade four mathematics books: "How many milliliters of water would be in the tank if it were completely full?" "If this pattern continued, how many people attended the last class?" "What sandwich and drink combinations could Marina have ordered with her money?" In young learner courses such structures are introduced much later, potentially complicating mathematics problem-solving for young second language learners who must learn mathematics in English. Stories can present conditionals in a meaningful context, preparing children for the grammatical awareness that will facilitate their understanding of word problems.

Integrating reading and writing with mathematics through storybooks not only helps children communicate mathematically, but stories can also help children see mathematics as a part of their everyday life (Whitin &

Gary, 1994). For interesting teaching ideas, see Welchman-Tischler (1992), and for K–3 classroom applications, see the delightful volumes of Burns (1992) and Sheffield (1995), both rich with student work samples.

Story and Science

The language of science is another potential problem area for young second language learners as it involves formulating hypotheses, proposing alternative solutions, describing, classifying, making inferences, predicting, and making generalizations (National Science Teachers' Association [NSTA], 1991). Just as mathematics, science uses everyday words with new meanings. For instance, the common words "table," "mass," and "force" have their unique meanings in the context of the science class (Uhl Chamot & O'Malley, 1986). Lemke (1990) points out also that the science discourse is characterized by use of passive voice and long noun phrases, making it difficult for young second language learners to construct meaning from their science texts. The following excerpt is from an American third-grade science text:

> Fuels can release energy that can be changed into electricity. Electricity is a form of energy that people make by using other kinds of energy found in nature.... Energy that comes into our homes as electricity can be used to light lamps, run computers, or cook popcorn. (Harcourt Science, p. F7)

It is easy to see the difficulties eight-year-old second language learners—or some first language learners, for that matter—might have in comprehending the concepts involved. Children may, in fact, develop erroneous conceptualizations as a consequence of limited language (Collison, 1974). Even when children might grasp the concept studied, they may lack the language to express their understanding accurately (Okhee & Fradd, 1996).

Literacy is now considered essential in acquisition of new knowledge in science (Freeman & Taylor, 2006), and 2001 witnessed the National Science Foundation-sponsored conference *Crossing borders; Connecting science and literacy*. Two decades before the conference, children's trade books had already begun to find their way into North American mainstream science classes to supplement the science textbooks, which Carlson (2005) argues to be often rather dry. Carefully selected, high quality nonfiction children's literature can enrich the science learning experience and enhance conceptual development, while also promoting language learning.

Provided the books are clearly related to the topic at hand, science trade books can "introduce children to the scientific method, transmit knowledge about the world, and give children the chance to experience the excitement of discovery" (Royce & Wiley, 1996, p. 18). Butzow and Butzow (2000) suggest that it is also possible to use fiction in conjunction with the science textbook. For example, the concept of buoyancy can become more real when the science book lesson is linked to Pamela Allen's (1982) simple but poignant *Who Sank the Boat?* The story begins when a cow, a donkey, a sheep, a pig, and a tiny mouse decide to go out to sea in a row boat. The illustrations show the boat gradually deeper and deeper in water until, at last, it is the little mouse's turn to get in, and then we do know who sank the boat.

The aim of using science-related literature—both fiction and nonfiction—in the language class is not to replace explicit teaching of science concepts with stories but rather to help children develop language that will facilitate their understanding of and communicating about the concepts at hand "by framing them within an applied setting" (Madrazo, 1997, p. 20). The story of the sinking boat is a good example of such framing.

Stories with science concepts are particularly useful for teaching young second language learners. For example, Eric Carle's masterfully illustrated books introduce essential concepts of life science in ways very accessible to even preschool children. His books, because of their simple, yet accurate text, coupled with highly skilled and aesthetically appealing illustrations, not only engage the young language learners but also provide them with a motivating context for learning vocabulary and formulaic chunks of language. In many primary school classes around the world, scores of children have enjoyed Carle's *The Very Hungry Caterpillar* (Carle, 1987) and learned about the life cycle of moths and butterflies, along with the relevant science vocabulary (e.g., Ghosn, 1997). Machura (1995) successfully used the story with a class of 12-year-old English language learners. Language of science and science skills of observation, prediction and hypothesizing can be enhanced through stories and story discussion.

The language skills and functions of the science class can be activated also through stories that are not necessarily involving science topics. Chamot and O'Malley (1994, p. 196), in their *The CALLA Handbook* identify a number of second language speaking skills associated with science that are similar to the language observable around story discussions: answering questions and asking for clarification, participating in discussion and explaining processes. Describing things, explaining and giving examples, giving reasons and identifying consequences, developing hypotheses and making inferences are some of the language functions associated with science. These, too, can be easily activated during story discussions and response tasks, even when the content of the story is not science-related.

Story and Social Studies

Social studies textbooks have been accused by some to lack personality and emotions (Vacca & Vacca, 1999), to be difficult to read and not engaging students (Brown, 2007; Villano, 2005; Ross, 1994; Hilke, 1999), particularly as regards students with below average reading ability (Howe, 1990). In contrast to textbooks, trade books come in a wide range of readability levels. Lamme and Ledbetter (1990) argue that children's trade books form a framework for exploration into the content and that "Textbooks in the content areas simply cannot match the flexibility, depth, or quality provided by trade books" (p. 736). Ross (1994) also points out that children's literature offers multiple perspectives to topics, as well as rich detail. Hence literature is likely to be emotionally arousing, create personal associations, and affect readers' attitudes. In the rapidly changing world, quality children's literature may also provide more up-to-date perspectives to some content than social studies textbooks (Thompson & Lehr, 2008). This applies to both fiction and nonfiction. When Richgels, Tomlinson, and Tunnell (1993) compared language in textbooks with language in children's trade books, they discovered that trade books were characterized by better structure, coherence and readability, and more elaboration. Consequently, trade books were more comprehensible than textbooks, an important consideration in the context of a second language class.

Since the early 1970s, the National Council for the Social Studies (NCSS) in the United States has published an annual list of notable children's trade books with social studies themes. The reviewers, among them McCarty (2007), believe that quality trade books can make a significant contribution to the social studies curriculum. Reading quality fiction and non-fiction literature widens children's knowledge about the history, daily life, customs, and concerns of other societies, providing a magic mirror which "gives children a window through which to see the traditions, visions, and contributions of individuals they might not otherwise encounter" (Goforth, 1998, p. 310).

Perspective-taking, whether historical, cultural, or gendered, is an important academic and real world skill that can be fostered by talking about literature (Raphael & Hu, 1998). When students have opportunities to talk about and reflect on characters' situations and actions, they begin to understand different perspectives. As Eve Bearne suggests, literature helps sharpen critical thinking skills and enables children to "read their own and others' representation of the world sharply and analytically" (Bearne, 1996, p. 318).

As the information technology and communications networks advance and travel to distant lands is now possible even for average people, our world is becoming smaller and societies around the world are increasingly characterized by diversity, it is important children develop appreciation and tolerance for different opinions, viewpoints, and perspectives. Thus, as Kincade and Pruitt point out, "learning to understand and appreciate cultural similarities and differences cannot be left to chance" (Kincade & Pruitt, 1996, p. 19). They argue that given children's unguided reading preferences, "exposure to different cultures might never occur without structured education intervention" (ibid), because left on their own, children are likely to pick what is familiar. Because exposure to diverse cultural beliefs, values, and traditions is of critical importance to our children, it cannot, indeed, be left to chance. Multicultural children's literature, whether fiction or nonfiction, offers many opportunities for children to explore other cultures.

In *Literature & the Learner*, Frances Goforth lists, among others, the following benefits from multicultural literature. Exploration of diverse groups through literature helps children "recognize similarities and differences among humans in all times and places" (Goforth, 1998, p. 311) and promotes "an appreciation for the common experiences that connect people from varied ethnic and cultural groups [which] produces a richer society" (ibid.). Literature raises children's awareness of feelings, emotions and needs shared by people everywhere, and helps children to "realize the imaginative, creative, political and social contributions of individuals in specific fields of endeavor" (ibid). Encountering diversity in literature also dispels stereotypes. Goforth further suggests that through literature

> Children realize the dynamic nature of culture. They recognize the conflicts that occur when old and new ways merge. This gives them a broader perspective and encourages them to look at the past to learn about the present and make predictions about the future. (Goforth, 1998, p. 311)

Finally, she argues that "literature gives children a sense of world problems and a more responsible attitude toward society" (ibid).

Interestingly, most—if not all—global coursebooks are devoid of content even remotely hinting at faith traditions. The Muslim headscarf, *hijāb*, the Jewish skullcap, *kippah*, and the Sikh turban are conspicuously absent from language teaching courses, although these items are worn by thousands, if not millions, of young English language learners around the world. Similarly absent are images or references to places of worship or religious festivals. Yet these concepts form an important part of the lives of many young learners. Undoubtedly, the diverse cultural contexts where the books are marketed pose restrictions on the content as publishers must ensure their books contain nothing that some groups may find unacceptable or offensive. Yet, clearly an opportunity for learning about other faith traditions is lost. Teachers wishing to promote tolerance for diversity of faith traditions can do so through carefully selected storybooks.

Well-written fiction provides children with vicarious experiences that enable them to "enter into the conflicts, the suffering, the joys, and the despair of those who lived before us" (Huck, Hepler, Hickman, & Kiefer, 2001, p. 464), and help children understand that "All people need and want respect, belonging, love, freedom, and security, regardless of whether they lived during the period of the Vikings or the pioneers or are alive today" (ibid).

Children's literature can support subject-matter instruction in mathematics, science, and social studies. In a second language class, storybooks provide a motivating medium to explore vocabulary and concepts related to school subjects, particularly in contexts where children must study some of the subjects in English.

THINK ABOUT IT

1. What is your view on integrating children's literature into subject matter classes?
2. Obtain one or more of the titles mentioned in this chapter. Examine its/their usefulness for language teaching.

5

Interest, Memory, and Language Learning Exploring the Connections

> *"But what did the Dormouse say?" one of the jury asked. "That I ca'n't remember," said the Hatter. "You must remember," remarked the King, "or I'll have you executed."*
> —Lewis Carroll, *Alice's Adventures in Wonderland* (1865/1974, p. 107)

Motivation and Interest

The relationship of motivation and language learning has been studied extensively, but much of that research has examined older learners. Young learner motivation has been investigated, for example, in Israel by Ohlstain, Shohamy, Kemp, and Chatow (1990), in Croatia by Mihaljevic Djigunovic (1993) and in Hungary by Nikolov (1999). According to the affective filter hypothesis (Dulay & Burt, 1977; Krashen, 1981), second language acquisition is either facilitated or hindered depending on the learner's level of motivation, self-confidence, and state of anxiety. The lower the affective filter, the more input is accessible to the learner. Although much of motivation, self-confidence, and anxiety can, of course, result from factors beyond the control of the classroom teacher, the learning environment and the lesson content undeniably play a role in young learner motivation. Motivation, in turn, determines how much time and effort learners are willing to spend on given learning tasks.

For young second language learners to be motivated and to engage in the lesson, they must find the material interesting and relevant. In Lugossy's (2006) longitudinal study of three groups of English language learners in Hungary between 1977 and 1995, an average of 90% of the children identified classroom-related reasons for their motivation in the English class. In a position paper of the Association for Childhood Education International, Jalongo (2007) stresses the profound influence motivation and interest have on academic achievement, while Artelt (2005) considers interest as the most important form of intrinsic motivation. It appears that interest is both a variable and a desired outcome of learning (Schiefele, 1991), comprising both situational interest and individual interest (Jalongo, 2007). Situational interest is based on novelty, curiosity, and the saliency of the information, and is believed to have a strong effect on engagement in learning. Because children typically do not have pre-existing interest in learning a foreign language they do not need on a daily basis, situational interest plays an important role in motivating them to engage in lessons.

Citing 20 years of research on situational interest, Hidi and Harackiewicz (2000) conclude that in the context of texts, certain text characteristics can evoke situational interest. According to them, interest-arousing texts are those that are easy to comprehend; present novel, unusual or surprising content; feature characters and/or topics with which the reader can identify; or involve high levels of activity or intensity (Hidi & Harackiewicz, 2000, p. 152). It is quite easy to identify a wide range of children's stories that match these attributes. Hidi and Harackiewicz further found that interesting texts result in superior reading comprehension as well as better recall, an important point to consider in the context of language learning.

Individual interest is the personal, unique interest individuals have in specific topics, activities, or concepts, and it appears that it is preceded by situational interest. In other words, situational interest can evoke personal interest. To illustrate how situational interest can influence motivation and generate personal interest, let us consider a primary school child with little or no intrinsic motivation to learn English. One day, the child listens to her teacher read a humorous story such as Slobodkina's *Caps for Sale*, for example. She finds the story amusing, the repetitious refrains captivating, and she eventually joins in. She then has a thoroughly enjoyable time during the TPR activities that the teacher generates from the story. Such enjoyable experiences, when repeated over time, can develop her individual interest in the English lessons.

An example of this is a nine-year-old second language learner, Alia. Alia was not interested in English, was a reluctant reader, and, therefore, was considered at risk for failure. Her teacher told me that when she introduced *pourquoi* stories to her class, Alia became interested in the genre. With assistance from the teacher and the school librarian, she read several different pourquoi stories and eventually constructed her own story. Her interest in English and reading improved significantly, and her achievement began to improve, albeit more slowly. This example resonates with research on individual and text-based interest reviewed by Hidi (1990) that shows individual interest to play a powerful role in learning. Interesting stories can both motivate and influence comprehension and learning.

Interestingly, when Adoniou (2001) explored the match between the language that a Greek seven-year-old English language learner *chose* to learn and what his coursebook taught, she discovered a correlation of less than 5%. In other words, coursebook language may not always reflect young second language learners' reality, needs or wants, a fact I have pointed out elsewhere (Ghosn, 2004). Motivation may be reduced when learners inhabit a different world than the one assumed by the coursebook authors, and language learning can be reduced to a drill with little or no personal meaning, as in the following example, where 11-year-old girls are engaged in a task of interviewing each other about seasonal clothing. The illustrations in their coursebook depict a girl wearing a sleeveless T-shirt and shorts in the summer, jeans in autumn and spring, and a warm coat in winter, and a boy wearing also shorts and a T-shirt in summer. Seemingly an interesting and relevant task, one might assume. However, the girls attend school in a very traditional Muslim community, where girls at this age typically wear a headscarf and an ankle-length coat, *jilbāb*, when outside the home. Because they are not expected to show bare arms or legs in public, meaningful choices for their summer clothing in this task were quite restricted. The summer sections of their charts thus consisted entirely of jeans, which produced rather monotonous exchanges:

    S1: What do you wear in summer?
    S2: I wear jeans and a coat.
    S2: What do you wear in summer?
    S3: I wear jeans.
    S3: What do you wear in autumn?
    S4: I wear jeans and a coat.

It was very evident to the observer from students' expressions and tone that the exercise had no personal relevance to them. As soon as their turn was over, students disengaged, with some exchanging whispers, leafing through their notebooks, or looking out the window.

In summary, anecdotal evidence clearly suggests that stories motivate and hold the interest of young learners. In contrast, the concepts and vocabulary of global coursebooks language practice may be foreign to learners, whose motivation is reduced when they find little that is familiar or important to them. Also, because story experiences are emotional experiences (assuming high quality storybooks are selected), they can influence individual interest, which is based, among other things, on the emotions associated with the learning experience.

Emotions and Learning

Neuroscience research tells us that learning is not only a cognitive process but also an affective one. Gilbert (2002), in fact, puts affect ahead of cognition, saying that "We have to play to the emotional brain; then and only then, will we open up the intellectual brain" (p. 2). Similarly, LeDoux (1993) considers emotions to be critical for learning. It appears that brain structures link perception, memory, and emotion (Sylwester, 1995).

In *Teaching with the Brain in Mind*, Eric Jensen (1998) explains how emotional states affect learning. The process he outlines can be related to story-based language instruction as follows. Story experience generates emotions, such as surprise, excitement, sadness, or joy. The emotions, in turn, generate thoughts, opinions and questions; "Why would he do that?" "I wonder how she would feel if . . . ?" The thoughts are followed by responses, such as anticipation, curiosity, or excitement that will influence student motivation to engage. Emotions can be engaged through storytelling or shared reading, by setting up a dialogue or debate between characters (student-generated, not memorized from a text), by putting up a play, and through emotion-evoking reader response activities, such as diary entries, or letters to characters, for example.

Because good literature provides emotional experiences, it helps children develop into thinking, feeling and expressive individuals. When children identify with story characters, they experience vicariously the same emotions, thoughts and situations as the characters. This develops their role-taking ability and the skill of empathy. There is hardly a child who will be left untouched by Andersen's *The Ugly Duckling*, Steig's *Sylvester and the Magic Pebble*, or Estes' *The Hundred Dresses*.

Memory

Because of the developments in brain-imaging technology in the late 20th century, we now have a fairly broad understanding of the learning brain. For example, a number of studies with both animals and humans have shown the importance of stimulation on dendritic growth in the brain (e.g., Diamond, 1988; Golden, 1994; Kotulak, 1996). But it appears not to be sufficient simply to be exposed to stimulating, enriched environment for learning to be optimized; learners should also participate in creating the environment, argues Sprenger (1999). In a language class, this could be realized, for example, by children writing dialogues for story-based plays, preparing props, posters, and invitations, and then presenting their play to peers or parents.

Recent brain research suggests that we humans have many types of memory, each located in a specific area of the brain, as well as separate areas for storing permanent and short-term memories. Semantic and episodic memories are two categories of what was earlier known as declarative memory (Sprenger, 1999). We rely on *semantic* memory to learn information from words, and Ullman (2001a), who has researched the memorization process associated with children's first and second language learning, concludes that children use their semantic memory when learning vocabulary. According to Sprenger (1999), for semantic information to be processed for long-term storage—in other words, for learning to happen—the information must be meaningful and processed repeatedly. The memory must be stimulated by associations, comparisons and similarities. Nummela Caine and Caine posit "The brain resists having meaningless patterns imposed on it" (Nummela Caine & Caine, 1990, p. 67), meaningless as in "isolated pieces of information that are unrelated to what makes sense to a particular student" (ibid). They suggest that grammar and vocabulary, for example, should be taught in context of genuine, whole-language experiences.

Repeated readings of a story—and meaningful follow-up work—can help process vocabulary from the semantic memory into the long-term memory, and that the practice of formulaic chunks of language, if meaningless and irrelevant to the children, may be less effective. An examination of young learner language courses suggests that while certain words and expressions are repeated in a number of exercises, the number of repetitions for an individual student may not be sufficient for long-term storage to take place, especially in the absence of multiple associations and comparisons or personal meaning. Although children may use their working memory, which can be useful for hours, to cram vocabulary for a test, for example, without adequate processing time, the vocabulary will not enter their long-term memory for later retrieval.

Episodic memory relates to location, or specific context. We remember information because we associate it with the context within which we learned it (Sprenger, 1999). A captivating story provides a meaningful context for learning, which helps explain the incidental vocabulary learning from stories described in Chapter eight. Repeated readings of a story, followed by story discussions and reader response activities will facilitate processing new vocabulary and phrases into episodic memory.

We rely on our *procedural* memory to learn to do things, such as riding a bike, swimming, or driving a car, and, according to Sprenger (1999), these behaviors become automatized when the procedure is stored in the cerebellum. Ullman's (2001a) research findings suggest that children rely on procedural memory to learn their second language grammar, while older learners rely on their declarative memory (Ullman, 2001b). This may help us understand how children can acquire grammatical awareness from story reading; repeated reading or listening to interesting stories facilitates the process, providing metaphorical "training wheels" to enhance the developmental process of grammar acquisition until the correct forms emerge and become automatized in the procedural memory. However, second language grammar learning, just as first language grammar learning, is a developmental process, and children can acquire given new structures only if and when they are developmentally ready for them.

According to brain research cited by Sprenger, we use the *automatic* memory to store things like the alphabet, multiplication tables, and songs, but not comprehension skills. This implies that when young language learners repeatedly sing a given song or chant a certain rhyme, the item can be stored in their automatic memory. However, it does not necessarily follow that comprehension is achieved. A case in point is a 6-year-old English language learner I met in one Lebanese school where children begin learning English at age five. During my visit to the school, the English language coordinator wanted to illustrate the success of the school's English language program and asked the girl to tell me a story in English. Promptly the little girl began reciting the classic story about the farmer and a beet, which she accomplished remarkably well, considering she had been learning English only for two years. When she finished, I asked her whether the story was one of her favorites. Receiving only a puzzled look, I paraphrased and simplified my question, at which point the girl turned to the coordinator and said in Arabic, "I don't know how to speak English." But she quickly added (in Arabic) that she could sing a song, which she did, again very successfully. Obviously, the story and the song had been repeated often enough to be stored in the cerebellum by automatic memory, which is, of course, important, but for language learners to make actual use of the new language, it is not sufficient unless it can trigger other memory paths.

The most powerful kind of memory is *emotional* memory, which stores emotional information in the amygdala, the two almond-shaped structures above the brainstem that are "the specialist for emotional matters" (Goleman, 1995, p. 17); Sprenger (1999) notes that it is so powerful that it takes priority over any other kind of memory. How can this be related to language learning? First, I believe that if we use stories that trigger positive emotional responses, the chances are that children will feel more relaxed and, thus, more receptive to learning as the affective filter is lowered. Second, powerful emotional experiences generated by a story might help children retain vocabulary and language presented in the story. For example, the joy a child experiences when listening to an amusing story may well facilitate acquisition of the story language, particularly when coupled with repetitious refrains that help process language into the automatic memory. Similarly, the empathetic emotions aroused by a story character's misfortunes may help children remember words of phrases from the story. When children hear or read about Alexander's miseries in Viorst's *Alexander* books, they empathize with him and quickly pick up some of his phrases.

Meaningful Materials and Rehearsal

Studies in memory show that meaningful material is learned faster and remembered better than information that is less meaningful to the individual (Anderson, 1995; Mayer, 1996). Novel, emotionally relevant, or personally significant information draws attention (Barkley, 1996; Voss & Schauble, 1992) and thus gets moved from the sensory register to the working memory better than information less relevant. To facilitate long-term memory storage, learners must engage in rehearsal, but rehearsal and repetition result in storage only if the information is associated with existing knowledge or is somehow elaborated. Teacher-led story discussions provide a context for such elaborated rehearsal.

In contrast to meaningfully rehearsed information, rote-learned information may be difficult to retrieve. For example, learners may appear to be able to learn by rote material such as vocabulary, for example, and keep it in their working memory for the next day's exam, but fail to recall it later. Retrieval of information is facilitated in a context similar to the one in which it was learned (Blaxton, 1989), which explains why students may be able to successfully complete vocabulary or grammar drills in class and in a test, but not be able to retrieve the material in real-life situation; knowledge acquired by explicit learning of rules or by drills is easier to access in tasks that resemble the learning activities (Gadbonton & Segalowitz, 2005). This suggests that learning vocabulary and syntax within a meaningful context of a story, and practicing them in activities that simulate real-life situations, such as role-play, drama and debates, might be more beneficial for recall out-of-class than the typical coursebook drills.

Learners must also process information in several ways in order for it to be stored into and retrieved from semantic memory, the memory holding information learned from words. According to Sprenger (1999), "semantic memory must be stimulated by associations, comparison, and similarities" (p. 51). She suggests some strategies how this can be accomplished, among them summarizing, student-generated questions and debates, all which can be applied in the context of story-based lessons.

Connectionist Theory

According to the parallel distributed processing, or connectionist, theory, language is partly learned in chunks rather than in single words, and sentences and phrases are not always formed word by word (N. Ellis, 2003). When children's language emerges, both first and second language learners begin to use formulaic chunks of language as a single word, such as *this-is-a* and *once-upon-a-time.* For example, in compositions collected from young Lebanese English language learners, I found several different spellings of *once-upon-a-time,* including *wansaponatime, onesoponotime, onciponitime, wansepon atime,* and *oncapone time,* which reflect an understanding of the expression as consisting of one or two words.

The connectionist view of long-term memory sees learning as resulting from a gradual strengthening of associations within a network of different pieces of information (Ormrod, 2013). Relating connectionism to language acquisition, Elman, Bates, Johnson, Karmiloff-Smith, Parisi, and Plunkett (1996) explain that when children are repeatedly exposed to a given linguistic feature in context, associations are formed between the linguistic element and what it represents and gradually also with other features that occur with them. Thus, an ever expanding network of association, or connections, is formed. In terms of second language acquisition, Ellis argues frequency of input to be the key determinant in acquisition, and the learner must have acquired "the appropriately weighted range of association for each element of the language input" (N. Ellis, 2002, p. 144). Fortunately there are numerous children's stories with enjoyable and repetitious refrains that would appear to offer sufficient repetition of meaningful chunks of language. When some of these chunks, or parts of them, are repeated in other stories and motivating follow up activities, meaningful associations or connections can be formed.

In summary, using literature in the language class makes sense also in light of what we know about memory, interest, emotions, and learning. For more about memory, see Marilee Sprenger's *Learning and Memory: The Brain in Action*. Zoltan Dörnyei's (2001) *Motivational Strategies in the Language Classroom* provides a wealth of motivational strategies for language teaching.

EXPLORING IT

1. Examine the target vocabulary in a young learner course lessons. How is it introduced? How often are individual words repeated? Consider a class of 25–30 children. How many repeated encounters with a given word might an individual student have in the course of the lesson? Is the vocabulary recycled in subsequent lessons?
2. Think about Ullman's research regarding second language grammar learning. What do his findings suggest about explicit instruction of grammar? What about Sprenger's notion of automatic memory and memorization of grammar rules?
3. What about the potential of the materials to evoke situational interest or emotional reactions from learners?

PART II

Expert Testimony Research in Support of Literature-Based Instruction

In Part II, research evidence is presented to support story-based instruction. Chapter six reviews anecdotal and empirical evidence on the motivating power of a good story and shows how stories captivate children around the world. It uses classroom vignettes to illustrate also the significantly different discourse generated in classrooms where children discuss stories and in classrooms where they engage in 'communicative' language practice. Chapter seven reviews the extensive research of the past 30 years that has examined the influence of story-based interventions on children's English language reading skills. Chapter eight presents research evidence on vocabulary learning and Chapter nine looks at grammar learning. In Chapter ten, children's writing samples reveal the qualitative differences between writing of children who have been exposed to literature as compared to those in traditional language classes. Chapter 11 examines the emerging evidence that points to the positive influence of literature on subject matter learning. Although some of the research is limited, such as the one on motivation and grammar, taken together, the six chapters testify to the power of literature in language learning and support the theoretical base laid in Part I.

6

Talking like Texts or Talking about Texts?

> *"No, no! The adventures first," said the Gryphon in an impatient tone: "explanations take such a dreadful time."*
> —Lewis Carroll, *Alice's Adventures in Wonderland* (1865/1974, p. 98)

Stories Captivate and Motivate

While empirical evidence focusing explicitly on motivation and literature is limited at best, several studies examining the influence of storybooks on various language skills have found that story-based instruction improves students' attitudes toward English and motivate them to engage in lessons. See, for example, the extensive *Book Flood* studies in Chapter seven.

In an experiment in two Taiwanese classrooms of ten-year-olds, Chen-Ying Li and Seedhouse (2010) found that story-based lessons generated more student initiation, more overlapping utterances, and broader variety of turn-taking moves than traditional language lessons. The authors interpret these as indicators of intrinsic motivation.

Belsky (2006) studied the effects of incorporating children's literature in the second language instruction of adolescents. In her semester-long study, she taught two groups of 15-year-old English language learners, using the same curriculum. In the experimental group, she supplemented the instruction with relevant children's literature of different genres. Her findings not only showed significantly higher gains in the experimental group in listening, speaking, reading and writing, but also in student attitudes towards English and reading. Students in the experimental group expressed their appreciation for children's books as valuable for their language learning and "cool" (Belsky, 2006, p. 81). Interestingly, both groups shared the opinion that textbooks are boring.

Similarly, Sullivan (1994) reports on adolescents' improved attitudes towards foreign language learning after children's picture books were used in instruction. Neither the proficiency level in the target language nor ethnic background had any influence on students' attitudes.

Eric Carle's (1972) *The Very Hungry Caterpillar* kept a kindergarten class of four-year-olds in Lebanon intensely occupied for over two weeks (Ghosn, 1997). The teacher read the story aloud several times, and children quickly began to join in. Many children sought the book out during their free time and learned to "read" the pictures. The influence of the story was evident from the second day into the story. At the writing table, children were drawing fruits and other food items, scribbling numbers next to them. During snack time, they inspected each other's lunch boxes to find "caterpillar food" and ate holes "through" slices of cheese and ham in their sandwiches. Some "popped" around as caterpillars emerging from their eggs, while others floated around the playground like butterflies, calling out, "Look, look, me butterfly!" A week into the unit, the book had become so popular the teacher decided each child ought to have their own copy of the story. Using the story as a language experience, the teacher elicited the story from the children and printed out copies of the text. Children then illustrated their stories, bound them and took them home. One copy was also made for the class library.

Machura (1995) provides a delightful anecdotal description of her experience with the same story in Hungary, where her advanced 12-year-olds enthusiastically worked through the story. The appeal of this story to such a large age span demonstrates the power of skillfully constructed narrative represented through the language that is both rich and predictable in its repetitious features. The superb illustrations undoubtedly add to the appeal as they not only clarify and extend the language but provide also a visually aesthetic experience.

Surprisingly, *The Realbook News*, a U.K.-based website dedicated to story-based instruction, warns that "for many children just beginning English there is too much" (Selecting, para. 5) in Carle's story, and that this may cause "some children to switch off and give up trying to understand beyond the information they can get from the picture" (ibid). However, during the past 20 years that I have observed teachers and children work on this story, I have never seen children "switch off" from it. On the contrary; children are highly motivated and pick from the story the language they want or need, which the teacher can then reinforce. It is not necessary for children to understand or acquire every word in the book. In my view, *The Very Hungry Caterpillar* exemplifies the kind of picturebook that is perfect for teaching English to young learners. While keeping children of diverse ages engaged, it introduces the days of the week, numbers from one to five, and useful food-related vocabulary. It also makes the past tense "ate" and the preposition "through" very clear. While the concept of the caterpillar metamorphosis into a butterfly captivates many children, others may be more interested in the variety of foods the caterpillar ate on day six. A wise teacher will select the instructional objectives according to the curriculum but allowing also for children's individual interests to be addressed.

Chen-Ying Li's (2004) classroom transcripts from a Taiwanese primary school class show the teacher engaging a group of 10-year old learners in a shared reading of a big book story *The Royal Dinner* (Parkes, 2001). Although there is much mother tongue talk from the children, there is no doubt about the enthusiasm with which they engage with the story (italics denotes reading from the story; underlining shows emphasis. Non-English script and some notes on teacher gesturing have been omitted here):

> **T:** He told the boys. *They all want something different. They all want something different or it's off with my head.*
> **G:** [G makes a sound.]
> **B1:** ((He can kill them one by one.))
> **T:** *So, he... puzzled... and he pondered.*
> **B:** ((Cool!))
> **T:** Okay? *He looked... and he read...* Okay? En, read, read, read (T takes a recipe book and pretends reading).... And *he found a perfect recipe...* Yes, *this is it.* This is it.
> **L3:** ((He found it.)) (Chen-Ying Li, 2004, para. 16, l. 55–66)

In the next episode, work on the story continues.

> **T:** *Then he mopped... his brow and said... I hope they all like it*
> **G:** ((She takes out the knife.))

T: *Or it's off with my head.*

B1: Yes, off with his head.

T: Okay, we need to stop here.

B1: <u>Why</u>? (Chen-Ying Li, 2004, para. 18, l. 1–7)

Throughout the transcript, it is very clear that children are highly motivated by the story, and disappointment is evident in the stressed "why?" when the lesson comes to an end.

Similarly, motivation is evident in a transcript presented by Tinker Sachs and Mahon (2006) from a fourth grade class in Hong Kong, where children are participating in a shared reading of *Pirate Adventure* (Hunt, 1988). The teacher is eliciting children's predictions while reading:

T: *"What an adventure!" said Biff. "What an adventure!"* What an exciting story. OK. So who comes? Who comes?

Ss: Pirate.

T: Pirates come?

Ss: Yes.

T: Yes, let see (turning the page). Well, a pirate...

S1: ((a big guy)).

T: OK, is this one the same as out book cover? Is this one the same as our cover?

S1: Yes, ((that big guy)).

T: He

Ss: ((oh, that big guy, that big guy)).

[...]

T: And what did the pirate say?

Ss: Children

T: Children! (in a dramatic tone)

Ss: Oh, that big guy)).

T: Well, why did he want the children? Why did he want the children? Yes, Tammy?

S2: Kill them.

T: Kill them.

S3: ((cut them into 18 pieces)).

T: Cut them into parts. Yes, Felix?

S4: Dump, ((throw them into the sea)).

T: Throw them into the sea.
S5: ((use them to make soup)).
T: Yes, what about Tony?
S6: ((throw them into rubbish pin)). (Tinker Sachs & Mahon, 2006, p. 211)

Although the episode implies a rather gruesome story, *Pirate Adventure* is actually quite a funny story and children end up in a party on the pirate ship. Needless to say, the teacher could make much more use of the children's first language utterances, but there is no question about children's level of motivation.

In Hungary, Lugossy (2006) carried out an experimental storybook-based project involving seven- to ten-year-old English learners in four schools. Twenty authentic picture books were regularly read aloud to children during English classes. Children were highly motivated by the read-alouds, perhaps in part because they were able to make sense of the text with help of the illustrations. In the words of a participating teacher: "Although the text is fairly long, the children could understand the story quite well on the basis of the pictures. As I was telling them the story, they kept commenting in Hungarian whatever they could make out of it" (p. 28).

In Turkey, Dann (2007) decided to replace the typical graded readers with an authentic story because of students' reactions to the readers. His students, aged 11 to 12, disliked the graded readers, labeling them as "based on boring stories" and complaining, "We always do boring questions with reader books!" (p. 6). Dann chose Roal Dahl's (1988) *Charlie and the Chocolate Factory*, a book typically read in American fourth or fifth grade classes. He reports that the motivational level of the students was high throughout the unit.

Similar high level of motivation was noted by Ng and Preston (1993) in the six- to ten-year-old children who participated in shared reading of "big books" in the Reading and Language Acquisition (RELA) project in Brunei Darussalam.

Classroom Interactions

A number of theories about second language learning have been proposed over the years. Reinforcement (Skinner, 1957), comprehensible input (Krashen, 1982), comprehensible output (Swain & Lapkin, 1995), and negotiated interactions (Gass, 1997) have all been suggested to be necessary for second language learning, but negotiated interactions are now viewed by many as the main vehicle through which language is most successfully learned. This is particularly true about young language learners who are still developing literacy and have limited ability to acquire language from reading.

In a language classroom, both teacher initiations and the textbook tasks elicit responses from learners. As learners attempt to produce comprehensible output, teachers employ a number of negotiation strategies to prevent communication breakdown. These strategies are very similar to what native speakers use when communicating with non-native speakers and include confirmation checks ("You mean she will be late?"), comprehension checks ("Do you know what I mean?"), clarification requests ("Do you mean *hop* or *hope*?"), repetition, expansions, and questions (Long, 1981). Language teachers use also repetition requests, self-repetition and decomposing of their utterances (Tsui, 1995). Researchers have identified three different types of negotiation, making a distinction between negotiation of meaning, negotiation of form (Lyster & Ranta, 1997), and negotiation of content (Rulon & McCreary, 1986), which often happen simultaneously (Gass & Varonis, 1985). Negotiations of form and meaning interrupt the flow of conversation, whereas negotiation of content—which is concerned with the topic of the conversation—enables discourse to continue. These negotiations improve communication, and Ellis (1985) and others argue that language learning happens as a product of such successful negotiated communication.

Discourse Around Stories

Because of a dearth of systematic research on interactions in primary school language classrooms, and because of the importance placed on interactions, I investigated discourse in six fifth-grade classes in Lebanon (Ghosn, 2001). The aim was to explore the role of instructional texts on classroom interactions and children's subsequent achievement. Three of the schools were using an American content-integrated, skills-based ESL course, while the other three were using an American literature-based reading anthology. With four exceptions, children were native speakers of Arabic. During one academic year, each class was observed and videotaped over different lesson periods, and segments of lessons were transcribed.

Teacher's talk in the six classes comprised nearly 70% of all transcribed talk, with children's talk consisting primarily of responses to teacher initiations. This was not surprising in light of previous classroom research around the world, which has found language teacher talk to constitute up to 60–90% of all interactions (Chaudron, 1988; Lightbown & Spada, 2006;

Tsui, 1995). However, a distinctive difference emerged in discourse between communicative language lessons and lessons around literature. Discourse observed during skills practice could best be characterized as "pseudo-communication" (Ghosn, 2001a, p. 152), whereas, discourse around stories was characterized by negotiation, particularly of meaning and topic.

   S1: [reads] *The gods talked among themselves and decided to leave the boy. The happy couple agreed that this boy should see a land of peace and*
   S2: and people who meet under it should exchange kisses [unsolicited contribution].
   T: So, I told you the mistletoe is used as a Christmas decoration, and I told you that when two people meet under the mistletoe should kiss each other. Now they tell us here, where did they get this habit from?
   S3: They said here that in Norse legends.
   S4: Miss
   T: Yes, Milad?
   S4: Miss, how can they bring him back to life?
   T: This is a legend, I'm telling you. Now a legend first, a legend is a story that is told from before. And it's not true.
   S1: Like fantasy?
   T: It's like fantasy, yes. They use magic. (Ghosn, 2001a, p. 196)

The following episode was recorded in a school where children study English as a second foreign language and other school subjects in French. Students in this grade five class have been studying English since first grade, using an American reading anthology. The teacher repeats and paraphrases her own questions to provide scaffolding and to help students understand the concept of "prediction" from the context of a story they are reading.

   T: How did she know that the roads were slippery?
   S1: The driver called the school.
   T: OK. So what was the prediction?
   S1: [no response]
   T: What did you think will happen? What did you <u>predict</u>? [several students raise their hands]
   T: What will happen? [maintains eye contact with S1]
   S1: The principal will close the school.

T: The principal will cancel school for the day. OK. Why did you think that she will cancel school for the day?
S1: Because the roads were dangerous.
T: The roads were dangerous. So, Ralph, read the next paragraph.
S2: [reads] *She called her little brother. Then they both put on warm clothes, scarves, coats, boots, and mittens.*
T: What do you think will happen next?
S3: What are mittens?
T: Mittens, like this [demonstrates] when you don't have the things for fingers.

In an animated, lengthy exchange, with some code switching between Arabic, French, and English, the class attempted to clarify exactly what mittens are, but the teacher eventually returns to the topic.

T: Now, Ralph, what do you think will happen next?
S2: She, they will go outside to play.
T: To play, OK. Why do you think that? Pamela?
S4: Because, they said that on the streets there were snow.
T: Why does that make you think they will go outside and play?
S5: Because there was no school so they can play.
T: We know that number one, there was no school, and number two, we know that Hannah doesn't have to get ready for school anymore because there was no school. Then we know something that shows they are going to play outside. Joseph?
S3: Because there was no school they going to put on warm clothes
T: Warm clothes, they put on warm clothes
S6: They will play in the snow and make a snowman.

Student six appears to have used also visual clues to help him predict what the children were going to do once outside as the illustration shows a glimpse of a child and a snowman visible through a window.

Very similar interactions were observed by Chen-Ying Li and Seedhouse (2010) in Taiwanese classrooms of ten-year-olds. After taking baseline data on interactions in two teachers' traditional language teaching lessons, the two teachers engaged their students with what appears to be the classic *We're Going on a Bear Hunt* by Rosen (1993), although the authors mention the title as *Bear Hunt*. When the researchers selected 17 extracts from the story-based lessons for analysis, they found story-based lessons to generate more student initiations than the traditional lessons. They also found more variety in turn-taking moves around stories, as well as more overlapping utterances. In other words, the interactions seem to reflect more natural discourse than the language learning activities in typical young learner courses.

Discourse Around Communicative Language Practice

In contrast to the connected, negotiated discourse around literature, in the three classes where a communicative ELT course was used, discourse was fragmented and conforming to the typical three-phase sequence of teacher initiation, student response, and teacher feedback. The following extract is illustrative of the interactions observed around communicative language practice tasks. Children are expected to talk about their favorite season and seasonal activities, with the text giving them the options of swimming, sailing, bike riding, playing in the leaves, and planting flowers.

    T: OK. Rami and Boutros. Please do the conversation.
S3: *What is your favorite season?*
S4: *My favorite* [pronounced as "fa'vrit"]
    T: My, Rami, my fāvðrite
S4: *My favorite season is spring.*
S3: *Why?*
S4: *I like warm, rainy days.*
S5: *What is your favorite season?*
S6: (unintelligible)
S5: *Why?*
S6: I want<
    T: Hady, when he asks you why, you will answer by <u>because</u>, <u>because</u>
S6: Because to swimming.
    T: Because I go
S6: I go to swim.
    T: I go swimming.
S9: *What is your favorite season?*
    T: OK. Now Rania, you answer him.
S10: *My favorite season is winter.*
    T: Why do you like winter?
S10: Because it's cold.

T: Because it's cold or because you like to play in the snow^

S10: I like to play in the snow.

T: Now, Hani and Zeina, you do the conversation.

S11: *What is your favorite season?*

T: [to S12] And don't say winter!

S12: [no response.] (Ghosn, 2003a, p. 295–296)

The class continued in the same manner, with children reading the responses from their books.

The below episodes are not very different. In the first example cited by Jayne Moon (2005), students in their second year of learning English engage in a practice dialogue (italics denote children reading from the board):

T: ...OK, Adam will ask and Evi will answer....

A: *May I borrow your pencil, please?*

E: Here you are.

T: Now come on, Evi, look at Adam. (Evi is looking fixedly on the board.)

A: Thank you.

...

T: ...Brenda. Come on, Shona, ask

S: May I borrow your pencil, please?

T: Brenda, look at Shona.

B: You are welcome.

T: welcome (teacher is not satisfied with pupil's pronunciation)

B: welcome. (p. 69)

In Moon's (2005) second example, a teacher is asking a ten-year-old student questions about a picture:

P: The man is sleeping.

T: And then?

P: The mango is fell down.

T: Then?

P: Two men is taking his drum.

T: Two...

P: Two men is taking his drum.

T: You say *two men*...
P: Two meen men...
T: No.
P: ...is taking his drum.
T: Again, do you say *is*?
P: Two men are taking his drum. (p. 5)

Patsy Lightbown and Nina Spada (2006) provide the following extract where French-speaking students are practicing simple present of English verbs:

S1: An uh, in the afternoon, uh, I come home and uh, uh, I, uh, washing my dog.
T: I wash.
S1: My dog.
T: Every day you wash your dog?
S1: No.
S2: *Il n'a pas de chien!* (=He doesn't have a dog!)
S1: *Non, mais on peut le dire!* (=No, but we can say we do!). (p. 139)

As Lightbown and Spada note, the correct verb use matters more than students' own experience.

Teacher Questions and Classroom Discourse

Teacher questions, which orchestrate classroom discourse, have been classified in several ways. Questions that are used to check student knowledge and to which the teacher knows the answer are generally referred to as display question, whereas genuine questions aiming to elicit information from learners are called referential or real questions (Long & Sato, 1983). Display questions and referential questions can be classified either as convergent or divergent and differ in the cognitive demand they pose on the learner. Convergent questions are of lower cognitive demand, typically having one correct answer and focusing on the lower levels of thinking, whereas divergent questions are cognitively more demanding, focusing on higher levels of thinking (Orlich, Harder, Callahan, Kauchak, & Gibson, 1994). Classroom research indicates that teachers tend to ask many more convergent display questions than real or divergent questions, as Long and Sato (1983) discovered when they examined teacher-student interactions in elementary schools in three U.S. states. Teachers also use more convergent, closed questions than open, divergent questions (Sirotnik, 1983). Although closed display-type questions are often viewed negatively, in a language class they can help develop formulaic speech and, thus, as Hatch (1978) has pointed out, may give the learner a short-cut into communication.

Classifying Teacher Questions

Classifying teacher questions is not straightforward, however. In her observations of Hong Kong language classrooms, Tsui (1995) noted several instances where language teacher questions appeared on the surface to be referential, but on closer inspection turned out to be either factual or display questions. The following examples from Lebanese classrooms help illustrate the difficulty:

T: Why did Tom not want to paint the fence?
S1: He like to play.
T: He would like to play, yes, but what else?
S2: The other boys will laugh.
T: Yes, the other boys would laugh at him.

Although the question seems on the surface to be a reasoning question, the teacher's feedback move indicates she is trying to elicit a specific answer (which was indicated in the teacher's guide). The following question about personal information seems also to be referential, but, again, the feedback move reveals something else:

T: Do you have any aunts?
S: No.
T: You have no aunts? How come? What about your aunt Zeinab?

The question turns out to be a display question, after all, as the teacher clearly knows the student's family situation and is asking the question to check whether the student understands the word "aunt."

Teacher Questions and Student Output

Different types of questions generate different learner output. Real questions tend to generate longer student responses than display questions as Brock, (1984) and Kubota (1989) have shown. Cognitively higher level questions increase both the length of student output and the syntactic complexity of output (Kubota, 1989).

Out of all the teacher questions recorded in the six Lebanese classes (Ghosn, 2001a), less than 20% were open, real questions, about a quarter divergent display questions, and the majority, over half, were convergent display questions. Significantly more real questions were recorded in the literature-based lessons than in the communicatively oriented lessons, where significantly more convergent display questions were recorded. These questions could often be answered with one or two words or by reading from a text.

Teachers' story questions resulted in syntactically more complex student responses than what was observed around language practice questions. The following episode comes from the class where students were introduced to prediction, cited above. Here students are discussing a story about Paul Revere:

> **T:** If you want to describe Paul Revere's character, who can give me some descriptive words that can be used?
> **S1:** Patient.
> **T:** He was patient. Why do you think he was patient? What made you think he was patient?
> **S1:** Because when he go to prison, when he went to prison.
> **T:** It's all in the past tense, be careful
> **S1:** When he went to prison he was patient.
> **S2:** When the officers caught him, he didn't try to run away.
> **T:** Right, he was patient. He took time. That wasn't a big problem. Other than patient?
> **S3:** Helpful.
> **T:** Helpful. Why?
> **S3:** Because he helped carry the trunk.

The next example is from a class where students have been studying English 6–7 hours a week for five years. They are reading Walter Farley's *The Black Stallion*:

> **T:** So what happened to Alec when he was on the ship?
> **S1:** They were going to America and a storm struck, so the ship split into two.
> **T:** Yes, and what happened to Alec?
> **S1:** He went to free the black stallion and they both went jumped into the ocean.

...

> **T:** So what did Alec do when he tried to ride the Black?
> **S2:** He leaned himself over.
> **T:** [nods] The horse was big, Alec was small, so what did he do?
> **S2:** He lead the horse to a sand dune and he [unintelligible] the horse slowly.
> **T:** And what did the horse do?
> **S2:** The horse waited a few minutes and then [unintelligible] he ran.

In contrast, student responses in the skills-based classes were typically brief, as the following three exchanges illustrate.

> **T1:** How many times a week do you wash the dishes, Zeinab?
> **S1:** Once.
> **T1:** Say it in complete sentence, please.
> **S1:** I wash the dishes once a week.
> **T1:** Ramzey, how many times a week does she wash dishes?
> **S2:** Once a week.

* * *

> **T2:** Do you have any sisters?
> **S1:** Two, Miss.
> **T2:** Two sisters. Do you have any brothers?
> **S1:** Miss, three.

* * *

> **T3:** Do you help wash the car?
> **S3:** Yes, Miss.
> **T3:** What about you, Ali? Do you help wash the car?
> **S2:** No, Miss ((my father takes it to the gas station)).

Examination of the teachers' guides of the coursebooks used in the six classes revealed all six teachers adhering to the suggestions in their respective teachers' guides. The recommended questions in the literature anthology included open divergent questions and questions at different levels of cognitive challenge. In contrast, the suggested questions in the communicatively oriented language courses included primarily closed, convergent questions and were limited to the lower levels of Bloom's (1956) taxonomy. Consequently, student output in the literature-based classes was more extensive and included more negotiation.

Teacher Feedback and Student Initiations

The above episodes point to another characteristic associated with skills-based lessons, namely teacher rejecting feedback. Although all six teachers observed provided overall more accepting than rejecting feedback, significantly more accepting feedback moves were recorded in the literature-based classes, whereas more rejecting feedback was recorded in the skills-based classes. The differences were statistically significant.

Closely associated with rejecting teacher feedback was the number and quality of student initiations. In all six classes, children initiated minimal discourse, but significantly more initiations were observed in the literature-based classes. Children asked questions such as "How did he die?" about Paul Revere, and "Miss, how can they bring him back to life?" about a character in a legend. In the communicatively oriented classes, student questions were mainly procedural, with very few exceptions.

Resonating with findings of Brown and Wragg (1993) and Jarvis and Robinson (1997), teacher feedback determined the course of the lessons observed, and the instructional texts were somehow associated with teacher feedback. It appears that the communicative tasks characterizing young learner courses focused teacher attention on accuracy of form, rather than on the content to be communicated. The teacher rejections, in turn, resulted in disconnected question-response-feedback exchanges and limited student initiations. In contrast, literature focused teacher attention to meaning, which resulted in connected, genuine negotiated discourse, more accepting feedback, and more student initiations.

Teacher Validation of Student Contributions

Teacher validation of a child's contribution to the classroom discussion is a powerful reward and source of motivation and continued engagement, as we can see in the following classroom episode. Here, a group of third-graders are preparing to read Judith Viorst's *Alexander and the Terrible, Horrible, No Good, Very Bad Day* (Viorst, 1972). We encountered this same group of children discussing the same story in Chapter four after they had read it. (Double brackets denote mother tongue utterances; italics denote student reading from a text):

T: OK, what is the title of our story? Rami.
S1: [reads] *Alexander and the Terrible, Horrible, No Good, Very Bad Day.*
T: Right. Alexander and the Terrible, Horrible, No Good, Very Bad Day It's about a boy who has a very bad day. Have you ever had a really bad day? A very bad day when many things went wrong?
S2: Miss! Yes me.
T: Yes, Rania. You had a bad day?
S2: Yes, Miss. Me and my friends we went to ((the amusement park)).
T: Ah! You went to the amusement park. What happened?
S2: Yes, Miss, and I ((lost)) my money.
T: Oh! You lost your money in the amusement park! You must have felt very bad.
S2: Yes, Miss. When my friends they buy ((cotton candy)) and Pepsi, me, Miss, I sit like this [puts on a sad face].
T: So you were sad because you could not buy any cotton candy or something to drink. So it was not a good day for you.
S2: Yes, Miss, but Zeina my friend, she give me some of her ((cotton candy)).
T: Oh, that's nice. Zeina gave you some of her cotton candy. It was very nice of Zeina to share it with you. So you felt better.
S2: Yes, Miss.

Linking content this way to children's personal experiences and emotions generates interest, because "personal and meaningful memories can be held in their brilliance while dry facts learned at school may soon fade away," as Gilbert (2002, p. 116) so elegantly states. What better than captivating stories to make the connection? There is hardly a child who could not identify with the experiences of Alexander, whether it is Alexander's miserable day or his reluctance to move in Viorst's *Alexander, Who's Not (Do You Hear Me? I Mean It!) Going to Move* (Viorst, 1995). It is more difficult to relate typical language teaching book's exercises meaningfully to children's emotions and personal experiences. One cannot also undermine the importance of the teacher approach in facilitating of interest and motivating learners. Note how the teacher in the above episode validates S2's mother tongue contributions, recasting them into English. Thus, the student continues to contribute to the discussion.

In summary, some research evidence as well as ample anecdotal evidence suggests that storybooks can motivate young learners as well as adolescents. In contrast, the concepts and vocabulary of global coursebooks' language practice can be less interesting and thus less motivating. This often leads to fragmented teacher-controlled "pseudo-communication" (Ghosn, 2001a), whereas motivated discourse around stories is more natural and involves students and teachers in genuine exchange of ideas. Teacher feedback and treatment of errors also differ between communicative language activities and story work, as do teacher questions and subsequent student output.

EXPLORING IT

1. Examine the content of some of the young learner courses marketed in your context. How relevant or familiar are the concepts to children in your country or society?
2. If you can access *The Very Hungry Caterpillar* or some of the *Alexander* series books, think about what could explain their motivational power. What is the critical difference between the coursebook narratives and these books?
3. If you are currently teaching a class, try out two lessons, one with a communicative language focus and another based on a children's trade book. Monitor your own questioning strategies, feedback and the ensuing discourse. Do they confirm or disconfirm the argument presented in this chapter?

7

Literature and Second Language Reading Development

> *"Consider the verdict," the King said to the jury. "Not yet, not yet!"*
> *The Rabbit hastily interrupted. "There's a great deal to come before that!"*
> —Lewis Carroll, *Alice's Adventures in Wonderland* (1865/1974, p. 105)

Reading Instruction in Young Learner Materials

Current language teaching coursebooks for young learners are limited when it comes to teaching children to read in English. Surprisingly, young learner courses—even those aimed at English language learners in the United States or the United Kingdom—lack explicit and thorough instruction in reading skills and strategies. There is a heavy focus on aural/oral language development, most likely as a legacy from the audio-lingual method. Yet, reading continues to be one of the single most important sources of knowledge, and, needless to say, English reading skills are critical for young learners who must study school subjects in English.

Passive, teacher-fronted instructional approach also appears to prevail, even in programs aiming to prepare young English language learners for the mainstream academic classes, as Ramirez, Yuen, Ramey, and Pasta (1991) discovered in their longitudinal study of ESL programs in the United States. They found that learners had little opportunity to develop complex language and reading comprehension skills crucial in the subject matter classes. Padrón (1994) arrived at a similar conclusion when comparing fourth- and fifth-grade reading instruction in inner-city schools enrolling Hispanic English language learners with instruction in other schools. In the inner city schools, English language learners spent little time actually reading during the reading lessons but were mainly listening to the teacher. Therefore, it is not surprising that primary school language learners use far fewer and less sophisticated reading strategies than their native-speaking peers (Padrón, Knight, & Waxman, 1986; Nagy, García, Durgunoğly, & Hancin-Bhatt, 1993).

Another factor influencing second language learners' reading performance is limited knowledge about the topics presented in their second language texts (García, 1991; Jiménez García, & Pearson, 1995). Delgado-Gaitán (1989) contends that teachers of ESL children do not always teach or invite children to use what background knowledge they do have when trying to construct meaning from texts. The lack of background knowledge, limited vocabulary, and limited repertoire of reading strategies help explain, at least in part, why so many English language learners in the United States and Great Britain do not achieve the expected levels of academic language competence, despite years of instruction.

Readers hold different perceptions about what constitutes reading, and these perceptions determine what they focus on when tackling a reading task. Devine (1988) found that readers who hold a sound-centered view of reading focus on the graphic information in the text; those with a word-centered view focus on the lexical items and syntax; and those with a meaning-centered view try to interpret the author's meaning. What readers focus on while reading ultimately influences their recall and comprehension. Through miscue analysis and recall tasks, Devine determined that readers who perceive successful reading as the ability to get the author's meaning, did best in recall and comprehension tasks.

Although Devine does not speculate where these theories originate, early classroom experiences in reading and the approach to reading instruction undoubtedly play an important role in the development of children's perceptions about reading. This is vividly illustrated by Gregory's (1996) study of young children learning to read in Sylheti, Bengali, Arabic, and Chinese, respectively, while simultaneously becoming literate in English. Her findings resonate with DeFord's (1981) study, which shows that children in traditional skills-based first language reading programs perceive reading as a letter-sound-related activity.

Similarly, second language programs that focus on practice of vocabulary words and small chunks of language may very well foster a sound- or word-centered perception about second language reading rather than one that is meaning-focused. In other words, learners will concentrate on decoding and pronunciation instead of meaning. This may be particularly true in the case of young learners who are also beginning readers in their mother tongue. In contrast, children's stories, with their familiar story grammars and themes close to children's life experience, coupled with comprehension-focused instruction can explain why story-based instruction supports children's L2 reading skills development.

Improving Reading Skills with Literature

A rich body of research unequivocally points to the benefits of storybook reading on second language reading development. Several studies demonstrate that extensive reading in the second language correlates with a positive attitude toward second language reading (Alshamrani, 2003; Renandeyas, Rajan, & Jacobs, 1999; Yang, 2001; Taguchi, Takayasu-Maass, & Grosuch, 2004). Positive attitude may, in part, explain the research findings described below.

Small-Scale Studies

Eade (1997) used *Look Out He's Behind You* (Bradman, 1989) with three bilingual learners in the United Kingdom over a period of four weeks. She generated a variety of activities from the story and found they had a positive influence on children's word attack skills, especially the use of picture and context clues. Eade notes the high motivational level of the children and suggests also that the story discussions play a significant role in the process of bilingual children's second language writing development.

In a study in India, Aranha (1985) investigated the influence of sustained silent reading on fourth-grade students' reading. The experimental group children engaged in sustained silent reading, while the control group children received traditional language instruction. She reports statistically significant gains in favor of the sustained silent reading over the traditional language program. The differences were significant not only in the reading scores, but also in children's attitudes toward reading.

In an experimental study in Lebanon, 92 children's (ages 9.5 to 12) reading comprehension was measured after 15 weeks of story-based interventions (Ghosn, 2003b). Children in the study had received 5–6 hr of formal English instruction since kindergarten, and, starting in grade four, were taught also mathematics and science in English. In the three experimental classes, one weekly English period was replaced with a story-based intervention, while the control classes continued with reading and writing tasks in their language books. Grade four and five children selected books from a given set of trade books. Grade four children then filled simple checklists, while grade five children completed written response tasks, which included letters to the characters, journal entries from the characters' perspective, newspaper reports about the story events, and so forth. Grade six children took chapter books to read at home and once a week engaged in small literature circles and teacher-led whole class discussions. Data were collected on children's vocabulary, grammar awareness and reading comprehension in pre- and posttests. The findings indicate that storybook reading, although only once per week over 15 weeks, had a positive influence on children's paragraph reading and sentence sequencing. Differences between the experimental and control classes were statistically significant. (Vocabulary, grammar and writing findings will be discussed in Chapters eight, nine, and ten.)

Large-Scale "Book Floods"

Storybooks are at the heart of a *book flood* (Elley & Mangubhai, 1983, p. 57), an approach developed in New Zealand. In a book flood, students are exposed to either extensive shared reading, an approach originally advocated by Don Holdaway in New Zealand (Holdaway, 1979; 2001) or sustained silent reading of target language storybooks. Central to the book flood programs is that teachers are trained to use storybooks as tools to teach new language through story reading, shared reading, and follow-up activities (Elley, 2000). The approach has proven to be one way to provide extensive exposure to second language in the challenging contexts where children are obliged to receive their schooling in a non-native language.

One of the most extensive book flood studies is an eight-month study of over 600 primary school children in Fiji (Mangubhai & Elley, 1982). The findings show that reading of storybooks resulted in significant gains in the rate of development of both reading and listening comprehension skills. Two experimental groups in the study were each subjected to a different intervention. The first group was taught using the shared book experience while the other engaged in sustained silent reading with no specific instruction. The control group continued with the traditional language program. At the end of the intervention, the researchers report bigger gains in both experimental groups than in the control group. In a one-year follow-up program with additional books, researchers found also significant gains in the two experimental groups' progress as compared to the gains of the control group. A total of seven language tests were administered to assess reading and listening comprehension, writing, awareness of structures, and oral repetition. These showed a statistically significant effect in favor of the experimental groups. What is particularly noteworthy is that Mangubhai and Elley (op cit.) report the positive effects on reading and listening having carried over to other subject matter areas.

Several similar projects have been carried out since the 1970s. Kuruppu (2001) describes a study in Sri Lanka, where a book-based pre-test/posttest project was initiated in 1995 in grades four and five in 20 disadvantaged schools, ten in the capital Colombo and ten in a rural area. Schools were provided with 100 quality children's books, and teachers were trained in the shared reading method, which they implemented 15–20 min a day. In ten control schools, classes continued with their communicatively oriented English language textbook and workbook. Grade four children were tested in reading and listening and grade five children in reading and writing. Kuruppu reports posttests showing that in all project schools, children's gains in reading were significantly higher than those in the control schools.

In Singapore, the Reading and English Acquisition Program (REAP) similarly produced statistically significant gains in reading (Ng & Sullivan, 2001). A total of 512 children in ten REAP and ten non-REAP schools were tested on four occasions between 1985 and 1987 in reading accuracy and comprehension, among other skills. The results were so significant in both reading and writing that the concept was adopted into the national primary education curriculum.

In South Africa, a Johannesburg-based organization, READ Education Trust, has supported book-based programs since the early 1980s to promote fluency in reading and confidence in using English and to improve classroom environment (Schollar, 2001). Elley, Mangubhai, Cutting, and Hugo (1996) report on one empirical evaluation of these programs, *Sunshine in South Africa*, based on the *Sunshine* story series published by Wendy Pye Ltd. Second and third grade students in 35 schools in six South African provinces were administered pretests of reading and listening. The intervention program was then implemented in 22 schools during nine months while the remaining schools continued with their regular programs. Posttests showed a statistically significant difference in reading gains between the two groups in favor of the story-based programs.

Schollar (2001) reports on two other three-year long projects implemented by READ in remote and poor rural areas of Eastern Cape, one involving 35 schools in the former Transkei and the other involving 37 schools in Kei-Komga. Out of the thousands of children in the programs, the researchers drew a random sample from both project and control schools. A total of 850 project students and 360 control students in grades three, five and seven were tested in reading comprehension and writing. Schollar cites significant gains in reading in the project groups, reports of which have resulted in a plan for a national pilot of 1000 schools.

In a longitudinal experimental project, *Read, read, read*, described by Sadowska-Martyka (2006), 240 children between the ages of six and nine in Poland were taught English through storybooks. Each year, children were exposed to between 70 and 80 books. In the first year of the three-year cycle, grade one children were exposed to 60 storybooks, which the teacher read aloud to the children. Children also produced 30 mini-books of their own based on the stories, and were encouraged to select books for individual reading and listening from a set of 20 books accompanied by audio cassettes. In the second year, children read 40 to 50 books with the teacher and took a book home once a week for a week. Children read about 20 to 25 books on their own at home. By the third year, reading aloud to children was reduced while the independent reading was increased. In the second and third year, children were also learning from a coursebook. At the end of the cycle, the children who took the Cambridge Young Learner exam *Movers* were only slightly below their international peers in reading and writing and actually outperformed the world-wide sample in listening and speaking. It is important to note that the children in the study were, on average, one year younger than the world-wide sample of test takers.

The Sadowska-Martyka study above supports also the argument regarding storybooks and motivation discussed in Chapter six. When the Polish children were surveyed at the end of the three-year cycle, their responses revealed enthusiasm about the program. The first graders' number one favorite activity was teacher reading stories aloud to them and the second was reading books on their own, whereas second and third year students' favorite activity was reading on their own. Interestingly, children's least preferred activity was reading books while listening to cassettes. Sadowska-Martyka considers the enjoyment factor experienced by children as influencing children's attitudes and motivation.

In Tunnell and Jacobs' (1989) book-flood type program in New York involved 225 predominantly non-native-English-speaking Kindergarten children, who were immersed in English-language children's stories for a school year. By the end of the year, children learned to read picture storybooks and class-dictated stories in English, with some of them reaching second grade reading level in English, their L2—a notable achievement even for mother tongue reading.

Shared reading, which is characteristic of book floods, produced improved reading comprehension in 105 L2 learners in a seven-month study conducted by Koskinen, Blum, Bisson, Phillips, et al. (1999) in the United States. Sixteen classes in seven schools were assigned to four treatment groups: small-group shared reading in a book-rich environment; small-group shared reading, with daily re-reading at home; small-group shared reading with audiotapes; unmodified reading instruction. The second language learners clearly benefited from the book-based intervention in terms of reading skills as well as an improved attitude toward reading.

Retrospective Studies

The Singapore REAP program, mentioned above under "Large-scale Book Floods," has undergone several evaluations since its inception in 1985, with REAP children consistently outperforming their peers in traditional language programs (Ng & Sullivan 2001). Based on the success of the REAP program, the Ministry of Education in Brunei initiated a similar program in 1989, developed by Ng Seok Moi. In the Bruneian *Reading and Language Acquisition* (RELA) program, children are exposed to a large number of illustrated high quality storybooks in big book format and participate in repeated shared reading of storybooks, dramatizations of the stories, and language experience approach activities. Ng (1994) has carried out two evaluations of the RELA program, and both studies indicate children in the story-based program outperforming their peers in all four language skills, including reading. RELA was initially introduced in grades one to three, but after its proven success was implemented also in the upper primary levels (Ng, 1994).

Several other retrospective book flood studies have been carried out since 1978, when a pilot study on the South Pacific island of Niue indicated benefits of a storybook approach on second language learning (de'Ath, 2001). After the successful pilot, a storybook-based program, *Fiafia* (fun; happiness) was initiated. Children, who had been learning English with structurally organized and highly controlled *Tate Oral English* (Tate, 1967) for two years, were instructed with 48 illustrated storybooks and a shared reading approach in their third year. The stories were specially written for the experiment by de'Ath, the Director of Education in Niue at the time. The books, which were A4 size and with large print, were illustrated by local artists and photographers, and featured themes fun and familiar to the children. Reading comprehension of 62 children was compared with that of 89 children who had studied with traditional *Tate Oral English* program for two years and with graded *Tate Readers* (Tate, 1967) for one year. Posttests revealed statistically significant differences between the *Fiafia* group and the *Tate* group in reading comprehension as well as in word recognition and oral language.

The impact of a storybook-based literacy program initiated in Solomon Islands and Vanuatu in the 1990s has been evaluated by Singh (2001) in two cross-sectional studies. In Solomon Islands, a total of 566 children (ages 9–10) in their third and fourth year of English learning were tested for reading comprehension and sentence completion. Children who had received storybook-based instruction performed twice as well in reading comprehension than their age peers who had received traditional English language instruction. Even when two of the highest performing storybook schools and two of the lowest performing control schools were dropped from the analysis, the differences remained statistically significant in favor of the book-based program. In Vanuatu, 662 children of the same age were tested in six book-based programs and three traditional programs. Singh (2001) reports similarly significant differences between the two groups in reading comprehension. Because children in Vanuatu were tested in the second month of the school year, the results reflect children's achievement after two and three years of English learning, further pointing to the positive influence of storybook-based instruction even within two years.

Children's reading achievement in literature-based programs and traditional structured traditional ESL/ELT programs have been compared in three retrospective studies in Lebanon (Ghosn, 2001a; 2006; 2010). In the three studies, reading comprehension data were collected from a total of 459 fifth-grade students in different schools. Towards the end of their fifth year of formal English language instruction, children were administered a standardized reading test consisting of subtests of general vocabulary, syntactic similarities, paragraph reading, sentence sequencing, and comprehension of science, mathematics, and social studies and vocabulary. Children in the literature-based programs outperformed their counterparts in all the subtests, except in mathematics vocabulary, with many of the differences being statistically significant.

Outcomes of Strategy Instruction

Chaaya (2006) followed six young Lebanese second language learners in her second-grade English-immersion class, where a guided reading program was piloted. In this approach, described by Fountas and Pinnell

(1996) in *Guided Reading: Good First Teaching for All Children*, children participate in teacher-led guided reading sessions in small, homogeneous groups and read trade books, both fiction and non-fiction, at their instructional level. During the guided reading sessions, the teacher explicitly teaches and models various reading strategies and closely monitors the children as they read books silently or in a low voice. The following transcript shows a typical session. LG and LB are two of the lowest readers in the target group of six children. Although the children are L2 learners, they have been in English immersion since the Nursery class (age four) and consequently have developed considerable verbal fluency in English:

>T: Today's story is a tale called *The Sky is Falling*, written by Katie Knight. It is about a nut that falls from a tree, hitting Rabbit on the head. Rabbit tells one friend that the sky is falling, and the story goes on.
>
>LG: I know I think I saw a video like it.
>
>LB: Can the sky fall?
>
>T: We will have to read to find out, but keep your thought. Let's do a book walk pausing on each page to point out what is happening and call attention to picture details and new words. (Children look through the pages.)
>
>S: What are those? (Points to quotation marks.)
>
>T: The quotation marks in this story tell us that someone is talking.
>
>LB: So Bear's words are in quotation marks because he is speaking to Squirrel?
>
>LG: Yes.
>
>T: [After the book walk.] Now we will start reading the book. But what do you think I can do when I come to a word that I can't read?
>
>S: [Shrugs shoulders] I don't know.
>
>LB: Oh I know, you can sound it out. Read the letters in the word.
>
>LG: Yeah you can do that, it helps you. Also you can look at the picture and try to look for details to help you....
>
>LB: [Comes to a word that is more challenging.]
>
>T: Okay [LB] I want you to pause and look for picture cues, what do you think this word is from the picture?
>
>LB: The picture is a squirrel, oh the word starts with 's' so it's squirrel!
>
>LG: Yeah, it is a squirrel I knew it from the picture also. (Chaaya & Ghosn, 2010, p. 333)

Children also read books at their independent reading level that they chose from their particular book bag containing three or four books selected by the teacher, as well as one book of the child's own choice. Children's reading levels were assessed every month using Running Records (Clay, 2002) and their reading groups were changed as indicated by the reading records.

According to Chaaya (2006), seven months into the academic year, the lowest readers, who had begun the year at mid first grade level, had achieved instructional reading levels of mid- and high second grade levels. The average readers, who had begun at mid second grade level, had reached third- and fourth grade levels, with the highest readers at fifth-grade level. Children's reading growth ranged from nine months to two full years. Chaaya reports that not only did the children make more than satisfactory gains, bearing in mind that all were second language learners, but their attitudes also changed during the year. The low readers, who had disliked reading at the beginning, were proud about being able to read what they considered "hard books." The average readers, who had expressed mixed feelings about reading, perceiving themselves as "not good readers," were enjoying reading and also proud about being able to read even "chapter books." The two good readers had gained confidence and were fluent readers.

Similar gains with the guided reading approach are reported by Suits (2003), who followed 39 second language learners in an international school in the Netherlands in grades one, two and three. During the school year, she provided children with explicit small-group strategy instruction daily in sessions lasting 15–20 min. She reports using a total of 61 books, both fiction and non-fiction. (Chaaya cited above does not report number of books children read.) At the end of the year, the young second language learners matched—even surpassed—their native speaker peers. The 14 first graders in Suits' study made the greatest gains, advancing an average of four reading levels, while their L1 peers advanced an average of only slightly over two levels. The 16 second graders and nine third graders advanced three levels, falling only slightly short of the progress made by their native speaker peers. Similarly to Chaaya (2006), Suits reports that children's perceptions about themselves as readers improved and they began enjoying reading.

Studies have shown that young second language learners do not employ reading strategies very effectively, and the less successful readers demonstrate the fewest and least sophisticated strategies. This is not very surprising, bearing in mind that the typical young learner ELT courses provide little, if any, explicit instruction in reading strategies. Yet, the Chaaya (2006) and Suits (2003) studies clearly point to the benefits of such instruction, not only in reading skills development but also the attitude towards reading and children's perceptions about themselves as readers. They resonate with Padrón's (1992) findings from third-, fourth- and fifth-grade classes in the United States, which revealed that cognitive strategy instruction in two weekly 30-min sessions over one month was sufficient to produce significant improvements in children's use of the selected strategies.

To summarize, extensive research on the influence of storybook reading has been carried out around the world, involving thousands of children in diverse learning contexts. Findings from these studies clearly point to the positive influence story-based instruction has on young second language learners' reading skills development.

EXPLORING IT

1. Examine the reading selections in a young learner coursebook series. How much time is allocated to reading? Is any explicit instruction provided in reading strategies?
2. Examine the teacher's guide of the series. Does it provide guidance on how to teach reading?

8

Vocabulary from Stories

> *"When I use a word," Humpty Dumpty said ...*
> *"it means just what I choose it to mean—neither more nor less."*
> Lewis Carroll, *Through the Looking Glass* (1865/1974, p. 197)

Vocabulary Challenge

First language research has shown that poor oral vocabulary skills are associated with later reading problems (Morgan & Meier, 2008; National Institute, 2005), and this appears to be true of second language learners as well (Grabe, 1991; McLaughlan, 1987). Reading problems are often followed by conduct problems (Bennett, Brown, Boyle, Racine, & Offord, 2003), making learners less receptive to instruction. Where subject matter is also taught in English, young language learners need to acquire a considerable vocabulary if they are to gain knowledge from textbooks and make academic progress. It has been suggested that second language learners need to have knowledge of at least 2000 high-frequency words if they are to be able to make sense of 85% of the texts they typically encounter in school (Nation, 1990; Coady, Magoto, Hubbard, Graney, & Mokhtari, 1993).

Vocabulary presents a major challenge to young second language learners' reading development in particular (e.g., García, 1991). Nation and Warig (1997) estimate that by age five, a native-English-speaking child has acquired a vocabulary consisting of about 4,000–5,000 *word families* (word family refers to the base word and all its inflected and derived forms, as in *speak, speaks, speaking, spoke, spoken, speaker*), continuing to add a thousand new word families a year. This means that by age seven, they will have accumulated 6,000–7,000 word families. Thus, by the time they finish school, they will have easily reached the 10,000-baseword target that Hazenburg and Hulstijn (1996) argue to be the minimum required for university studies. In contrast, young English language learners in Indonesia and India, for example, acquire only about 1,000–2,000 word families during *five* years of English instruction (Nation, 1990). Presumably they acquire this knowledge following a traditional, structured syllabus. If it takes learners five years to acquire 2,000 word families, the challenges children will face in academic subjects taught in English are formidable.

What It Means to Know a Word

What constitutes knowledge of a word is far from simple, and Cameron (2001) provides an elegant and very befitting metaphor of words as flowers that illustrates the complexity of word knowledge: "All we see above ground is the flower, but that flower is kept alive and growing by roots that spread underneath it. Underneath the flowers of spoken words lie the roots, a connected web of meanings, understandings and links" (Cameron, 2001, p. 74). She contends that children use words without fully understanding the underlying complex meaning system.

To know a word implies many types of knowledge (Nation, 1990, 2001; Richards, 1976; Schmitt, 2000). To be able to understand and use a word in its correct meaning requires *conceptual knowledge*, which can be either receptive knowledge, as in listening or reading, or productive knowledge, being able to use the word when speaking or writing (Schmitt, 2000, p. 4). Since many words have more than one meaning, knowledge of a word involves polysemy, the understanding that words can have multiple meanings (Nagy & Scott, 2000, p. 271).

Metalinguistic awareness involves *morphological knowledge*, which will help determine meanings of inflections and derivational affixes (Nagy & Scott, 2000); to know that "talk" becomes "talked" in the past tense, but "bring" becomes "brought," that "helpful" becomes "helpfulness" when used as a noun but "difficult" does not, or that "humble" becomes "humility," and so on.

Grammatical knowledge of a word means to understand its function in a sentence and be able to use it in a grammatically accurate way; to know, for example, that a word can function both as a noun and a verb, as in "We keep records of student attendance" and in "The teacher records student attendance every day." Morphological knowledge is also related to grammatical knowledge, particularly in the case of derivational suffixes (Nagy, Diakidoy, & Anderson, 1993).

Because words are interrelated (Nagy & Scott, 2000), to know a word means also to have *semantic knowledge* of it. This implies collocational knowledge, the knowledge of what other words can be used with a given word; for example, that we say "beautiful flower" and not "handsome flower," or "aroma of coffee" and not "perfume of coffee." It means also to know how the word may be used metaphorically, as in "Beware of loan sharks," or "Tom is a real chicken." Collocational knowledge means also to know what other words are associated with a given word (that "farm" is associated with "farmer," "tractor," "barn," "shed," "paddock," "fields," for example). Semantic knowledge implies also connotational knowledge; what positive or negative associations the word has (while "frugal" and "slim" have a positive connotation, "stingy" and "skinny" are negative).

Pragmatic knowledge refers to knowing how to use a word in a right situation in the real world and to know the difference between formal and informal uses, the style and register of the word. It means, for example, to know that while among friends the greeting "Howdy" is acceptable, it is not when greeting a school principal or a visitor.

Finally, being able to pronounce a word or to recognize it in spoken and written language implies phonological knowledge, which does not necessarily mean that the learner is able to read the word when encountering it in a text. For example, a young learner may understand and use expressions such as "thisisa" (this-is-a) or "wansaponatime" (once-upon-a-time), but not be able to decode them in a text. This is a formidable amount of knowledge for a young language learner to accumulate. For more detailed discussion about word knowledge, see Nation, 1990, and Nation, 2001.

Vocabulary Learning

Scott and Nagy (2004) claim that word consciousness, alertness to words, is "essential for comprehending the language of schooling" (p. 201). Developing complex word knowledge, or consciousness, is not a one-step process, but happens gradually over time as learners see and hear a given word and use it in their own communication. The likelihood of gains is higher when the target words are repeated more than once in a meaningful context (Beck & McKeown, 1991). Laufer (2005) believes that the learner typically must encounter a word several times in order for it to be remembered, and Nation and Wang (1999) suggest a minimum of ten encounters with a word are needed for acquisition to be likely. Zimmerman (2009), however, argues that the more salient the word is the fewer repetitions are needed for it to be learned, suggesting that gains can be made even with fewer than three encounters, provided the word is central to the given context. Nation and Wang's (1999) claim about ten encounters is based on a study involving graded readers, which are simplified in structure and lack elaboration, thus possibly reducing the contextual saliency of words.

Tatiana Gordon insightfully points out "It may be hard to learn the meaning of new words intentionally, because the meaning of most words is very difficult to describe or explain" (Gordon, 2007, p. 67). Story context can illuminate word meanings often much better than dictionary- or teacher-provided definitions. Take the word "crossly" from Nick Butterworth's *One Snowy Night,* cited in Chapter two. Trying to explain that to be cross means to be annoyed is not going to help children much, since they are unlikely to know that word either. The facial expression of the squirrel in the illustration offers the first clue to the meaning, and if a teacher reads the squirrel's question with appropriate verbal and facial expression, the meaning will become quite clear. Through reading, learners can process unfamiliar words within a meaningful context and register.

Coady (1997) further contends that extensive reading is an important source of words that are not typically encountered in daily discourse but are part of advanced learners' lexicon, and Ellis considers reading as an ideal medium for vocabulary learning also because in speech, words pass "ephemerally" (N. Ellis, 1994, p. 40), while text enables learners to take time to process unfamiliar words.

Warwick Elley, who has conducted extensive research on the influence of story reading on children's second language skills, argues that "much of our vocabulary development is a result of incidental learning from silent reading" (Elley, 1997, p. 6). He suggests that

> When exposed to a number of unfamiliar words, in a comprehensible story or passage, the typical reader appears to make tentative hypotheses about meaning, based on the surrounding context, and is apparently able to retain this hypothesis until subsequent encounters allow for confirmation or revision. (Elley, 1997, p. 6)

Learning Words from Stories

Research conducted since the 1970s clearly points to the positive influence reading of enjoyable storybooks has on incidental vocabulary learning. In a 1978 study, Saragi, Nation, and Meister had college ESL students read *A Clockwork Orange* by Burgess, a book that contains a large number of special made-up slang words. After students had read the book, they were given a surprise multiple-choice test on 90 out of the 241 slang words in the book. As hypothesized by the researchers, the students had figured out the meaning of 50 to 96% of the slang words, the average being 76%. Nagy, Herman, and Anderson (1985) and Nagy and Herman (1987) found similar results with grade eight students, confirming that even a single reading can result in vocabulary gains. Although a number of other studies have investigated college students' vocabulary acquisition from reading, they are beyond the scope of this book.

Collins (2005) examined the effects of storybook reading on 80 native Portuguese-speaking kindergarten children learning English as a second language. Experimental group children were read eight stories, three times each over a three-week period. The readings were accompanied by rich explanations of target vocabulary through pointing at illustrations, definitions and synonyms, gestures, discussion questions, and using the target words in a sentence. The control group children were read the stories, also three times each, but without vocabulary explanations or discussion questions. Findings revealed a strong statistically significant effect of the explanations and questions on children's vocabulary learning, even when controlling for home reading practices.

Roberts (2008) exposed 33 preschool children (average age four) to storybook reading in the children's mother tongue (Hmong and Portuguese) and in English. A total of 12 storybooks were used in the study, and versions in the children's mother tongue were developed for each. Children took books home for one week at a time and the home reading was followed by two classroom lessons consisting of interactive big book reading of the English versions of the books, explicit instruction of six target words at a time, and "pretend-reading." A picture vocabulary test and oral language proficiency test were used to assess children's vocabulary learning. Repeated measures tests revealed that children learned vocabulary encountered in the storybooks, retaining most of the vocabulary even after two and a half months (Roberts, 2008). A study by Roberts and Neal (2004) similarly found that interactive storybook reading and explicit vocabulary instruction combined helped preschool-age English language learners acquire vocabulary from storybooks.

The positive effects of a storybook are further demonstrated in Carger's (1993) study of three five- and six-year-old Spanish-speaking Kindergarten children in a low-income section of Chicago. The children were identified by a standardized assessment measure as having little or no knowledge of English grammar and vocabulary. The researcher used a picture storybook where the main character discovers the pleasure of pretend-reading. Through the story, the three subjects were introduced to the concept of pretend-reading. In the following week, another picture storybook, Ezra Jack Keats' *Louie*, was read to the children three times. After each reading, the children worked to make a puppet from the story and pretend-read to the teacher. The pretend-readings were done individually in a separate room and audiotaped. The results showed significant increases from the first pretend-reading to the third in children's total word counts, in two- and poly-syllable words, meaning units, and target vocabulary. The meaning units of the children nearly doubled, displaying growth in their ability to express thoughts about the story.

Elley (1989) reports on a class of Fiji Indian children of 11–12 years of age, who were read one picture storybook, *Three Ducks Went Wandering* (Roy, 1987), three times over a period of one week. Though no explanation or instruction was provided on the six target words, children's mean gains in the target words ranged from 7 to 52, with an average of 20%. Elley then used the same story in two other studies, one in Niue and the other in Kiribati (Elley, 1997). He reports gains of 26% in the first group and 38% in the second. Based on these studies and studies with first language learners, Elley concludes that words which occur more than once in a meaningful context and are accompanied by illustrations are more readily acquired. Elley's findings are supported by Lambert's (1991) similar study.

The Fiji book flood study (Elley & Mangubhai, 1983; Mangubhai, 2001) was conducted in grades four and five in 12 primary schools. Children in the eight experimental groups read 250 illustrated story-books over a two-year period. At the conclusion of the study, their general vocabulary scores were 10% higher in a 30-item test than those of the children in the control groups. Elley (1991) reports similar results from a three-year study in Singapore, in which 500 children in grades one, two, and three participated. Two different vocabulary tests showed the experimental group's vocabulary gains to be significantly higher than the gains made by the control group children.

Verhallen and her colleagues have investigated the potential of multimedia storybooks in remedying young children's vocabulary deficits with promising results. Children in their studies were learning Dutch as a second language and read digital storybooks on the computer screen. In one study of 92 children (age five), the experimental group children improved their expressive vocabulary significantly by reading both static and animated storybooks (Verhallen & Bus, 2010).

In a small-scale study of three young English language learners, Ariaz (2010) exposed the children to shared storybook reading at home. Children were read electronic bilingual Spanish/English books and conventional English and Spanish books. She concludes there was a significant increase in children's English vocabulary, regardless of the reading condition.

Studies in Lebanon resonate with the above findings. In one of the retrospective studies cited in Chapter seven, the English language achievement of 106 children (ages 9.5–11) were compared after five years of formal study of the language in two different programs (Ghosn, 2010). Two of the schools in the study used a North American ESL text while the other two used a literature-based reading anthology. The number of weekly instructional hours was seven in all four schools, and children in all schools were also taught mathematics and science in English from American textbooks. Data were collected on children's general and subject-specific vocabulary knowledge. Children in the literature-based programs scored significantly higher than children in the ESL program in general vocabulary as well as in science and social studies vocabulary.

In Ghosn's (2003) experimental study, described in Chapter seven in detail, 92 children in grades four, five, and six were randomly assigned to experimental and control classes. Children in the study had received 5–7 hours of formal English language instruction since kindergarten, and had begun to learn also mathematics and science in English in grade four. In the experimental classes one weekly English language period was replaced by story intervention during 15 weeks. The control classes continued with their English language course. Age-appropriate books were selected for each class, many of them award-winning titles. The titles were not specifically chosen with vocabulary in mind as the main aim of the study was to see whether the intervention had any influence on children's reading and writing. However, several of the test items did appear in the books, some as many as five or six times. In the vocabulary subtests (general vocabulary, mathematics, science, and social studies vocabulary), the experimental group made greater gains than their control group peers in all but the mathematics vocabulary. The gains were statistically significant, supporting Elley's (1997) and Krashen's (1989) argument about incidental word learning from reading.

To conclude, acquisition of vocabulary is crucial for young second language learners, and is particularly important for children who are preparing to access academic subject matter in English. While vocabulary learning is a complex process, available research evidence indicates children can acquire new vocabulary from storybooks, whether through reading or listening. Because vocabulary in stories is presented within a meaningful context, learning does not necessarily require several repeated encounters but can result even from limited exposure.

EXPLORING IT

1. Examine vocabulary in a young learner course. How important is the target vocabulary for learners in your context? How contextually salient are the key vocabulary items? How many times are they repeated? On average, how many times would an individual student have an opportunity to use the word during the lessons within which the words appear?
2. How does the coursebook promote the different types of word knowledge: phonological, morphological, grammatical, semantic, and pragmatic?

CHAPTER 9

Learning Grammar from Stories

> *They've a temper, some of them—particularly verbs, they're the proudest—adjectives you can do anything with, but not verbs—however, I can manage the whole lot!*
> —Lewis Carroll, *Through the Looking Glass* (1865/1974, p. 197)

A debate exists about explicit and implicit acquisition of L2 grammar. Studies examining explicit and implicit learning of grammatical rules of both artificial and natural languages suggest that explicit instruction yields superior results, although some learning can take place implicitly (e.g., DeKeyser, 2000; N. Ellis, 1993; Robinson, 1996, 1997). Implicit knowledge is knowledge acquired over time without the intention of learning (Ormrod, 2013). Although implicit knowledge is difficult to explain, we rely on it daily; we tie our shoelaces, ride a bike, or speak in grammatically correct sentences in our L1 without giving thought to *how*. Explicit knowledge is acquired intentionally, and in terms of grammar involves awareness of rules or attention to form. The grammar-translation method of teaching is an example of a very explicit approach, whereas the communicative approach relies on implicit learning. Schmidt (2010) sites the case study of an adult Japanese English language learner, Wes, which suggests that implicit learning without attention to form may leave learners with fossilized errors even after years of exposure and achievement of acceptable communicative competence. Despite being a quite fluent communicator, after years in the United States, Wes would frequently make statements such as, "Yesterday I'm go beach" and "Tomorrow I'm go beach" (Schmidt, p, 723). Krashen (2003) identifies two components in explicit grammar instruction: focus on form and presentation of the rule (p. 30), suggesting it is possible to focus on form without presenting the rule.

Studies supporting explicit teaching of L2 grammar have involved adult learners, and Krashen (2003) argues they show effects of explicit teaching to be "peripheral" (p. 30), despite researchers' claims of significance. Explicit teaching of grammatical structures in young learner classes can be expected to have similarly peripheral effect, if, indeed, any. First, explicit learning of grammar requires the ability for abstract thought, which, on average, begins to develop at age of nine or ten. In their seminal study of nearly 300 young English language learners' syntactic errors, Dulay and Burt (1973) found that the errors children (ages 5–8) made were mostly similar to those made by children acquiring English as their first language. Their analysis suggests L2 children use universal language processing strategies similar to L1. In other words, they draw on Universal Grammar (UG), "the innate, biologically determined principles, which constitute one component of the human mind—the language faculty" (Chomsky, 1986, p. 24).

Dulay and Burt (1973) suggest that focus on target structures often results in "the message of sentences taught, if there is one, [to be] meaningless for both teachers and children" (p. 257). For young learners, rich exposure to grammatical structures in a meaningful context can lead to implicit learning, in a way similar to L1 learning, particularly in the case of children between the ages of four and seven, whose performance in aspects of grammar have been found comparable to those of native speakers (DeKeyser, 2000; Johnson & Newport, 1989). Yet, it would be wrong to say that young children can learn a foreign language quickly and easily, because many complex factors, from psychological and social to experiential, will affect the process. Successful learning depends on the quality of L2 input and instruction (Marinova-Todd, 2003).

Many second language specialists have long emphasized the need for authentic texts and connected discourse for both reading comprehension and grammar instruction (e.g., Celce-Murcia, 1991). Yet, many, if not most, young learner courses still reflect a bottom-up approach to grammar, presenting fragmented discourse and artificial exercises. I concur with Adair-Hauck and Donato (2002), who contend that stories provide "multiple passes" (Adair-Hauck & Donato, 2002, p. 271) to language, and recycling of the language of the story in a variety of activities will result in better comprehension, as the "framework of the story provides a continuous flow of mental images that help the learners to assign meaning and functions to the forms they hear" (ibid).

For new knowledge to be processed to the long-term memory, attention is necessary, but attention need not be *intentional*. In other words, when children attend to an amusing or interesting story, the predictable refrains they repeat can get processed into their long-term memory. As noted in Chapter five, children's second language grammar learning occurs through procedural rather than declarative knowledge used by older learners (Ullman, 2001a; 2001b). Yet, instruction in most coursebooks is still based on principles of "imitation, repetition, reinforcement, immediate correction of any errors" (Tarone, 1974, p. 5). Interesting storybooks provide the kind of authentic, connected discourse associated with grammar instruction in whole language and content-based approaches. There is a wide range of predictable books for children in English, from very simple stories with one or two repetitious structures and limited vocabulary to more sophisticated ones with more complex and varied, but still predictable structures.

Experimental Research

The earlier cited book flood studies have contributed not only to children's reading and vocabulary, but also to their learning of syntactic features. In one of their studies, Elley and his colleagues (Mangubhai, 2001) involved 535 Fijian children in 12 schools in a year-long book flood of some 250 storybooks. In the experimental group children had 20–30 min of their regular ESL program replaced by reading of storybooks. In one group 166 children participated in shared reading program, while in the other group 172 children read books silently. Neither group received specific instruction on grammar, whereas the control group did. Mangubhai reports that at the end of the year, children in the experimental groups demonstrated better awareness of the target structures than their counterparts, who had received systematic instruction. The differences were statistically significant. The researchers then extended the project for another year with the same children (grades five and six) with similarly successful results.

Elley (1982, cited in Elley, 1997) then identified 24 grammatical structures that were part of the Fijian sixth-grade curriculum, and investigated whether grade five students would be able to understand the structures they encountered in their reading before they had received formal instruction.

Two thirds of the fifth-graders were able to understand 18 out of the 24 target structures, although they had not received instruction in them yet.

In the experimental study (Ghosn, 2003) described in Chapter seven about reading, 92 children in grades four, five, and six were randomly assigned to experimental and control groups at the beginning of the school year. During the 15-week story-based intervention, one English language class period a week in the experimental group was replaced by story reading and written follow-up activities, while the control group children worked with lessons in their communicatively oriented coursebook. A test of syntactic similarities revealed statistically significant differences between the experimental and control groups in grades four and five. In grade six, where children had been exposed to explicit grammar instruction longer than their younger peers, the differences did not reach statistical significance (Ghosn, 2003).

In Wai-King Tsang's (1996) study of 140 high-school language learners in Hong Kong, one group received reading enrichment consisting of reading eight books and writing reviews of them, another group wrote weekly essays and received teacher feedback, and the control group did no additional reading or writing. After 24 weeks of intervention, the enrichment group wrote grammatically more correct essays than the other two groups.

In their study, Bus, deJong, and Verhallen (2006) used digital storybooks with 60 five-year-old learners of Dutch as a second language. Experimental group children read digital stories on the computer screen. Some groups read static stories while others read animated stories. In both cases, story reading had a positive influence on children's syntactic awareness as compared to the control group children who played non-text videogames.

Retrospective Studies

In a retrospective study, Ng and Sullivan (2001) compared the achievement of 256 year one children in a book flood program to that of 256 children in a regular structural language program in Singapore. In the Singapore Reading and English Acquisition Program (REAP), which was introduced in 30 schools in 1985, children are exposed to a large number of illustrated high interest storybooks, and participate in shared reading and follow up activities. Children in the study were tested four times, once in 1985, twice in 1986 and once in 1987. Statistically significant differences were found in the variety and accuracy of grammatical structures between the REAP and non-REAP children' writing in favor of the REAP group.

A comparison of 190 fifth-graders' grammar awareness in Lebanon (Ghosn, 2006) revealed that children who were taught with literature-based materials outscored their ESL course counterparts in grammar awareness, with differences being statistically significant. In the literature-based classes, children's grade levels in syntactic similarities test ranged from fourth to high fifth grade, while scores of children in traditional skills-based classes ranged from high second grade to beginning third grade. An interesting finding emerged from two classes, where children were learning French as the first foreign language and English as a *second* foreign language, 2–3 hours per week. Being both part of the same parochial school system, the curricula in the two schools were identical in all aspects, with the exception of the English language textbook. Children learning from a literature-based anthology were at grade level in English grammar, whereas their age peers in the other program were three grade levels below.

Transcripts collected from six grade five classrooms over one academic year (Ghosn, 2001a) reveal significant differences between children's oral language and written output in literature-based classes and classes using communicatively oriented ESL texts. After five years of formal English language instruction 6–7 hr per week (and exposure to English in kindergarten), children in the literature-based classes produced not only more output but also much more grammatically accurate output. The following five utterances reflect the output typical in the literature-based classes. The first three are from a class where children studied also science and mathematics in English: "One day I climbed, I climbed in [rock-climbing center]. It was fun"; "Once I was climbing [location] with my two friends in the snow"; "...and people who met under [the mistletoe] should exchange kisses" (Ghosn, 2001a, p. 196). The other two are from a class where children studied English as a subject from an American reading anthology and most other subjects in French: "When [Paul Revere] went to prison, he was patient"; "When the officers caught him he didn't try to run away."

In the "communicatively" oriented classes, students' discourse consisted mainly of reciting textbook dialogues or brief answers to teacher questions. In one class, the coursebook featured highly simplified story excerpts as part of the end-of-units assessment, and the teacher tried to use the excerpts to generate output from children. The first utterance is related to an excerpt of *Moby Dick*, and the other two to an excerpt from *Tom Sawyer*. All three illustrate the difficulty children had with putting to use any syntax they may have been taught: "The whale shake the boat surprise them"; "The boy look stand like this [demonstrates] and say for the boy and say for him 'do you want to eat'"; "The boy are fighting who want to paint" (Ghosn, 1999).

Children in literature-based programs also produce grammatically more accurate writing than their age peers in communicatively oriented programs.

Although research in grammar learning from stories is limited and not conclusive, it does suggest extensive reading of storybooks can have a positive influence on children's second language grammar acquisition. Research also indicates that children do not need to be taught grammatical structures *before* they encounter them in books; children can acquire grammatical structures incidentally from interesting books they read, just as they can acquire vocabulary. Storybooks can also be used to teach grammar with carefully planned focus on form.

Kretzschmar (2011) proposes to employ children's literature in grammar teaching while following the PACE model (Adair-Hauck & Donato, 1994, 2002). In this four-phase model, a given grammar point is presented in the context of the story and is then reinforced by a variety of activities aimed at getting learners to pay attention to the form and to deepen comprehension. Afterward, the teacher guides the learners to construct their understanding of the grammatical patterns. In the extension phase, children are encouraged to use the newly acquired structures in a variety of ways that will help them integrate them to their existing knowledge. Figure 17.1 in Chapter 17 presents a brief sampling of storybooks that feature repetitious and predicable language, including grammatical structures, in a clearly meaningful context. Although some of these stories are intended for native English-speaking children who are learning to read, they are pedagogically sound also for young second language learners.

EXPLORING IT

1. Examine the first three levels of a current young learner course. How carefully sequenced are the grammatical points presented? Are any past tense verbs introduced? Are any future tense verbs introduced?
2. Examine the coursebook dialogues and reading selections. Does the language sound natural or artificial? What role does the presented grammar play in the quality of the texts?

10

Writing from Reading

> ... *he was obliged to write with one finger for the rest of the day; and this was of very little use, as it left no mark on the slate.*
> —(Lewis Carroll, *Alice's Adventures in Wonderland,* 1865/1974, p. 105)

Writing Instruction for Young Learners

Writing is a skill given very little emphasis in young learner English language courses; writing here defined after Sarah Hudelson as "the creating of original text using the individual's intellectual and linguistic resources rather than copying someone else's text, using prepared lists of words to create sentences or stories" (Hudelson, 1989, p. 5). Instead, writing tasks in primary ELT courses rarely call for creation of original texts, consisting mainly of filling in the blanks, compiling lists, and constructing short messages and letters. Explicit focus on organization and idea development is rare, if it exists at all. Samway (1987) found that writing tasks in primary school English as a second language texts served an exercise function and that even "the most advanced levels of most ESL texts for elementary grade children present writing in an artificial way" (p. 3). A look at some young learner texts published by the largest international textbook publishers between 2000 and 2010 confirms this to be true still at the time of this writing. For example, the highest level of one five-level globally marketed ELT course contains a total of 72 thematically grouped lessons, but only 20 writing tasks *in all*, ten of which are either poems or letters. One unit has no writing tasks at all. Teachers' guides of four courses examined reveal no explicit writing instruction is expected (Ghosn, 2013). The underlying assumption appears to be that a single example, such as a letter or a simplified newspaper article provides a sufficient model for students to be able to learn to compose their own texts.

Yet, assigning writing tasks is not *teaching* writing and presupposes that students somehow know *how*, when, in fact, they may not have a clue. Donald Graves, whose work has significantly shaped our understanding of how children develop as writers in their native language, contends that without modeling of how the writing process happens, children perceive it rather like magic, as if "We only hold the pen and a mysterious force dictates stories, poems, and letters. The better the writer, the less the struggle" (Graves, 1983, p. 43). He suggests that teachers actually model writing in front of the class, going through the choice of the topic, the actual composing and then soliciting children's feedback and revising the text. He also points out that "There is no one-to-one expectation: here it is in the modeling session, now do it" (ibid, p. 49). Writing is a craft, and as with any craft, we cannot produce quality results if we have not developed control over the medium. Yet, the great majority of the writing tasks in primary school ELT materials seem to echo children's perceptions about writing as "magic."

When young second language learners engage in writing, they have to make decisions about the purpose of the text, the sequence and language. This helps them develop an understanding of how and why texts are written and what the writer does in order to make the text say what is intended. Thus, writing gives young learners insight into the goals, constraints, and concerns of authors, insight which they can apply to their own reading. In Zamel's (1992) words "Writing, because it gives rise to our own ways of probing and working with texts, is thus a way out to construct, to compose the reading" (Zamel, 1992, p. 469). This argument echoes Halliday's (1975) and Kamii's (1991) claims that children construct language by interacting and manipulating language and by engaging in meaningful use of language within a community of language learners. In other words, they must be actively involved in producing language and examining the results. Maguire and Graves quote Heddie, a nine-year-old second language learner who brings her experience to bear upon the L2 writing theory in this poignant statement: "The more you write, the more you learn how to write. It's like speaking, the more you speak, the more you learn how to speak" (Maguire & Graves, 2001, p. 561). In reverse, the less one writes, the less one learns how to write.

Writing may also facilitate other schoolwork (Hudelson, 1984), and thus deserves special attention in the challenging contexts where children must tackle school subjects in the second language and be able to communicate their learning in the second language in written tests and examinations.

The limited attention to writing in young learner ELT courses is rather surprising in light of what is known about both what young children are capable of and the role of writing in children's L2 development. Research shows that young second language learners are quite capable of producing texts that express their ideas and experiences even when their oral language is not yet well developed (Hudelson, 1983; Samway, 1987; Samway & Taylor, 1993). It appears also that, contrary to a prevailing belief, reading skill is not a prerequisite to writing (Rigg, 1981; Edelsky, 1982; Hudelson, 1984; Zamel, 1992), as pointed out earlier. However, because second language writers have limited control over the language, their writing often lacks clarity and fluency (MacGowan-Gilhooly, 1996), with lack of adequate vocabulary in particular hindering fluency (Arndt, 1987; Raimes, 1987). Thus, young learners must depend on the few limited second language structures they can acquire from the often limited input they receive in their language class.

Instructional Texts as Models for Children's Writing

The available research indicates that when young language learners write, their writing resembles the texts they read. In other words, children use instructional texts as models for their own writing.

Hudelson (1989) reports on observing two second grade English language learners over one school year. The writing children produced was a reproduction of the language they encountered in their skills-based language book. Even when they were given an opportunity to draw and write what they wanted, children's writing consisted primarily of simple, list-like series of sentences, rather than cohesive text. Samway and Taylor (1993) found that English language learners who read a variety of texts, including storybooks, wrote more diverse texts that resembled the texts in their reading materials. Learners borrowed plot elements, characters, and themes from the stories they read, and were also influenced by the literary techniques and mechanics of texts. Their findings resonate with the extensive research into children's first language writing, which shows chidlren's writing to be modeled after the style and structure of their reading materials (e.g., DeFord, 1981; Dressel, 1990; Mikkelsen, 1984).

When Huie and Yahya (2003) compared writing samples of non-native and native English-speaking children in the United States, they came also to the conclusion that the type of writing materials and tasks children are exposed to significantly influence the style of their writing. The writing of second language learners, who were exposed primarily to "fill-in-the-blanks" type of worksheets, differed significantly from the writing of native English-speaking children, who were exposed to rich texts in diverse genres in their reading programs and had opportunities to generate texts of their own as opposed to filling in the blanks.

In her insightful book, *When English Language Learners Write*, Samway (2006) illustrates the processes and practices that facilitate children's writing and language development through the voices and writing samples of five learners. She identifies two contrasting approaches to teaching writing to English language learners: skills-based and communicative. The skills-based approach rests on the assumption that language learners must develop their oral fluency before they can begin to write. Writing instruction based on this philosophy, therefore, focuses on discrete skills, sentence-level exercises, fill-in-the blanks, and practice of grammatical structures. These are precisely the kind of writing activities that predominate in current young learner ELT courses. The diametrically opposite communicative approach, which Samway argues for, is grounded in the belief that the message is the most important aspect of writing, and skills are not taught in a predetermined sequence, but rather as the need arises. Children's writing is not predicated on their oral fluency, and the belief is that writing will facilitate children's reading development.

Writing in Story-Based Programs

Retrospective Studies

Children's writing has been assessed in some of the earlier cited book flood studies. In the longitudinal REAP study in Singapore, fifth-grade children were assessed four times over a three-year period (Ng & Sullivan, 2001). Children's writing was evaluated on correct words and sentences, sentences relevant to the given picture stimulus, and a variety of grammatical structures. In all four writing tests, REAP children, who were in a storybook-based program, outscored their non-REAP peers, with the differences statistically significant.

Books in Schools program in Sri Lanka, mentioned in Chapter seven, grade five children in 20 schools (ten book-based and ten traditional ELT programs) were given pictures of "some mischievous pigs" (Kuruppu, 2001, p. 187) and were asked to write sentences about them. The combined means in both the urban and rural experimental groups were significantly higher than the means of the control groups. The urban experimental groups' mean was four times that of the control groups and the rural experimental groups' mean was close to double that of the controls. Kuruppu notes that the best writers in the experimental schools wrote "some clear fluent sentences" (p. 188), whereas the best writers in the control schools wrote sentences that were "shorter, more stereotyped and often lacking coherence" (ibid).

Singh (2001) study in Solomon Islands and Vanuatu, (described in detail in Chapter seven) assessed children's writing after three years of English learning. Grade four children were given a sentence-completion test, with many of the items designed so as to assess children's awareness of grammatical structures that were focused on in the control group program. Sentences were assessed based on grammatical accuracy and on whether the sentences made sense or not, with no penalty for spelling errors or poor handwriting. Singh found the best writing came from the project schools, where 27 children scored more than five out of possible ten, while only three children in the control schools were able to do so. According to Singh, the best writers wrote sentences that were "interesting, grammatically correct, and quite mature for young children writing in their second language" (Singh, 2001, p. 235). Among his examples are the following sentences (italics denote a child's writing): "Next week *my father and I are going to Santo*. When it rains heavily *I think about swimming in the rain*. The food is too *hot for little children like me*." (Singh, 2001, p. 235).

In a retrospective study (Ghosn, 2012), 100 written narratives were collected from children in two schools, one using a literature-based reading anthology for English instruction and the other using an ESL text. In both schools, which cater primarily to middle class families, children learn English 7 hours a week and study also mathematics, science and information technology in English. Compositions were collected in the spring of grade five. Children were given a picture stimulus depicting a prehistoric scene of mammoth hunters and were told to write a story about the picture. The narratives were evaluated based on literate language features, including lexical complexity, coordinating and subordinating conjunctions, and mental and linguistic verbs. The narratives of children in the literature-based school were superior to those in the ESL course school in terms of lexical complexity and other literate language features.

Experimental Studies

The earlier cited Fiji book flood (Mangubhai, 2001) collected writing data from 145 fifth-graders in two experimental groups (silent reading and shared reading) and a control group. A series of pictures served as the writing stimulus. Mangubhai contends that the differences between the experimental and control groups' compositions were "quite dramatic" (Mangubhai, 2001, p. 152) and provides examples to illustrate. Mangubhai identifies this sentence as "typical of the modal score" (p. 152) of the book flood group: "One morning when Luke's mother was washing, and the men were drinking yaqona, Luke was boiling the water" (ibid.). In contrast, the following is typical of the control group: "Is there was a woman in the tree. Mothe sitg in the tree there was a looking at hes mother" (Mangubhai, 2001, p. 152). Clearly there is a significant difference between the two texts in syntax and spelling.

In an experimental study in Lebanon, 140 compositions were collected from children in grades four, five, and six (ages 9–12.5) (Ghosn, 2007). Once a week, the experimental classes spent one lesson period reading and working with storybooks. For details of the intervention, see Chapter seven. Picture stimuli were used to generate compositions. Children were given a brief review of the story elements before both tests and were then instructed "to write a story that goes with the picture." As in studies by Samway (2006), Samway and Taylor (1993) and Hudelson (1989), children in the experimental classes borrowed many literary elements from the texts they read, and they also borrowed authors' techniques. They wrote longer compositions than their ELT course counterparts, more interesting sentences with adjectives and adverbs and coordinating conjunctions. They used more effective opening sentences and included more dialogue in their writing. Their narratives were also qualitatively more interesting because of their use of more descriptive vocabulary, better organization and use of strategies that contributed to coherence. Their increasing awareness of syntax was also evident in their attempts to use grammatically more sophisticated sentences.

The first example from the post-test, despite grammar, spelling, and punctuation errors, illustrates the level of sophistication in the compositions of children in the experimental classes. Note some of the cohesion devices (emphases and frames mine):

> There was many people wants to go to space. They go in _groups_ and _every group_ wants to take things with them. The _first group_ take clothes, _second group_ brings shevel, _Third_ brings a map to tell them the way. The next Saturday They went they go up by airplanes and fly. Only They have 3 months . When They arrived they saw many people diging and the airplanes, and a very big people, The eliens also, and traines. _Every group_ put his thing on the ground. And they started to work. they want to find How many stars, and moon, and if they have more spaces. One of the _group_ find a very big train

they go a faraway with it. The other group dig in the ground. The 3 months go on and They have to go. The next Monday They whent in the airport and all the people go to see them they take all of the story to them and whent they did and They were very happy. (J. K., 10) (Ghosn, 2007, p. 181)

The following two texts were generated by a 12-year-old female, identified by the teacher as one of the weakest students in her sixth grade class. There was a 15-week time span between the pretest and the posttest, during which time the class read storybooks once a week and completed written reader response tasks.

> I am see in the pickesher the people hit the elephant because the elephant atacked to the people there are eight people is hit the elephant and the elephant is very big the people is hold a big roll to hit him and the threes is put new [end of writing]. (Ghosn, 2007, p. 181)

The following paragraph was written by the same girl fifteen weeks later, after the story-reading intervention (italics mine):

> **Discovery the moon**
>
> Long ago we have many astronauts went to the moon to discovery, they went to bring the petrol, they went with him three Garph to dug the rock to discovery the patrol, then they arived in the rocked to the moon, then they bring all the tools to dug the rock, they bring to the moon ten astaudents to discovery, then they start there warek very well, they have Garph to dug, they have astronauts to dug the rock with shovel, when they warek one astaudent when they warek they see under he rock a petrol then they showet *I found the petrol I found the petrol* then the friends tell *yes, yes, yes,* alvehim very happy then they went to the America strat, and they have the petrol. (Ghosn, 2007, p. 182)

Although the text is a long run-on, and suffers from problems of grammar and spelling, it is clear that the student has picked up some basic elements of narrative. The sequence of events is clear, with a clear beginning and a satisfying conclusion, and she is also attempting to provide transition signals that contribute to coherence. The word "Garph" is her invented transliteration of the Arabic word *jarraf*—a bulldozer, while "alvehim" seems to be her interpretation of "all of them." The dialogue (in italics) adds to the story quality of the text.

In contrast, narratives of the control group children were shorter and lacking in narrative structure as in this sample:

> I see in the story the moon and people running to the person whos sit on the rock and the airplain going down to the ground and the tree and the

train is working and the person is drove the bus and there is night and the sea and the person is working in the sea and the stars in the wind and the axe and the person was happy.

The following reader responses were generated by two fifth-grade children during the experiment to *Children Who Hugged the Mountain* (Ghosn, 1998), a story in which a group of children wants to stop a quarry operation. The first is a letter to the main character, and the second is a diary entry from the same character's perspective.

> Dear Omar
>
> I am happy about you, because you are a good person. You take responsibility of the <u>invironment</u>, because if they destroy the mountain it will be the <u>invironment</u> withoute trees, flowers and a home for the animal, and even the air will be <u>polluted</u> and the people will be sick. Omar you are a <u>smart</u> and you have a good idea.
>
> good luck
>
> Zeinab

It is worth noting that although nearly 90% of the words in the text fall within the first 1000 level words in Laufer and Nation's (1999) Lexical Frequency Profiler, the words "environment" (classified as an academic item), "polluted," and "smart" are beyond the first 2000 level. Both environment and pollution appeared in *Children Who Hugged the Mountain*.

The second sample is a diary entry from the perspective of the main character, Omar (emphases and frames mine):

> Dear [Diary],   Dec. 23, 2003
>
> Today, I had a very big <u>responsibility</u>, one person his name Mr Anazar, he wanted to destroy the mountain where is the <u>nice</u> [cave] that have the [drawings] of the historic people and the [pine] tree where the [owl] have it's <u>nest</u> they will all be gone. Then after a 5 minutes I remembered [Indian] story where a person talled the [villagers] to [huge] the trees then nobody can cut them, I talled all the children to hug the mountain and no body can destroy it then we told Mr. Anazar that if you destroy it your children can't have a nice place to play and keep remembering it and also no plants and no animals to have, and he said stop! Doing this and we had happy
>
> Your friend
>
> Omar

Here, the four underlined words are 2000 level words, while the seven framed words are off-list words in the Lexical Frequency Profiler.

Clay (1991) reports interesting findings from New Zealand, where she compared the reading achievement of young Maori and Samoan children. Although the Maori children entered school with higher oral proficiency in English than the Samoan children, by age six and seven, the Samoan children were outperforming their Maori counterparts in English reading performance. Clay concludes that the difference was a result of the Samoan children's frequent observation of adults' letter-writing practices and their subsequent awareness of writing as an important and valued means of communication. In other words, their view of written texts as meaningful communication had a positive effect on their development as readers.

In summary, second language learners' development as writers will be enhanced when they have plenty of opportunities to write and when writing happens in a warm and supportive environment, where they also receive extensive modeling of writing as a process. One cannot, indeed, over-emphasize the importance of support the young L2 learner must have in order to develop as a writer.

EXPLORING IT

1. Again, examine a young learner ELT course. How many writing tasks are there in each lesson/grade level? What kind of texts are learners expected to produce? Can you think of other types of writing that could be generated from the lessons?
2. Is writing integrated with reading? Is any explicit writing instruction suggested?

11

Literature and School Subjects
Emerging Evidence

> "There's more evidence to come yet, please your Majesty,"
> said the White Rabbit... "this paper has just been picked up."
> —Lewis Carroll, *Through the Looking Glass* (1865/1974, p. 105)

Literature and Mathematics Learning

Although the empirical evidence on the influence of literature on mathematics learning is still fairly limited, it is quite promising, albeit in the first language context. Research in second language settings will be needed to confirm these findings.

Experimental Studies

Jennings, Jennings, Richey, and Dixon-Krauss (1992) conducted an experimental study to teach mathematical concepts and vocabulary to five-year-old kindergarten children. They used 20 children's books in the experimental groups, while the control groups were taught the same concepts and vocabulary using a mathematics textbook. Posttest scores showed experimental groups' gains in concept acquisition were significantly higher than those of the control groups. Observation data revealed experimental groups' children used significantly more mathematics vocabulary from the target list during free play time than the control groups' children. The researchers also report story-group children's interest in mathematics increased.

In another experimental pretest–posttest study, Cordova and Lepper (1996) investigated the effects of computer fantasy on children's intrinsic motivation, task involvement and mathematics achievement. A total of 72 fourth- and fifth-grade children in two schools in San Francisco participated in the study. The experimental group children played math games on the computer involving four different fantasy conditions while the control group children played the game without fantasy context. Cordova and Lepper found statistically significant differences between the experimental and control groups in student enjoyment and willingness to stay on task after class. They also found that the experimental group children used complex operations, such as use of parenthesis, negative numbers and division, significantly more often than the control group children. Moreover, they found a significant effect of experimental treatments on the learning as demonstrated in the posttest.

Casey, Erkut, Ceder, and Young (2008) conducted two experimental studies in the United States to assess the influence of story-based instruction on kindergarten children's development of geometry skills. In the first study, 12 kindergarten classes were randomly assigned to experimental and control groups, with 76 children in the story-based group and 79 in the control group. The second study involved 63 children in four kindergarten classes. The same procedures were applied in both studies. Experimental group teachers were trained to use an adventure story and supplementary materials designed to develop children's spatial reasoning, particularly their ability in spatial visualization and mental rotation, skills that have been associated with mathematical achievement. In the story, characters faced mathematical problems that required children to solve them. Experimental classes received eight story-based lessons with related follow-up activities over a 4-week period, while the control classes received only their regular mathematics curriculum. Analysis of pre- and posttest results yielded statistically significant gains in favor of the story-based group, with the approach particularly beneficial for girls (Casey et al., 2008).

Morgan's (2007) experimental pretest–posttest study involved 72 third-graders in four different classes, two in a school in Texas, and two in Maryland. Thirty-six children were taught multiplication and division using literature and storytelling while the control group received the same content instruction, but without literature. There were two goals set for the groups: (a) multiplication of 2- and 3-digit numbers and (b) division of 2- and 3-digit numbers. Morgan reports that the great majority in the experimental group (84%) benefited from the literature-integrated approach, which also increased children's interest in mathematics.[1]

Beard (2003) investigated the influence of literature-based mathematics instruction on fourth-grade students' mathematics achievement and anxiety. While she found no significant difference between the experimental and control groups' achievement, students who received literature-based instruction indicated they "enjoyed the use of books to teach mathematics concepts" (Beard, 2003, p. 2).

In their two-year study, O'Neill, Pearce, and Pick (2004), investigated the relationship between early narrative ability and later academic achievement. The pretest–posttest study involved 41 three-year-old children. Children were given an adaptation of Mercer Mayers' (1974) picture book *Frog Goes to Dinner*, with no text. Children were first asked to preview the book and tell what was happening in the pictures. Children were then asked to tell the story to a "naïve listener," in this case a Sesame Street character puppet, who had not heard the story before. Children's preview comments and their storytelling were transcribed. Two years later, the same children were assessed on seven measures of narrative ability: mean length of utterance, vocabulary diversity, complex syntax (conjunctions and subordinate clauses), event content, theory of the mind understanding, and perspective-taking/shifting. O'Neill, Pearce, and Pick (2004) report the main findings showing children's narrative ability, particularly event content, perspective-shifting and theory of mind understanding, were significantly correlated with mathematics achievement, while vocabulary diversity correlated with later reading recognition.

Non-Experimental Studies

Ten Black Dots (Crews, 1995) was used by Weinberg (1996), who describes second graders' enthusiastic and thoughtful responses to the story. When children were invited to write their own "ten dots" stories, they had to figure out how many dots they would need for their book if each set of dots could appear only once. This was an easy task for the children, who were then challenged to think how many dots total they would need for their class of 20 children (55 × 20). This proved a more difficult task, but children found creative ways to solve the problem (1,100 dots). Children observed each other's approaches to solving the problem and listened to their reasoning. Weinberg concludes that students are able to solve complex problems at an earlier stage of development than one might assume, provided the problems are presented in the context of a story.

In an after-school day-care setting, Ameis (2002), worked with 13 children (grades one to four) over a period of seven months, during which he used a fictional story to expose the children to mathematical problems. In the story (which Ameis wrote for the study), the characters encounter mathematical problems that children needed to solve before the story could continue. Although most of the problems were very challenging for the children, Ameis did not adjust their difficulty level, as children's self-esteem did not appear to be adversely affected by the task difficulty (Ameis, 2002, para.11). Because children identified with the story characters, they took ownership of the problems, which became authentic for them, and enthusiastically set to solve them and were "ecstatic when they solved one" (ibid). Children's views about the activities were expressed by one of the third-graders: "I love math because you taught it with a story. At school, we just learn it without a story" (Ameis, 2002, para. 10). After the initial confusion Ameis describes, the children were motivated and eagerly participated in solving the problems they encountered in the story.

Jenner (2002) uses storybooks in order to find out what mathematics children discover in the books. She selects books without a specific mathematics focus but that have rich potential for mathematics. She describes the response of a group of second graders to *Selina and the Bear Paw Quilt* (Smucker, 1995). The story presents patterns composed of tessellating geometric shapes. Contrary to Jenner's expectations, children's responses did not center on the patterns, but rather on transformational geometry. Children "squeezed," "squished," and flipped the shapes mentally: "If you were to squeeze these ones back together, that'd make a square" (Jenner, 2002, p. 168), said one student, while another noted "If you put two more triangles there, it'd make a square" (ibid, p. 169). Although the story did not involve explicit mathematics, the children discovered the math in it. Jenner contends that the shared reading experience she employed, in particular, created a safe environment within which children could extend their understanding of geometry. In this case, they were developing the skills Casey and her colleagues (Casey et al., 2008) targeted in their study, namely mental visualization and mental rotation. Jenner also notes that use of literature encourages creativity and reduces anxiety, while offering children highly personal learning experiences and enabling them to "enter a story at their own levels of mathematical curiosity" (Jenner, 2002, p. 167).

Martinie and Bay-Williams (2003) used three different stories to stimulate middle school students' proportional reasoning: *Animal Farm* (Orwell,

1946) for percent increase; *Wilma Unlimited: How Wilma became the World's Fastest Woman* (Krull, 1996) for algebra, and *Jim and the Beanstalk* (Briggs, 1970) for measurement and geography. From their description it is clear that students were highly motivated and rose to the challenges posed by the tasks arising from the stories.

In a kindergarten study, Hong (1996) exposed a group of children to mathematics-related stories through storytelling and another group to non-mathematic-related stories. The results showed that mathematic-based storytelling resulted in better mathematics aptitude, as well as a more positive disposition toward mathematics.

Story-based mathematics instruction appears also to influence teachers' instructional approach and classroom discourse, as Pettig (2002) discovered when she observed three elementary school teachers over one academic year as they integrated literature into their mathematics lessons. She came to the conclusion that when teachers incorporated stories into their lessons, they employed more constructivist, student-centered practices than they did when no literature was involved. She also discovered that discourse in the literature-integrated lessons was more interactive and more aligned with the discourse she observed in the teachers' language arts lessons.

The above evidence suggests that it might be useful to integrate mathematics-related literature into the English language classes where children must study mathematics in English. Even when children study English only as a subject, exposure to mathematics-related literature can enhance their cognitive development.

Literature and Science Learning

Empirical evidence to support the role of literature in science achievement is still surprisingly scant, but children clearly enjoy science literature (Mechling & Oliver, 1983). As Butzow and Butzow note, "A story puts facts and concepts into a form that encourages children to build a hypothesis, predict events, gather data, and test the validity of the events... Using fiction, the lesson becomes relevant and conceptually in tune with the child's abilities" (Butzow & Butzow, 2000, p. 4). They also point out that "well-chosen fiction reinforces the idea that science is part of the lives of ordinary people" (ibid).

In a pretest–posttest experiment DeSpain (1997) exposed two groups of fourth-grade children to a six-week unit on rain forests. The experimental group's instruction was augmented with literature (five non-fiction and five fiction), while the control group was taught using only the textbook.

Examination of the pre- and posttest results revealed that there was no difference in content retention between the two groups, but DeSpain reports children in the literature-incorporated group having enjoyed the stories used. However, it is not clear from her paper exactly how the literature was used, particularly to what extent the teacher helped children relate the fictional stories to rainforests. While three of the non-fiction texts used have explicit information about rainforests, two do not, and only one of the five fiction titles used (*The Great Kapok Tree* by Cherry, 1990) reinforces understanding of the content assessed in the science test. Results may well have been different had the literature selected been more relevant.

Similar findings are reported by Royce (2002), who investigated the effects children's literature on third-graders learning in a six-week unit on invertebrates. Four classes participated in her pretest–posttest study. One group received instruction using a textbook, the second group received instruction using a textbook supplemented with two non-fiction trade books, and the third group received instruction using only four non-fiction trade books. All three groups participated in hands-on activities as well. A control group received no instruction on invertebrates. While Royce found no difference in achievement, she found a significant difference in children's attitude toward science and tradebooks in favor of the literature groups.

Two retrospective studies in Lebanon (Ghosn, 2001a, 2010) found that children in literature-based classes recognized science-related vocabulary significantly better than their age peers in traditional language teaching programs, even when children in both programs were learning science in English. Examination of the literature-based reading anthologies used by some of the schools in the studies revealed several lesson units featuring science-related reading selections, both fiction and non-fiction, about rain forests, weather, pollution, and so on.

Lauritzen and Jaeger (1992) used *The Green Book* by Jill Paton Walsh (1982) with different groups, from fifth-graders to adults. In the story, a group of humans must escape the dying planet Earth to a new planet. The authors report that the motivational appeal of the story gets readers of all ages interested in the science concepts presented in the story, albeit each at their own level. They conclude story "helps us remember; it parallels life; it fosters meaning making; it provides a meaningful context..." (Lauritzen & Jaeger, 1992, p. 10).

Literature and Social Studies Learning

Despite the recommendations by professional social studies organizations and compelling arguments by children's literature experts about use of literature to support the social studies curriculum, there are not many studies on the relationship between student achievement and the use of children's literature in teaching social studies. However, most studies have found literature increases positive attitudes toward social studies.

Howe (1990) examined the effect of historical fiction and the social studies textbook on elementary school students' social studies achievement and attitude toward social studies. Her experimental study involved 168 fifth-grade students in two schools. During American history lessons, the experimental groups' teachers read relevant selections from historical fiction, while in the control classes only the history textbook was used. Howe found that the experimental group did significantly better in a measure of social studies achievement than the control group. She also found a correlation between social studies achievement and attitude toward social studies (Howe, 1990).

Guzzetti, Kowalinski, and McGowan (1992) taught a unit on China to two groups of American sixth graders, one of which was taught with the social studies textbook and the other with children's literature. Both groups received instruction on China for 12.5 hours over a five-week period. Each day's lesson in the literature group began with the teacher reading aloud a narrative selection about China and followed it up with a discussion about the story. The posttest measured concept acquisition and attitude toward social studies and reading. Students taught with children's literature did significantly better in concept acquisition than those taught with the traditional textbook. Interestingly, Guzzetti et al., (1992) report that both groups listed social studies as their least favorite subject, but when they interviewed students, they discovered that the literature group did not consider the unit on China as social studies since no textbook was used.

Other studies have found positive effects primarily in student attitudes. In Swift's (1993) experimental study, four third-grade classes of 75 students were randomly assigned to experimental and control classes for a lesson on American history. In the experimental classes, the teacher read a historical fiction book over four days and discussed the story with the children. The control classes studied the same subject from the textbook. While there were no differences between the groups in the history test, a difference was found in children's attitude toward social studies, with children identifying the subject as "interesting" and "exciting" (Swift, 1993, p. 40).

Reynolds (1995) studied the achievement and higher order thinking skills in a group of 38 fifth-grade students during 15 class periods on the American Revolution. One group was taught using children's books (both fiction and nonfiction), while the other was taught with the regular social studies text. Although the study found no statistically significant difference between the two groups, the literature group consistently had a better attitude toward the class, with the other group frequently complaining about the work they were required to do in their workbooks. Reynolds speculates that the small size of the sample might help explain why no differences emerged. It is possible that with a larger group, more differences would have surfaced. She also points out that since the pre- and posttests included only material that was covered in the textbook, it was not possible to find out what additional content beyond the textbook the literature group might have acquired, a point well worth considering.

Similar results emerged from Corbin's (1990) 12-day study involving 85 fifth-grade students in four schools. While the control classes studied the American Civil War era with a history text, the experimental classes studied the same period with three historical fiction books. The two groups did not differ in their achievement, but Corbin found a significant gain in the literature group's regarding interest in the subject.

Demircioğlu (2008) used historical stories to teach tolerance to Turkish eighth grade students. A teacher-constructed story about life in Ottoman Turkey had students interested and enjoying the story, which Demircioğlu states had a positive impact on students' thinking about diversity and the importance of tolerance.

Walling (1994) conducted a study involving three groups of fifth-graders. The first group was taught social studies with nonfiction materials, the second with both fiction and nonfiction, and the third with only fiction. Although all three groups made gains, Walling asserts that children's literature "satisfies cognitive and affective goals of social studies through expository as well as narrative writing...a combination of children's literature, both fiction and nonfiction, may be utilized effectively in the social studies classroom to teach not only facts but also concepts" (Walling, 1994, p. 75). McKinney and Jones (1992) arrived at similar conclusions with a study involving nonfiction literature.

A retrospective study in Lebanon (Ghosn, 2010) supports Walling's assertion about concept learning. The study compared 10–11-year olds' vocabulary and reading comprehension in six schools, three using American literature-based reading anthologies and three using a traditional skills-based ELT course. After five years of study, children were administered a reading test, which includes a subtest of social studies vocabulary, with some concepts specific to American society. For example, children needed to be able to associate "candidate," "governor," and "congressman" with "politician" and "congressman"; "outpost," "pioneer," and "westernmost" with "settler" and "trapper"; and "Comanche," "Mohawk," and "Sioux" with "Chippewa" and "Cherokee." Children who were taught with literature-based anthologies were able to make such associations significantly better than their counterparts in the traditional language program, as many of these concepts appeared in their literature selections.

In summary, although experts recommend the use of literature to complement mathematics, science, and social studies textbooks, empirical research is limited, particularly in science and social studies. However, the research cited above consistently shows that (a) children learn mathematics, science, and social science from literature and from textbooks *equally well* and sometimes better with literature; and (b) literature has a positive influence on children's attitudes toward these subjects. These two findings are important; if literature improves attitudes without any detrimental effect, its use is well justified. The above cited research has investigated children's subject matter achievement primarily in first language settings, and it would, therefore be important to extend studies into contexts where English language learners must access school subjects in English. Exposure to mathematics, science, and social studies related children's literature, when used in an English class, can introduce students to concepts they will need to study in English later on.

EXPLORING IT

1. Talk to the math, science or social studies teacher of your English language learners to identify some of the learning objectives set for them in these subjects. Obtain one of the trade books mentioned in Chapter five that matches with the learning objectives. Read the story to your students and engage them in a discussion about the concepts and plan for some follow-up activities.
2. If you are the classroom teacher in charge of other subjects as well, plan a complete math or social studies lesson unit around one of the trade books mentioned that is aligned with your learning objectives.

Note

1. One must take Morgan's report with some caution, as his literature review presents some inaccurate accounts of prior studies.

PART **III**

Eyewitness Accounts
One Story, Different Paths

From the classroom vignettes in this part, a practical model for literature-based instruction emerges, which is sufficiently general to be applicable in a variety of cultural contexts and within the many curricular constraints that teachers in different parts of the world operate. Literature- or story-based instruction observed typically occurs in four phases, somewhat analogous to a journey. First, the teacher prepares the children for their journey to the story world, and in Chapter 12 we will see different teachers do that using often very different approaches. In Chapter 13, we observe teachers guide their students through the story and see how teachers invite children to reflect on their experience and respond to the story. Finally, in Chapter 14, children are given meaningful reasons to re-visit the story, and in Chapter 15, we find out how some teachers link stories to school subjects. The vignettes illustrate the adaptability of the approach to diverse contexts. Just as one can choose to take a brisk, guided tour through the main sights of a new town or take one's time exploring the winding narrow alleyways, teachers can structure the journey through a story in multiple different ways. Figure P3.1 shows the stages in the process, and the classroom vignettes illustrate the diversity of possibilities for application.

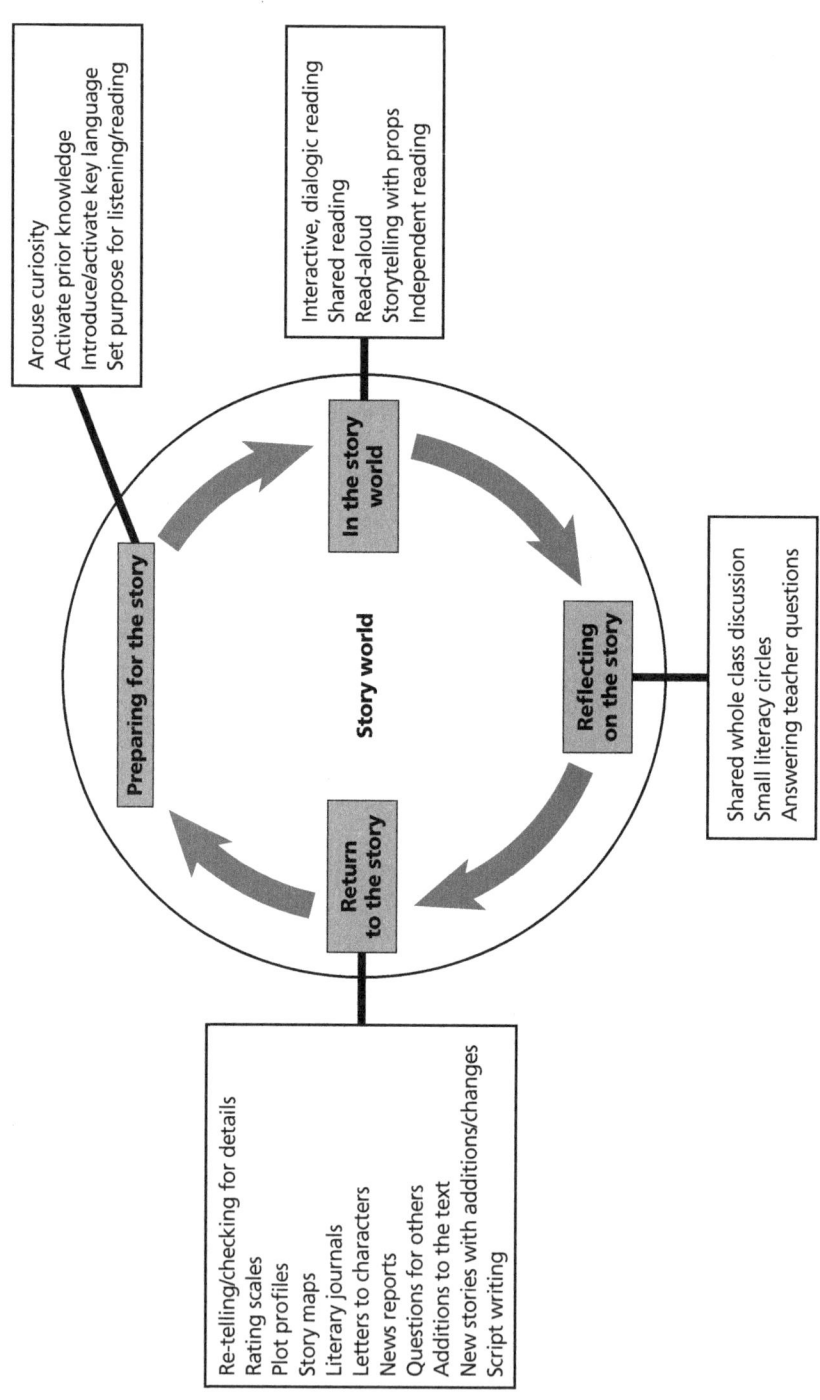

Figure P3.1 Journey through a story.

12

Preparing for the Story Journey

"Would you tell me, please, which way I ought to go from here?"
"That depends a good deal on where you want to get to," said the Cat.
—(Lewis Carroll, *Alice's Adventures in Wonderland*, 1865/1974, p. 61)

Teachers and Their Classes

In this part of the book, we will visit classrooms of ten different teachers who either use literature-based programs or who supplement their language teaching courses with trade books. Five classrooms are in English-as-the-first-foreign language (EFL1) schools. In three of them, children study mathematics and science in English from the onset of schooling. In the other two, children study English 7 hours a week and other school subjects in Arabic until grade three, when partial English-medium instruction is introduced in mathematics and science. Five classrooms are in English-as-the-second-foreign language (EFL2) schools, where children learn English as a subject two to 3 hr a week and study content area subjects in French. All teachers have a minimum of three years of university education and some hold also additional teaching credentials. Table 12.1 presents a brief description of the classes visited.

TABLE 12.1 Teachers and Their ELT Programs

Teacher	Program	Grade Visited	Hours of English Language	Onset of English Instruction	Type of Texts
Daisy	EFL1	KG	7	KG	"Big books" Picturebooks
Zinnia	EFL1 English math, science, IT	1	7	KG	Literature-based reading anthology
Marigold	EFL2 French math, science, IT	1	1	1	"Big books" Picturebooks
Jasmine	EFL2 French math, science, IT	3	2	2	Content-integrated ESL course
Rowan	EFL1 Arabic math, science in grades K–2 English math, science from grade 3	3	7	1	ESL course Trade books
Dahlia	EFL2 French math, science, IT	4	2	2	ESL course Storytelling
Lily	EFL1 English math, science, IT	4/5	7	KG	Literature-based reading anthology Trade books
Violet	EFL1 Arabic math, science in grades 1–3 English math, science from grade 4	6	7	1	Literature-based reading anthology

English as a First Foreign Language (EFL1)

Daisy teaches second-year kindergarten in a small rural EFL1 school. Her students, who are five years old, began English language and literacy learning in their first kindergarten year at age four, 7 hr a week, simultaneously with Arabic literacy instruction. *Zinnia* teaches grades one, two, and three in the same school as Daisy. Children have seven weekly hours of English, 5 hr of math, and 2 hr of science in English. We will visit her first grade class. *Rowan* teaches English and science in grades three and four in a small-town EFL1 school, where children begin to learn English as a subject in kindergarten but learn other subjects in Arabic until grade three, when English-medium instruction (EMI) is introduced in math and science. We will visit his third grade class. *Lily* teaches English and mathematics in grades four and five in an EFL1 school in the capital, Beirut. Children begin learning English in kindergarten and EMI in mathematics and science is introduced in grade one. We will visit both of her English classes. *Violet* teaches English in grades six, seven, and eight in an urban EFL1 school with a similar program to that of Rowan's school. We will visit her sixth grade class.

English as a Second Foreign Language (EFL2)

English as the second foreign language programs in Lebanon are similar to typical EFL programs, where children study English as a subject and other school subjects in their mother tongue. However, in Lebanon, many EFL2 schools teach school subjects in French, a legacy of the 23-year French mandate in the early 20th century. Hours of English language instruction in EFL2 schools typically range from one to three weekly hours. We visit five EFL2 classes, all in schools where children study most academic subjects in French.

Marigold teaches grades one, two, and three in a suburban EFL2, and we will visit her first grade class. *Jasmine* teaches also grades one, two, and three in an urban EFL2 school, and we will visit her third grade class. *Rose* and *Iris* teach grades two and three in small-town schools. We will visit Rose's second grade class and Iris' third grade class. *Dahlia* teaches English in grades four, five, and six in an EFL2 school in a suburban community. We will visit her fourth-grade class.

Getting Ready for the Story

Visiting a storyworld—whether it will be by listening or by reading—is not unlike embarking on a journey; some preparation is needed for a successful and satisfying trip. Student engagement with the story is often, if not always, influenced by the way the story is introduced. The "luggage" learners bring with them include knowledge, or schemata, about language and how it works, about the topic at hand, and what they know about different types of texts. Well planned introductions help activate the schemata and any key language, facilitating engagement and comprehension. Stimulating introduction is particularly critical to motivate children who have experienced limited success in language learning or reading.

When proficient readers prepare to read a book, they first look at the cover, reading the title and the author's name. They read any information available on the book jacket, and often also flip through the beginning pages, before they decide whether to read the book or not. Surprisingly, a three-year study conducted by the National Language Research Center in the United States shows that very few primary school children in second language immersion programs pay attention to the title of storybooks they are about to read. Yet, the title, alongside the cover art, usually offers the first clue as to what the story might be about and thus also the first opportunity to activate any prior knowledge and to set expectations. A good example of a "clue-rich" title and cover is Judith Viorst's *Alexander and the Terrible, Horrible, No Good, Very Bad Day*, in which the cover illustration complements the title. Young readers will be eager to read the story in order to learn the exact nature of Alexander's misery and how it might compare with their own experiences. "Picture walk" examination of story illustrations is another way to get children to make predictions about stories. However, the picture walk should not reveal any surprise ending of a story, which should be left to be discovered.

Pictures and objects can be used to introduce key vocabulary and concepts, while brainstorming is a useful way to activate prior knowledge or to arouse curiosity. Let us visit three teachers' classrooms to see how they use distinctly different approaches in preparing their students for a journey to the story world.

Jasmine's Third-Grade EFL2 Class

Jasmines third-grade EFL2 class is in a school in Beirut, a cosmopolitan city rich in environmental print in English and French. Thus, although children learn French as the first foreign language, many would have encountered some English outside the class. This is the eight-year-olds' second year of learning English 2 hours a week. Jasmine describes herself as a traditional language teacher and says she makes frequent use of pictures, vocabulary cards, and *realia*. She likes to run an orderly class, where she is in total control of what goes on. She has a rigid schedule and high expectations of her 28 students, and they seem to respond well to her approach. She is preparing her class for *The Doorbell Rang* by Pat Hutchins (1986).

Jasmine has twelve large chocolate chip cookies on a tray on her desk. The cookies are spread out for easy counting.

> **T:** Grade 3, what do I have here? [points to the cookies]
> **Ss:** ((cookies!)) ((Biscuit! Biscuit!))
> **T:** ((Biscuit)) in French. In English we say <u>cookies</u>, <u>cookies</u>. I have some cookies here.

[Jasmine puts up a card with the word "cookies" printed next to a photo of a plate of cookies cut from a magazine.]

> **Ss:** Cookies!
> **T:** How many cookies do I have here? Who wants to come and count the cookies?
> **Ss:** Me! Miss! Please, me Miss! [Several hands go up, children eagerly bidding for turns.]

The teacher selects three children, one after the other, to come and count the cookies. She repeats the word "cookies" several times, alternately sweeping her hand under the word on the board and pointing to the cookies on the tray. Next, Jasmine introduces the word *share*, which is problematic for many Arabic speakers, who tend to use it as students one and two in the following transcript.

> **T:** Would you like to taste the cookies?
> **Ss:** Yes! Miss, yes! Oui, Miss!
> **T:** Very well, we will <u>share</u> the cookies. Each one will have some. We will <u>share</u> them. [Puts up a card with a picture of two children sharing an ice-cream sundae and the text They share some ice-cream.] We will <u>share</u> the cookies. Who can give me a sentence with the word <u>share</u>?
> **S1:** I share my sister ((my chocolate)).
> **T:** You <u>share</u> your chocolate <u>with</u> your sister. That's nice of you, Raya, to <u>share</u> your chocolate <u>with</u> her. The two of you share the chocolate. Anyone else? Yes, Patricia.
> **S2:** My brother ((never)) share me his candy.

T: Your brother never <u>shares</u> his candy <u>with</u> you. ((Are you sure? I think he does sometimes.)) We say we <u>share</u> something <u>with</u> someone. We can also say we share something <u>between</u> us, or just we <u>share</u> something. [Jasmine solicits few more sentences about sharing and continues]:

T: Mmm! Delicious! Good, these cookies look delicious. Delicious. We are all going to <u>share</u> them. Each one will have a piece. Who would like to come and taste the cookies?

Jasmine breaks the cookies into pieces, and when each child has had their share, she points to the empty tray and says, "What happened to the cookies? Where did they go? We shared the cookies!" The children chorus, "We shared the cookies!" She confirms it by repeating "Yes, we shared the cookies between us." She then tells the class that they will read a story about some children sharing cookies. She has the full attention of the class, with several children calling out "Story! Story!"

Zinnia's First-Grade EFL1 Class

Zinnia offers a very different introduction to *The Doorbell Rang*. The 25 first-graders in her EFL1 class have been introduced to English in kindergarten and are now also learning math and science in English. The class has 7 hr of English a week. Zinnia says she rarely pre-teaches vocabulary when using storybooks but prefers rather to work on vocabulary within the story context and during follow up activities. She draws children's attention to the author, with whose work children are already familiar. Children in literature-rich classes eagerly look for titles by authors whose work they have enjoyed.

T: OK, grade one. It's story time. Are you all ready?

Ss: Yes, Miss! Yes!

T: Let us see the cover. [Shows the cover to the class.] The title of the story is The Doorbell Rang. The Doorbell Rang [pointing to the words]. The author is Pat Hutchins, Pat Hutchins. Do you remember any other stories we read by this same author, Pat Hutchins?

S1: Miss! The story ((where the wind blew everything)).

T: Very good, Hala. That story was The Wind Blew, and it was also written by Pat Hutchins. Now, grade one, look at the|

S2: |Miss! Who make the pictures?

T: Oh, you mean who illustrated the story?

S2: Yes, Miss.

T: The illustrator is also Pat Hutchins. She did the story and the pictures, she made the illustrations.

S2: Oh, ((she is very clever!))

T: Yes. She is very <u>talented</u>. OK, now. Look at the cover illustration. What do you see?

Ss: Children!

T: Right. There are children. How many children are there? Wissam?

S3: [Goes to the teacher and begins counting.] One, two, three, four, five, six, seven, eight, nine, ten, eleven, twelve. Twelve, Miss.

T: Very good, Wissam. There are twelve children. What about the lady?

S1: ((She is the maid, because she has a broom)).

T: So you think she is a helper?

S1: Uhuh.

S4: No! She the mother. Look! She white. Maids they are ((dark skinned)).[1]

T: Hadia, let's use the word "helper," OK? We will find out who she is when we read. Now, look at the children. What do you think they are doing?

S1: Miss! They ((they are peeking through the door))!

T: Right. It looks like this boy here is peeking through the mailbox. See the mailbox? What do you think|

S5: |Miss, what's a mailbox?

T: Oh, yeah, a mailbox. A mailbox is this opening in the door. The mailman puts in letters, magazines and whatever mail you get. Well, we don't usually have mailboxes in our doors ((because we have no mailman [laughs] we must go to the post office to get our mail)). Anyway, what do you think is on the other side? Let's find out. Are you all ready?

Ss: Yes, Miss!

Notice how student S1 resorts to her mother tongue and how Zinnia validates the contribution, recasting it into English. Thus, the student continues to participate in the discourse. We will return to the class later to see how Zinnia takes her class through the story experience.

In Rose's Second-Grade EFL2

In the next episode, grade two teacher, Rose, is preparing her students (ages 7–8) for a trickster tale, their second such story of the month. The class has received English language instruction for three years, and the following discussion was recorded towards the end of the school year. Rose displays on the board pictures of a tiger, a rabbit, a monkey, a turtle, a mouse, and a toucan, and labels them.

    T: What did I write? [points to the words]
    Ss: Tiger, rabbit, mouse, monkey, turtle, toucan!
    T: What are all these?
    Ss: Animals!
    T: Remember not to talk without raising your finger. Take one minute to think about these animals, and when you finish I would like each one of you to give me only one word describing each animal.
    T: Let's begin with the tiger.
    S1: Mean
    T: That's great [writes the word on the board]
    S2: Strong
    T: Good. What else?
    S3: Striped
    T: OK.
    S4: Big
    T: OK. That's enough. Let's move now to the rabbit.

Children describe all the six animals and the teacher lists their descriptions on the board. Twenty-two children contribute a word each during the first part of the lesson.

    T: Who knows what a toucan is?
    S3: It's a kind of birds.
    T: Bravo. It's a bird. Who can describe the toucan [point to the picture]
    T: [some students raise their fingers] Yes, Tara
    S2: Lazy?
    T: Nice description. Why lazy?
    S2: [shrugs and smiles]
    S3: Flies high

T: Good going. Birds fly high.

S4: Long beak

T: Excellent, it does have a long beak. These are the characters that you will be seeing in your story today [writes "rabbit" and "tiger" on the board].

T: Open your book on page 49, flip through the pages and tell me what is the difference between this story and the one we read before.

T: [Several students begin talking excitedly] Yes, Rami.

S1: The characters are different.

T: Good, Rami. You noticed that the characters are not the same as in the other story.

S2: Many animals in the story.

T: That's right, Jasmina. There are many animals in the story.

S3: The name of the animal and what is saying

T: Excellent, Jawdat. We know what each animal is saying. So, it is a? [looking around the class]

T: [no response from the class] This is a dialogue and the story you will listen to in a few minutes is a play. In this play, we have characters they are animals.

S4: It's a trickster?

T: Ah. So, you think it is a trickster tale. And, Joseph, who do you think will trick the other?

S5: The rabbit will trick the tiger.

T: Why do you think so?

S5: Because the rabbit is smarter than the tiger.

T: OK. We will see if the rabbit is smarter than the tiger. You might be right.

T: Before I play the tape, I want you to know that the black sentences [in the book] refer to each animal speech and the red ones explain how the animals are acting. Did you understand me? Now, listen carefully.

The class is now ready for the story. We will return to this class later on to see what happens.

In Iris' Third-Grade EFL2 Class

Iris's students have received formal English instruction for three and a half years, and study mathematics and science in French. Here, Iris is encouraging children to make predictions from the title and cover art before reading to them Andersen's familiar classic, *The Ugly Duckling*. Iris has prepared a "big book" version of the story by enlarging it on A4 size pages, with large print and enlarged photocopied illustrations from her original trade book. She has simplified the story by reducing the number of events and sentences, and she has also simplified the grammar, but has retained the simple past tense verbs. While young children may not use the story title for predictions, they often use pictures to predict story events and also to elaborate on the text

    T: Let's take a look at the title of our story. Who would like to read it?
    S1: [reads] The ugly duck..duck.ling
    T: Very good. The ugly duckling. Let's look at the picture on the cover here. What do you see?
    S2: A bird
    S3: A bird and ((a rock))
    T: Yes, there's a bird [points], and there's something behind the bird. Jesse said it's a rock.
    S2: No, the bird it come from the egg
    T: Ah! So you think that this [points] is an egg and that this bird came out of the egg. What makes you think that?
    S2: There [points] it is break
    T: Yes, it looks like the egg is broken, like there's a crack here [points]
    S1: Miss the Pokemon it [makes a smashing sound and hits one fist with another]
    S3: Miss, the bird it it is ugly?
    T: What do you think? Is it an ugly bird?
    Ss: No!
    S2: Miss, the bird it [makes a sad face]
    T: You think that the bird is sad?
    S4:   sad!
    S2:   Yes, Miss.
    T: Let's read to find out why the story is called The Ugly Duckling, OK.

Predictions provide a purpose for listening, as children will want to check whether their predictions were accurate. When inviting predictions, it is important to keep in mind that all predictions are of equal value; there are no "right" or "wrong" predictions, as long as one has some basis for making them. Asking for justification also gives the teacher an opportunity to model questioning. When there are many different predictions, they can be listed on the board, and after reading, students can examine the various predictions. Some of the predictions that are not confirmed in the story might have been valid as well. While the primary goal is to develop language, students' thinking skills are fostered as well. Students begin to realize that there are often many possibilities, many different hypotheses, and that, while some are more plausible than others, all need to be tested or verified.

In a language class, predictions offer an ideal, natural opportunity to introduce and/or review the use of future and past tense verbs, and as children offer their ideas, Iris records their predictions on the board:

> T: [writes on the board]
>
> *Jumana thinks the bird came out of the egg.*
> *Rania thinks the bird is sad.*
> *Wissam thinks the bird is sad.*
> *Samer thinks a Pokemon broke the egg.*

Since it is important to record all offered predictions, in a large class of 35, it might be wise to ask for a fixed, reasonable number of suggestions and not try to record 35 of them! Note that Iris accepts Samer's suggestion about "Pokemon" and lists it as equally valid with the other ideas. As often happens, more than one similar suggestion is offered, and the teacher combines the suggestions, at the same time modeling compound subject use and singular/plural verb use:[2]

> T: Uhm. Let's see what you have predicted. Here, *Rania thinks*... and *Wissam thinks*... We can combine them, so we'll have more space here. Let's see... [edits the text on the board] So, we can say *Rania and Wissam think the bird is sad.* See, we don't need the –s here anymore, because we have Rania and Wissam, we have two persons.

In Dahlia's Fourth-Grade EFL2 Class

In the following episode, Dahlia prepares to take her 11-year-olds into the classic trickster tale, *Stone Soup*. Children have been learning English as the second foreign language for three and a half years. Dahlia frequently supplements her ELT coursebook lessons with storytelling and occasional trade books. Now, she begins by showing the class a round, smooth stone:

> **T:** What do I have here? What is this? [showing the class a stone]
> **Ss:** ((a stone))
> **T:** That's right. It's a <u>stone</u>, a nice, white round <u>stone</u>. What can, what could we do with this stone?

Some of the boys immediately propose a number of ways to use the stone as a weapon, but Dahlia challenges them to find other, non-violent uses for the stone. As children brainstorm different possible uses for the stone, Dahlia lists their suggestions on the board. Most of the suggestions are in French and Arabic, but the teacher recasts them into English, thus validating all contributions. Some of their suggestions were to use the stone as a paperweight; secure the beach towel with it when it's windy; crack almonds with it; use it as a doorstop; use it in a stone-kicking competition; use it as a marker in ball toss; paint it and use it as a decoration. Dahlia then poses the question that hooks the class:

> **T:** Do you think we could use, use this stone to make food?
> **Ss:** ((Food?)) No! No! ((Nobody can make food with a stone!))
> **T:** Well, guess what, today I'm going to tell you a story called *Stone Soup*.
> **Ss:** Stone soup? ((Stone soup?))
> **T:** Uhuh, yes. Let's see how someone can make soup with a stone.

Children are all ears as Dahlia begins to tell the story.

<u>THINK ABOUT IT</u>

1. Which teacher's approach to introducing a story appeals to you most? Why?
2. Do you think some of these approaches would appeal to your students? Why or why not?

Notes

1. Lebanese middle and upper class families typically have live-in domestic workers, the majority from the Philippines, Sri Lanka and Ethiopia. Socially conscious teachers are trying to get children to use the term "helper" rather than "maid."
2. While the National Curriculum in Lebanon does not recommend explicit teaching of grammatical structures before Grade four, in many schools grammar instruction begins in Grade two.

13

The Story Experience

> *Alice started to her feet... and burning with curiosity, she ran across the field after it... down a large rabbit-hole under the hedge.*
> —Lewis Carroll, *Alice's Adventures in Wonderland* (1865/1974, p. 10)

In the Story World

When reading picture storybooks with young learners (or older beginners), an interactive, "dialogic" approach enables teachers to emphasize new vocabulary and structures and to clarify meanings naturally in context. During reading, children are invited to affirm or negate teacher comments, make predictions, and point to the illustrations. The approach works well with beginners of all ages. The teacher ought to be tuned to student leads, however. While predictions, questions and examination of illustrations will help children maintain attention, attempts to engage them in a dialogue when they are intensely involved with the plot can be frustrating for them.

In Zinnia's First-Grade EFL1 Class

Let us return to Zinnia's first grade class, where she engages children in dialogic reading of *The Doorbell Rang*.

> **T:** [reads] *"I've made some cookies for tea," said Ma.*
>
> **S1:** The lady she the mother ((not the maid like Hadia said))!
>
> **T:** Right, she is Sam's and Victoria's mother. See the cookies she has made [points to the illustration]. Mmm! That's a big plate of cookies.
>
> **S1:** [Several children lick their lips and make "mmm" sounds.] Miss! Me, my mother she make cookies ((very tasty)).
>
> **T:** Oh, your mother makes delicious cookies too! Did you hear that grade one? Ruba's mother makes delicious cookies, just like Sam's and Victoria's mother. [Several more children offer information about their mothers' and grandmothers' cookies and cakes, and Zinnia briefly entertains their contributions.]
>
> **T:** [reads] *"No one makes cookies like Grandma,"* when the doorbell rang. Who do you think that is? Let's see who is coming [. . .] [after two more doorbells] *"Nobody makes cookies like Grandma,"said Ma as the doorbell rang.* Oh-o! Who do you think it is?
>
> **Ss:** More friends! ((more friends!))
>
> **T:** OK. Let's see who is coming.

The dialogic, interactive approach engages the children, and Zinnia skillfully paraphrases and recasts children's Arabic utterances, modeling correct English without overt correction. Children's mother tongue contributions provide her with a resource to draw on. She pays particular attention to a typical error her Arabic-speaking students make: "My mother *she* makes cookies" and "The book *it* was on the table."[1] Recasting does not necessarily result in immediate self-correction, as Lyster and Ranta (1997) have pointed out, because children will need to unlearn the forms transferred from their mother tongue. Exposure to rich, natural language typical of quality children's literature will facilitate the procedural memory's processing of the correct structures to the cerebellum.

In Jasmine's Third-Grade EFL2 Class

Jasmine reads the same story to her third graders, but, unlike Zinnia, she stops at the end of each page to ask comprehension questions:

T: So, what did Sam and Victoria's mother make? What did she make?
Ss: Cookies!
T: Correct. She made some <u>cookies</u>. Here are the cookies [pointing to the illustration]. Did she make little or plenty of cookies? Little or <u>plenty</u>?
Ss: Plenty!
T: Right. She made <u>plenty</u> of cookies, she made many cookies. Where are Sam and Victoria sitting? Where are they?
Ss: ((Kitchen!))
T: Yes, they are sitting in the <u>kitchen</u>. What is Sam holding [points to the illustration]?
Ss: A cat! ((a cat!))

Children are clearly enthusiastic and participate eagerly, using both their mother tongue and French as need arises.

Marigold's First-Grade EFL2 Class

Marigold employs a dialogic approach in reading *The Rabbit and the Turnip* to her first graders. This delightful "big book" story is from Addison Wesley's out-of-print ESL series, *Amazing English*. The story, although written with language learners in mind, is aligned with the definition of children's literature posited by Goforth (1998) and cited in Chapter 1. The theme of sharing is relevant and meaningful to young children; the use of past and future tense verbs renders the language more natural than in typical ELT coursebooks of this level; and the repetitious refrains offer immediate short-cuts to the new language.

T: *Little Rabbit found two turnips.* See, here [pointing] are two turnips.
S1: ((What is)) turnip?
T: Uhuh, turnip, let me see, yes, it's ((turnip)), ((turnip)) is turnip in Arabic. I don't remember what the French word is. So, here's the turnip.
Ss: Turnip!
T: Yes. He is gobbling up the turnip ((gobbling it all up)). Who can come and point to the other turnip? [A child gets up to point]. Right. That's the turnip. *He gobbled one right up. He wanted the other turnip. Then he thought* [puts index finger on her forehead] *about his friend Little Donkey.* [turns the page] *"Little Donkey is probably hungry, too. I'll take this turnip to him." Little Donkey was not at home.*

Little Rabbit left the turnip on his doorstep. See, here is Little Donkey. He is coming home. What is this here on his doorstep? [Points to the turnip.] What is this?

Ss: Turnip! ((turnip))

Throughout the reading, Marigold uses gestures to help clarify meaning.

In Rose's Second-Grade EFL2

Let us return to Rose's class to observe how the children work through their story. The teacher plays the tape while students follow in their books. She stops the tape at the end of each page to ask questions, following what is reminiscent of Stauffer's (1969) Directed Reading and Thinking Approach (DR-TA), originally developed for native English-speakers' reading instruction. This approach lends itself particularly well for story reading in second language classrooms where children are not yet independent readers. The approach is similar to the dialogic approach but much more structured, with the teacher in control of the discourse. The aim is both to get children to think about the story and to introduce, activate, or reinforce key language. The approach must be used with caution, however, as stopping at too many points or asking too many questions can destroy the flow of the story. This is how it worked in Rose's class:

T: So, now what are the characters?
S1: Tiger, rabbit, turtle, monkey, mouse, and toucan.
T: What is the problem?
S2: The tiger bulling [sic] them.
T: Yes, Kamal. The tiger is bullying them. What is the meaning of bullying?
S3: Tricking?
T: Not exactly. It means bothering, scaring, being rude to them, chases them.
T: [students listen to the second page] Who do you think will help them?
S1: The rabbit.
T: Why do you think the rabbit will help?
Ss: [unintelligible]
T: Do you still remember the word "bargain"? What deal did the rabbit make with the tiger? If . . . ? [no response]

T: It means a "deal" and people shake hands when they make a bargain [shakes some students hand] Who knows what the bargain was?

S4: If the rabbit rides on the back of the tiger before sun set the tiger will leave Puerto Rico.

T: Fantastic! But what else?

S5: But if he doesn't do this he will eat the rabbit.

T: Good remembering, Ghassan. What do you think will happen now?

In Dahlia's Fourth-Grade EFL2 Class

Dahlia uses storytelling to take her fourth graders through the *Stone Soup*, following an approach demonstrated by Ghosn (2005). She has prepared laminated picture cards of a variety of local vegetables (tomatoes, potatoes, carrots, onions and turnips), and pictures of a man and an old woman.

T: Let us see if we can make some stone soup. [Children giggle.] Long, long time ago, a tired and <u>hungry</u> man [tapes the picture of a man on the board] came to a village [draws some houses and trees on the board next to the man]. The man was <u>very</u> <u>hungry</u> [rubs her stomach], very <u>hungry</u>. He saw an old woman [tapes a picture of an old woman and her house on the board]. Here's the old woman in front of her house.

Dahlia tells the story with much expression. When she gets to the part where the old woman brings out a kettle, Dahlia sets a cooking pot and a wooden spoon on her desk, puts the stone into the pot, and continues the story:

T: "The soup <u>would</u> <u>be</u> better <u>if</u> <u>we</u> <u>had</u> some potatoes," said the man. "But we <u>don't</u> <u>have</u> any." And he stirred the water in the pot [stirs the imaginary soup in the pot with the spoon]. "I think I have some potatoes," said the old woman and went into her house [moves the picture of the woman towards the house and back]. "Here are four potatoes," [picks up laminated pictures of potatoes] said the old woman. One, two, three, four potatoes. She put them into the pot [puts the potato pictures into the pot one at a time].

She continues in the same manner with the rest of the vegetables, carefully repeating the key vocabulary. She stirs the pot and sniffs at the imaginary aroma of soup. Soon many of the children are joining in repeating "But we do not have any" and "I think I have some..." The class is thoroughly enjoying the experience.

In Iris' Third-Grade EFL2 Class

Using the "big book" she has prepared, Iris leads the class through the story. She reads the story sentence by sentence, using a ruler to point to the words. She invites the class to repeat each sentence. She takes the class through a second choral reading, and then invites children to take turns to read the sentences. This may resemble the old *round-robin*, identified and named by Austin and Morrison in 1963, where students take turns reading a few sentences, which the teacher follows with comprehension questions or questions about vocabulary. But, Iris does not stop to ask comprehension questions at this stage, and children appear comfortable with her approach and eagerly wait for their turn to go to the front to read their sentence. The story is read this way a number of times.

When she finishes, Iris checks the predictions children generated earlier, and uses this context to introduce the past tense of verb "think":

> T: Let's take a look at our predictions. *Rania and Wissam think the bird is sad.* So, they <u>thought</u> [corrects the verb, underlining it] the bird was sad. Was their prediction OK? Was the bird sad?

In Violet's Sixth-Grade EFL1 Class

Violet's sixth grade EFL1 students are independent readers and need a purpose for their reading to help them maintain focus and facilitate their comprehension. To guide her students through Sharon Bell Mathis' (1975) *Hundred Penny Box*, Violet provides them with the following questions:

1. Why is Aunt Dew living with Michael's family?
2. Why does Michael's mother want to throw Aunt Dew's hundred penny box away?
3. What does Michael want to do with the box and why?
4. How is Aunt Dew's box like Michael's teddy bear? How is it different?

Students are expected to jot down the answers in their notebooks for a later discussion in class. The purpose of the questions is not to test students but simply focus their reading and provide guidance for the discussion and other tasks to follow. Violet circulates among the students, and when she notes that the slowest readers have begun to work on the questions (by this time, the fastest readers are usually working on the last question), she calls the class together. It is not necessary for everyone to finish answering the questions in writing, because the questions will be answered during the discussion that follows. Instead of questions, she sometimes gives students a table to fill, a list to compile, or some other task associated with the class objectives. For example, when the class was reading Moskin's (1978) *Day of the Blizzard*, she asks the class to make a list of all instances where Katie, the main character, showed courage.

Teachers in the above examples use very different approaches when guiding their students through the story, and each seems to be working.

Reflecting on the Story Experience

When we return from an enjoyable trip, we reflect on the experience and usually share it with others, but children need time to think before responding and sharing their reflections. In beginning level classes, children should not be expected to respond in English, of course. A meaningful discussion is possible even with young beginners if we allow children to use whatever language they have as we have already seen in the earlier classroom vignettes. (This is possible only when teachers share children's L1 or have at least some level of command of it.)

Research shows that, when faced with questions that can be answered in one or two words, that is precisely what students do. Hence "Did you like the story?" will probably generate either *yes* or *no* answers. In contrast, open-ended questions generate longer and syntactically more complex responses (Kubota, 1989; Ghosn, 2001). "What do you think (about the story)?" will allow for each child's own interpretation, what they thought was meaningful or important, or what they found confusing. Open-ended questions will invite children's own thoughts and ideas to come forth. At times, a brief silence following the reading will elicit more interesting responses from the class than teacher questions. After children's responses, any remaining predictions and pre-reading questions can be discussed. Throughout the discussion, children's interests and concerns guide the discourse. Needless to say, teacher-provided questions that address predictions made before reading or questions about characters, setting and plot are equally appropriate as determined by the intended learning outcomes.

Readers' Aesthetic Responses

The teachers featured in this chapter provide a variety of reader response activities, both efferent and aesthetic. Rosenblatt (1991) defines efferent responses as those where the reader obtains information from the text, while aesthetic responses imply reader's emotional and intellectual involvement with the text. Sebesta, Monson, and Senn (1995) have categorized aesthetic responses into a nine-level hierarchy. In the first level response, children *re-live the story* when they remember a vivid or a cozy scene. For example, one of Zinnia's first graders said she could still smell the cookies Sam and Victoria's mother made. *Imagining or picturing* characters, setting, or events from the story is another basic response. An example of this is provided by a student, S2, in the episode from Lily's fifth grade class, where another student (S1) is sharing a personal story with the class:

S1: One day I climbed a high wall in [a place with a climbing wall]. It was fun! But it was also ((scary)). They put ((a rope)) on me like|

S2: |Miss! He was talking about a parachute? It has a [unintelligible] and he does like this [waves arms indicating gliding motion].

A story can also remind the reader about a *personal experience*. The following two examples illustrate this level of response. McConaghy tells of a little six-year-old girl's response to the story *Bus Ride* (Jewell, 1978), in which an elderly woman and a child develop a friendship during a bus ride and part company, knowing that they probably will never see each other again. After hearing the story, the little girl said:

> That story reminds me of when I go to the doctor's office. Sometimes I meet a friend and we play and then she goes into her doctor and I go to mine and we never see each other again. (McConaghy, 1990, p. 36)

In Violet's sixth grade class, a student applied his personal experience to *The Hundred Penny Box* the class was reading:

T: Yes, Hassan?
S1: Miss, my grandfather he live with us. He always forgets things.
T: What kind of things?
S1: [laughing] he always forgets my name, Miss.
T: He forgets your name?
S1: Yes, Miss. Me and my brother's ((he calls me Hani, that's my brother, and he calls him Hassan)).
T: You mean he confuses the names of you and your brother?
S1: Yes, Miss.

S2: He has five brothers, Miss! That's why.

T: So you think he forgets because they are five boys?

S1: No, Miss. He forgets because he is old, like Michael's grandmother.

Teachers can encourage children to relate the story to their own life experience by asking questions such as the following: "Has anything like this happened to you?" "Have you ever seen something similar?"

Applying other reading or media to the story is the fourth level response in Sebesta et al. (1995) hierarchy. For example, children might compare a story with other stories that have a similar theme, or a different theme but similar characters or setting. An example is offered by one fourth grader in Lily's class when children were discussing Steptoe's *Mufaro's Beautiful Daughters*. She said "Manyara is like the bad sisters of Cinderella." Fourth level aesthetic reflection is also encouraged when children write about stories, as in the following two examples.

Lily's fifth grade students compared Alexander in Viorst's *Alexander and the Terrible, Horrible, No Good, Very Bad Day* and Ahmed in Perry Heide's *The Day of Ahmed's Secret*. After completing a Venn Diagram, students used it as a guide to compose their paragraphs. The features they compared included home country, family, daily life, and emotions. This is what one fifth-grader wrote:

Two different days
by Hani M.
Miss [Lily's] Grade 5

Alexander and Ahmed both had a special day, but they were special in a different way. Alexander woke up and went to school, and he had a very terrible day. His brothers were not very nice with him and his teacher did not like his picture. Ahmed lives in Cairo, Egypt. He did not go to school. He went to work. But he was very happy because he had a secret. He told his secret at home to his parents. It was that he knows how to write his name. So one boy had an unhappy day and one had a happy day.

That's life! (Ghosn, 2003c, p. 19)

Following is one girl's reflection on Steptoe's *Mufaro's Beautiful Daughters* and San-Souci's *The Talking Eggs*. Note the very insightful advice she gives to Manyara.

Talking Eggs and Mufaro's Beautiful Daughters

The two stories are similar by that Nyasha and Blanche escape from home, but they different that Nyasha went to the King. But Blanche goes to an old woman's house and help her. Manyara should learn that not to be show off because maybe she would have good luck without cheating. Z. F. (age 10)

On another level of aesthetic response, students should be able to share their responses with others and discuss their *interpretations*. In Violet's sixth grade class, these reflections were voiced in a literature circle after *The Hundred Penny Box*:

> **S1:** Michael knows that if Aunt Dew loses that box, it be like losing a part of her life.
> **S2:** Yes, I think so, too. I think it's 'cause she collected the pennies all her life.

Level six response is to examine the text from *other perspectives* or points of view, as in "How do you think the mother hen felt when everyone made fun of her chick because it looked so different from the other chicks?" Letters to characters provide an opportunity for students to reflect more deeply on the story content and different points of view. The activity also provides a natural context to teach conventions of letter writing. The following letter was written to a character in *Mr. G. Reed Makes a Deal* (Ghosn, 1999) who exhibits excessive greed:

Mr. Reed,

The money is nothing it's not important. One day God will let you bring more money. You have three cars why you want to bring more? What happened its not good. Please don't do it again. R. R. (age 11)

Another letter from the same class is addressed to a character in *The Dragonfly Surprise* (Ghosn, 1999) who is facing discrimination at school, but ends up winning an art contest, albeit with some questionable help from a friend:

Dear Mallika,

Don't care about what the teacher and children talk about you, because you are black and they are white. They are like you. I want to say what a nice prize you win! And your friend Heba is a nice friend and nice, brave and good friend. At last you and Heba are best friends.

Your friend B. R. (age 11)

Letters from characters to their friends or family are another way to get children to reflect on different viewpoints. They are more demanding in that they will require more sophisticated perspective-taking than letters to characters. Here is a letter from the above character, Mallika, to her sister:

> Dear Sister,
>
> I miss you very much. You is my best sister. I enter in the contest and they gave me money 1000 dollars. I'm going to give you them. My friend Heba told Miss Randa to enter me in the contest I make a dragonfly. My friends always make fun at me. Tomorrow I will send it.
>
> Your sister Mallika J. K. (age 10.5)

Writing literary journal entries from the point of view of different characters also helps children develop perspective-taking ability, which is an essential aspect of empathy. Children take on the role of a character or an object in the story and write a journal entry using the first person voice. The following journal entry from the main character's point of view was generated by a fifth grader after reading *Children Who Hugged the Mountain* (Ghosn, 1999) where a group of resourceful children save a mountain from destructive quarrying by resorting to a strategy they learned from an old Indian story:

> Dear Diary:
>
> Today I have a very big responsibility. Me and my friends are going on a nice trip but I will tell you what happen. A greedy man Mr An Nzar he is going to destroy our mountain. But he will have a big surprise. I told my friends we make like Indian peapol in the story they hug the trees. We will sleep on the ground and hug our mountin. I am going now. R. H. (age 11)

Although the language leaves much to be desired, it is clear that the student has reflected on and understood the sense of responsibility the main character demonstrates in the story. Written responses give children time to reflect on the story events and themes and to develop deeper and more sophisticated understandings about the connections between the story and their personal experiences.

It has been suggested that young children typically respond at the basic levels of the nine-level hierarchy; however, primary school children are capable also of interpreting or *generalizing* about the meaning of their literary experience, Sebesta et al. (1995) level seven. One 11-year-old in Violet's class, after listening to Shel Silverstein's *The Giving Tree*, noted that the tree was "like a mother, always gives and gives what her child asks." Similar generalization ability is illustrated in the coda, "That's life!" in the comparison of life experiences of Alexander and Ahmed quoted above.

It has further been suggested that *evaluating* what has been obtained from the experience or evaluating the quality of the work itself, level eight and nine Sebesta et al., responses, respectively, are beyond young learners, but with teacher guidance young learners can engage in such evaluation, albeit at their own level. I have observed some of the most delightful "critique" discussions in English-immersion kindergarten classrooms, where five-year-olds have evaluated Leo Lionni's and Eric Carle's works and discussed these authors' use of words. With guidance, children are also able to discuss what the story experience meant to them personally.

Oral Reading

Unlike many teachers I have observed over the years, Violet and Lily do not engage their students in *round-robin* (Austin & Morrison, 1963) reading, in which students take turns reading a few sentences, which the teacher follows with comprehension questions or questions about vocabulary. The process is repeated until everyone has had a turn, the text is finished, or the bell rings! Round-robin is really a complete waste of time. First, when one student reads, most others, although supposedly following along, may in reality be disengaged and listening only for their own turn. Once their turn has passed, students typically lose interest and tune out. John Savage, Professor Emeritus of reading and literacy instruction, points out that round-robin will actually "hamper listening, because following the lines of print and looking ahead to see one's passage to read can be a distraction instead of an aid to listening" (Savage, 1998, p. 330).

More importantly, perhaps, brain scans have shown that when a student is reading silently, much more frontal lobe activity is taking place than when he or she is reading aloud. In contrast, when a student is reading aloud, brain activity is concentrated in the motor area governing speech, with little activity in other areas of the brain. This implies that more comprehension is taking place during silent reading than oral reading (Wolfe, 2001).

Yet, oral reading has its place in the instructional cycle, primarily because it helps develop fluency, but many more meaningful approaches are available than round-robin. Zinnia, Violet and Lily have learned a number of strategies that not only engage students but also help them assess students' comprehension. For example, to encourage aesthetic responses to *The Hundred Dresses*, while also engaging her students in oral reading, Violet employs a useful strategy acquired in her teacher education class:

T: How did Maddie feel about Peggy teasing Wanda about the hundred dresses?

S1: She, Miss, she didn't like it.

T: Uhuh. She didn't like it. Can you read aloud a part where it shows she didn't like it.

S1: On page 33 it says [reads] *even if you felt uncomfortable as Maddie had* and then on page 34 it says [reads] *Maddie was glad she had not had to make fun of Wanda* and then, Miss she started to write Peggy a letter to say [read] *let's stop asking Wanda how many dresses she has.*

T: Right. She did not like it. She was uncomfortable.

T: Did Maddie have any regrets about her own behavior?

S2: Yes, she was sorry because she ((did not defend)) Wanda.

T: Where in the story does it tell us she was sorry, that she had regrets?

S2: Miss, on page 47, it says [reads] *She had a very sick feeling in the bottom of her stomach. True, she had not enjoyed listening to Peggy... She had stood by silently, and that was just as bad as what Peggy had done. Worse. She was a coward.*

Other possible purposes for oral reading during the story discussion are to read aloud the part where the author foreshadows an event, where something is funny, sad, or exciting, or where a meaning of a word is made clear. This approach is more interesting than round-robin, and it allows for different interpretations and extension of the same question to others. If no fixed questioning routine is evident, students are also more likely to stay tuned in.

To develop reading fluency, children in Zinnia's, Violet's, and Lily's classes read poems chorally, with appropriate expression, and read aloud play scripts and dialogues in stories. Teachers might want to consider the advice from Savage, who suggests teachers develop "one-liners" by selecting lines spoken by story characters but adding instruction for different ways to read, such as "read sadly," "read eagerly," and "read pleadingly," and so on (Savage, 1998, p. 331). Children then practice their lines in small groups before reading to the class.

THINK ABOUT IT

1. Which teacher's approach appealed to you the most? Why?
2. Do you think some of the approaches would work with your students? Why or why not?

Note

1. In Arabic, which is a pro-drop (pronoun-dropping) language, verbs are inflected to show gender and number of subjects: "She went to school" = *Dahabat* (went she) *ila al-madrasa*. Verbs are inflected to show gender and number of subjects. For example, "Layla went to school" = *Dahabat* (went she) *Layla ila al-madrasa* (Layla to school), while "Sam went to school" = *Dahaba* (went he) *Sam ila al-madrasa*. In less formal register of everyday language, the subject may precede the verb: *Layla dahabat ila al-madrasa*. Thus, an Arabic speaking child will say "Layla she went to school" or "My mother she bakes cookies."

14

Revisiting the Story World

> *"Make a remark," said the red Queen. "It's ridiculous to leave all the conversation to the pudding!"*
> —Lewis Carroll, *Through the Looking Glass* (1872/1974, p. 245)

In order for children to internalize vocabulary and structures from a story, they need to revisit it several times and use the story language in meaningful contexts. The reader responses described above often create a need to return to the story, but teachers can also set many other meaningful purposes for students to return to the story to read it again. The following are just some examples.

Storymapping

Story mapping is a visual depiction of the setting, characters, and the sequence of events of a story. The strategy helps students to increase their comprehension of stories and facilitates retelling. Story maps are also excellent tools for story writing. There are numerous models of story mapping (see http://

www.ReadWriteThink.org; http://fcit.usf.edu/fcat/references/strategies/pc4.htm; http://olc.spsd.sk.ca?DE/PD/instr/strats/storymapping/index.html; or do a Google search on "storymapping" to find a rich sampling suitable for all age and proficiency levels). Dahlia wants her students to focus on the most important events in the beginning, middle, and end of the story. She draws a story map template on the board (See Figure 14.1), with the empty boxes for listing of the main events. (For more complex stories, the map will need to have space for all the major events at each stage of the story.) Dahlia guides her students through the story, and as they note events, she inserts them into the story map. Dahlia then has children copy the story map in their notebooks and illustrate the main events. Children will then use the story map to retell the story.

Choral Reading

The simplest way to revisit the story is for children to read the story chorally. Choral reading creates a low-anxiety environment, within which learners can take risks without fear of failure, a central aspect of many

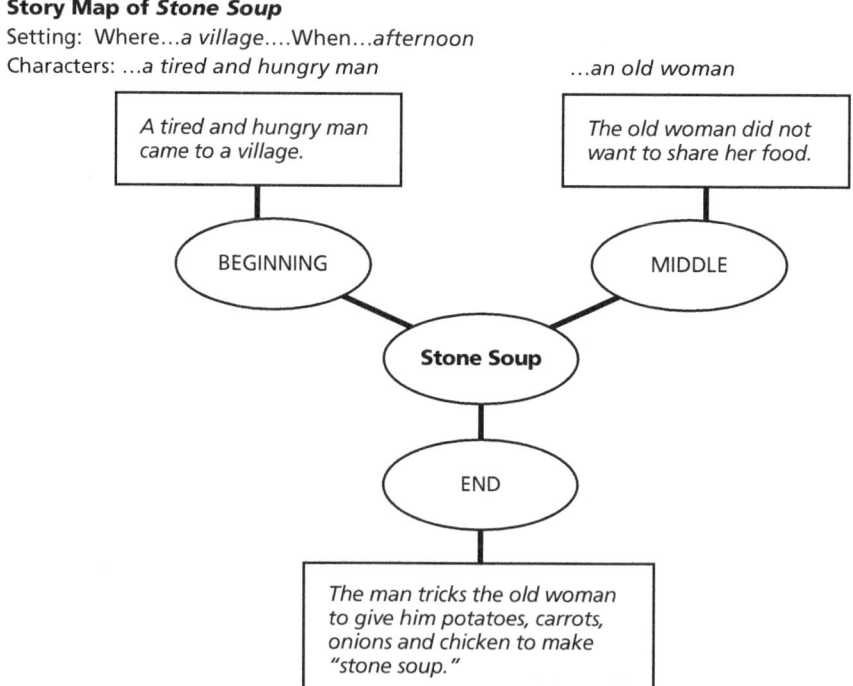

Figure 14.1 Story Map of *Stone Soup*.

language acquisition theories (e.g., Krashen, 1982; Ovando & Collier, 1985). In choral reading, children are able to participate according to their individual abilities, and the chorusing hides any mispronunciations. Reading is practiced several times, first with the teacher modeling appropriate expressions. Joyce and Daniel McCauley, who have worked with young language learners using choral reading, state that "choral reading never fails to excite children's interest in reading regardless of their age, reading level, or level of language proficiency" (McCauley & McCauley, 1992, p. 527). The repeated readings facilitate language acquisition when the words children read become part of their language repertoires, as Richard-Amato (1988) points out. Research also shows that repeated readings improve reading fluency (Hasbrouck & Tindal, 2005), an important consideration where children must access subject matter content through reading. Zinnia and Daisy, introduced in Chapter 12, use choral reading frequently with their young learners in their EFL1 classes, but refrain from participating in the reading as soon as children are catching on. This enables them to observe children's performance and to identify children who might need special attention.

Language Experience Stories

An adaptation of the classic Language Experience Approach (LEA), developed originally by Van Allen and Allen (1967) for first language reading and writing instruction, works well with young L2 learners. LEA is based on the notion that anything that can be spoken can be written down, and that what has been written can be read. The experiences the teacher creates range from cooking and science activities to field trips. A story provides an excellent experience, and children create their own books to take home. In a second/foreign language class, the teacher needs to consider the target vocabulary and structures and then construct the text to be elicited from children. After the story has been read a few times, children re-tell it as the teacher guides them, eliciting the targeted language. The teacher writes children's dictation on the board or on flip chart paper. With beginning learners, contributions will often be in L1, and allowing children to use their mother tongue helps the teacher to determine what and how much children have understood. The teacher restates children's contributions in correct English (without overt corrections), recasts mother tongue utterances into English, and then writes them down, reading each sentence aloud before moving on.

LEA Story in Dahlia's Fourth-Grade EFL2 Class

Dahlia employs the language experience approach with the *Stone Soup*, using the story as the experience. She reminds the class about the story, inviting them to tell what they remember. She re-tells the story, using some of her props. She then suggests that the class write the summary of the story so that they can read it themselves.

> **T:** Now this is a story from long ago. How do stories often begin?
>
> **S1:** Once upon a time, Miss.
>
> **T:** Very good, Tony [writes] *Once upon a time*. What happened at the beginning of the story? Who can tell?
>
> **S1:** A man came to ((the village)).
>
> **T:** OK. A man came to the village. Is that how you would like to start our story? OK. But do we say "a man came to the village, or to a village"? Do we know this village from before?
>
> **S2:** Miss, a village?
>
> **T:** Right. We say a village because this is a new village to us. So, *a man came to a village* [writes] OK. Now the man, what do we know about this man? Wissam.
>
> **S3:** The man he hungry.
>
> **T:** He was hungry. OK, but Wissam, do we say "the man he," or "the man was hungry"?
>
> **S3:** The man was hungry.
>
> **T:** OK. A hungry man [inserts "hungry" to the text] What did he see? Yes, Rayan.
>
> **S4:** He see, he see
>
> **T:** Rayan, remember it's a story. A story is always in the past.
>
> **S4:** He, he saw a woman.
>
> **T:** Excellent. He saw a woman. What did he ask the woman?

When the story is completed, she invites children to read the sentences they had contributed. Once the story is finished, the class reads the story twice chorally. (Some teachers accommodate children's suggestions that deviate from the original script, while still making sure the target language is included.) For the upcoming session, Dahlia types the jointly constructed story on sheets of A4 paper, with blank space for illustrations, and makes copies for her students. Students will illustrate their own copies and make covers for their books. In the illustration process, the story will be read many times.

LEA Story in a Pre-Service Teacher Education Class

When I introduced the LEA approach to a group of pre-service teachers, their response demonstrated its potential at diverse age levels. In the episode below participants are taking turns to re-tell a simple story I (referred to as IG) had read to them, *A Story without End* (Butterworth, 1994). The story tells of a king who loved stories and promised a bag of gold to anyone who could tell him a never-ending story. A clever little girl tells him a story about ants and some grains of sugar. The task generated considerable exchange of ideas with the adult participants and illustrates how this approach not only creates a purpose for revisiting the story but also how it activates critical thinking.

S1: Once upon a time there was a king who liked stories.
IG: [begins to write on the board]
S2: Don't you think we should say his name?
IG: Rana suggests that we should mention his name? Does anyone|
S2: King Harry!
IG: [adds *Harry* to the text and re-reads the sentence]
S3: I think we must say who <u>loved</u> stories.
IG: Oh. What should we say, liked or loved?
Ss: Liked! Liked!
IG: OK. Let's come back to this later [circles the word *liked*]. What's next?
S2: People came every day to tell him stories.
S4: Many people came every day.
S2: It did not say many people. It said <u>people</u> came every day.
IG: OK. It seems we need to check this.
Ss: People!
IG: [gives the book to a student] can you please find the place and read to us what it says.
S5: [reads] *People came every day.*
IG: OK. So it says people.
S4: But every day <u>is</u> many people, because if they came every day and many days, it means there were many people.

We had to return to the story several times. Returning to the text to verify ideas or details provides students with a meaningful purpose to re-read parts of the text. It can also create an opportunity to examine how language means what it means. The enthusiastic engagement of a group of adults around a very simple story demonstrates the power and potential of the approach at different levels.

Summarizing

Young learners will need guidance and plenty of practice in learning to distinguish between the main ideas and details. The re-telling is also useful when teaching the important skill of summarizing the main ideas. After students have finished their dictation, the teacher guides them through the process of editing to remove any unnecessary detail. Alternatively, students work in pairs or small groups to write story summaries. To challenge students' thinking and language skills, and sharpen their main idea recognition skills, the number of sentences in their summary can be limited. The shorter the summary, the more challenging is the task and the greater the need to use compound, complex and compound–complex sentence structures. Here is a summary of *Harry the Dirty Dog* (Zion, 1956), produced by Rowan's third graders after the class dictation and revisions:

> Harry was a white dog. He did not like a bath. He ran away. He was very dirty and black. His family did not know he was Harry. Then Harry wanted a bath. The children washed him. Then Harry was white and they knew he was Harry. Harry was happy.

Comparing Stories

Lily uses a wide variety of trade paperbacks from the school's well-stocked library to supplement her literature-based reading anthology. In the following episode, she is guiding her fifth graders to identify the criteria for comparing and contrasting five Cinderella stories: the classic Grimm brothers' *Cinderella*, *The Egyptian Cinderella* (Climo, 1989), *The Persian Cinderella* (Climo, 1999), *The Golden Sandal* (Hickox, 1998) set in the Middle East, and *The Enchanted Anklet* (Mehta, 1985) set in India.

Lily draws a chart with five rows and six columns on the board, asking students to copy the chart in their notebooks and to write the story titles in the first column. She then continues:

> T: When we are going to compare and contrast something, what are we thinking about?
> S1: Miss, what is same and different.

T: Correct. We compare what is similar and contrast what is different. We can also simply say we are comparing, and that can mean we are thinking of both similarities and differences. OK. But when we are comparing, we must know <u>what</u> we are going to compare, we cannot just compare and contrast every single thing in the story, can we? No, we must have <u>criteria</u> [writes "criteria" on the board]. Criteria means on what we base our comparison, like a standard. What exactly we will we compare. OK? So, if Hani and Youssef, if you are going to compare two basketball players, would you compare their eye color and the cars they drive?

Ss: No, Miss! Their baskets! ((How many baskets! How many 3-pointers!))

T: Right, you will think, you will think what is important in basketball. So, when we want to compare the five Cinderella stories, we should all think about the same important things, to use the same <u>criteria</u>. OK? Good. Now, where do these stories take place?

Ss: Egypt! India!

T: OK. What do we call the <u>place</u> where the story happens? Raymond.

S1: Setting, Miss.

T: Setting [writes the word at the top of the second column]. Very good. We can compare settings. What else do we have in a story besides setting? Elsie.

S2: Miss, we have characters.

T: Very good, Elsie. Characters [writes the word on top of the next column]. Now, in these Cinderella stories we read, there is something special. What is special in them?

S3: They have magic.

T: Magic... uhuh, yes, they have magic. What else?

S3: Miss! ((something is always lost))

T: Good, Youssef. In each story, there is a lost object [writes "lost object" on the chart]. Good. Now we have three <u>criteria</u> [writes "criteria" above the chart]

S5: Miss, you forgot to put the 's'

T: Excuse me? Oh, yes, no we don't need 's' here, because criteria is plural, if we had only one thing to compare, we would say criterion, OK. So, three criteria.
So we have now three criteria for comparing the stories. Is there anything else we could compare, anything other than setting, characters, and the lost object? Another criter<u>ion</u>?

S4: Miss, there are the ((parties)).

T: Uhuh, parties, parties.

S4: Yes, where the things get lost.

T: Yes, but they are not all <u>parties</u>, are they?

S5: Miss, can we say the place?

T: What do you mean, Heba, the place?

S5: I mean the place where the thing gets lost.

T: Excellent, Heba. Yes, we can say the <u>place of loss</u> [writes on the board]. Now, we have, let's see, four criteria. In your groups, fill in the chart. Put the title in the first column. Each group will work with one story and then exchange with another group. OK?

Lily distributes the books, and students work in small groups of four. One group asks if they can add more criteria, and, after some negotiation, they add *personal attributes* (of the main character), and *punishment* to their list of things to be compared. When finished, groups share their lists and discuss any discrepancies. During her next session, Lily planned to review compare and contrast vocabulary, and have students work in groups to compose a draft text comparing the five stories. The drafts would be shared and discussed, with revisions and editing left as homework.

Script Writing

Preparing a script to dramatize a story or parts of a longer one is another task that requires many purposeful re-readings. Children will need to verify the sequence of events, the characters' actions and mood, and what each one was saying and when and how. I have witnessed numerous times children huddled in small groups discussing how to structure their skit. Naturally, in a homogenous language group, much of this discussion often takes place in children's mother tongue. However, the outcome will be in English. The use of mother tongue will facilitate discussion and debate about the correct English to be used, which might be more difficult for beginning learners to do in English. Here, the teacher has a monitoring role; circulating among children, listening to their L1 comments and affirming them by recasting them into English, while also seizing any "teachable moments." In an ESL class with many home languages, children will need to communicate in English, and only teachers versed in children's home languages will be able to take advantage of children's first language input.

Here is a partial script a group of Lily's fourth graders produced after reading the *Children Who Hugged the Mountain* (Ghosn, 1999), set in the local context and featuring some resourceful children (text left unedited):

Setting: Cave Mountain

Characters: Omar, Mazen, Ziad, Nisreen, Mr. Al Nazar, Principal

Omar: My friends, you know that we have a big responsability.

Mazen: Yes, Omar. We must protek the mountin and trees.

Ziad: Yes. We cannot let Mr. An-Nazar destroi the prehistoric cave.

Omar: I think I have an idea. Remember the story Mr. Daher read to us about Indian peoples and the trees?

Nisreen: But how can that help us, Omar?

Omar: We will get our mates from school and we will make like the Indian peoples.

Nisreen: Oh, Omar. You are a very ingenes boy!

Writing up a scene that might have taken place before the story begins, or one that might take place after the story ends, will require fairly sophisticated inferential skill, and adding dialogue between characters will foster perspective-taking skill.

Rating Scales

Literacy through Literature by Johnson and Louis (1987), although written with first language learners in mind, presents a rich selection of enjoyable reader response activities that are appropriate also for second language learners. Character rating scales are created by making a list of contrasting characteristics such as *beautiful/ugly, brave/fearful, honest/dishonest* and placing them on a grid. Figure 14.2 is a rating scale for Manyara in *Mufaro's Beautiful Daughters* filled by a group of fifth graders. Children first worked in pairs to rate the character and then shared their ratings and justifications with the class. The rating task can be completed even by children whose limited oral language hinders expressing of their ideas but who have some familiarity with the vocabulary. The activity facilitates inferential thinking and skills of analysis and evaluation.

Manyara	Very	Quite	Neither Both Don't Know	Quite	Very	
beautiful	x					ugly
kind				x		unkind
hardworking			x			lazy
brave		x				fearful
friendly				x		unfriendly

Figure 14.2 Character rating scale for Manyara in *Mufaro's Beautiful Daughters*

Plot Profiles

Plot profiles, also from Johnson and Louis (1987) cited above, help children sequence and evaluate events. The teacher prepares a grid and selects the key incidents from the story to be plotted along the horizontal scale and the level of excitement of each incident on the vertical scale. Students then rate the excitement levels, either in pairs or within a whole-class discussion. This is how it worked with Zinnia's first graders (Figure 14.3):

> **T:** OK. Grade one, we are going to talk about the plot of *Goldilocks and the Three Bears*. Plot means what is happening, what the action is. We call this a <u>plot</u>, a plot, what happens in the story. What is the plot in Goldilocks? [Several children call out parts of the story.]
>
> **T:** OK, So, you all know what happens, what the plot is. Now, I want to find out which parts of the plot you think are exciting, exciting, like you really want to know what's going to happen next! OK. See the graph I have here [puts the graph on an easel]. How many events have I put here? Tanya.
>
> **S1:** [counts] Seven, Miss.
>
> **T:** Right. I have written here seven events from the story. Who would like to come and read the first one? Sabine.
>
> **S2:** [goes to the chart and reads] *Goldilocks goes for a walk.*
>
> **T:** Very good thank you, Sabine. Now, let's look at the chart. Goldilocks goes for a walk. Is that very exciting [points to the top of the chart]? Like up here, really, really exciting? Yes, Roy.
>
> **S3:** No, Miss! Me, I go, I walk every day. ((There is nothing special about walking.))

Revisiting the Story World ▪ 157

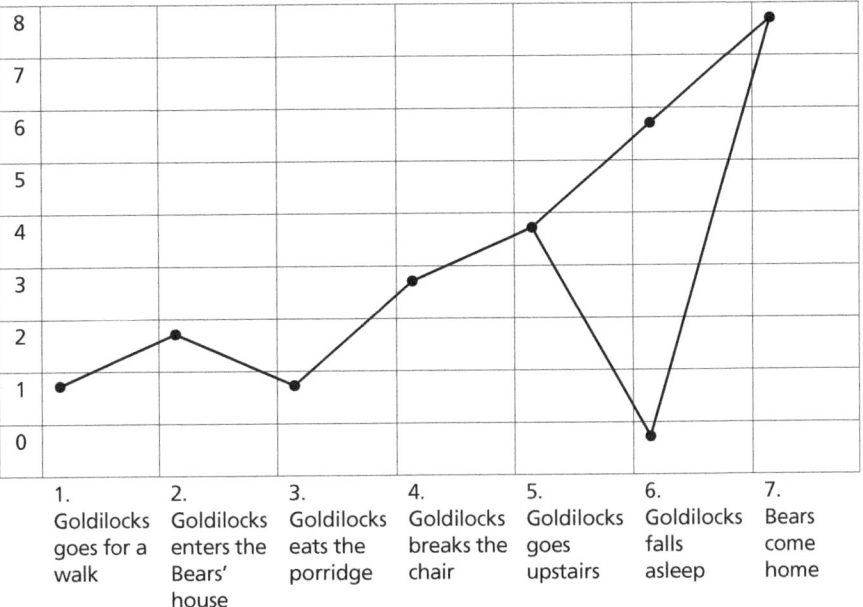

Figure 14.3 Plot profile for *Goldilocks and the Three Bears*.

    T: OK. Roy says it's not exciting, he goes walking every day. We all do. So we put an X here, in number 1. You all agree? It means not exciting at all.

    SS: Yes, Miss!

    T: Next. Who will read number two? Hammoudi.

    S4: [goes to the chart and reads] *Goldilocks en-enters the Bears's house.*

    T: She enters the Bears' house. Is that exciting?

    S4: Yes, Miss ((a little)).

    S2: ((But the bears are not at home!))

    S4: But ((maybe they are just coming back)).

The class continues until the plot profile is complete. Note the incident, where Goldilocks falls asleep. About half of the children in this class thought Goldilocks falling asleep was a very tense moment, with the bears perhaps returning any minute. Others argued that Goldilocks sleeping was not exciting at all.

News Reports

Writing news reports is a good way of getting children to develop multiple perspectives to events (Ghosn, 1999). News reports can be generated from any story where something "newsy" happens. Children should first be able to explore sample news articles and understand that newspaper articles are usually short and tell only the main ideas; the *what, where, when* and *why*. There is also often a quote from someone involved in the events.

Writing newspaper reports for different audiences will require children to take on different perspectives, which will develop their ability to recognize bias in reporting. For example, trying to write up the *Little Red Riding Hood* events first for *Parenting Magazine*, then for *Woodcutters' Weekly*, and, finally, for *The Wolf Protection Society* or *Wolf Village News* is likely to be an eye-opener (Ghosn, 2003). Below is a news report from one of Lily's fifth graders.

Sri Lanka girl wins contest!

> Yesterday Mallika from Sri Lanka win a big art contest. Her friend Heba put her dragonfly in the contest. But Heba put it without her permishon, she put it without her permishon, because she want to help her best freind. "This is a very big surprise" said Mallika. H. Z. (age 11)

Different groups of children can also be assigned different newspaper audiences. Writing reports for TV news is even more challenging, because TV newscasts must include many items in a short period of time, and, therefore, each report will only have about one minute, sometimes even less. So the TV news reporter has to limit his or her report to the most important ideas and use language very carefully.

Examining Author's Craft

Students can re-visit the story to examine the author's craft and literary strategies. How does the author build excitement during the story? How does the author help readers guess what might happen next? What did the author do that made us think the character was not really happy? How does the author use words to help us *see* what is happening? When Violet asked her sixth graders when they figured out something bad might happen in a story where a greedy man dumps toxic waste into a mountain lake, one girl said

> When I read that Ramzy's school was going on a trip to the mountain, and his father has putted the barrels ((of chemicals)) in the water in the moun-

tain, I was scared. I think something bad will happen. Then when the author she make Ramzy drink the water and I think the ((chemicals)) they are in the water, I think Ramzy will ((be poisoned)).

In Zinnia's first grade class, children explored Judith Viorst's use of language to show Alexander's mood in *Alexander and the Terrible, Horrible, No Good, Very Bad Day*. Children concluded that the best part was the repetitious "terrible, horrible, no good, very bad day."

The following two quotes from Samway imply that the young writers have examined their stories closely. She quotes Shanti, who says "In the beginning of the books I pay attention to what kind of writing that is... sometimes I try to use that kind of writing" (Samway, 2006, p. 121), and Rubé, who says "I think reading, it helps me, you know when I write my sentences, like the punctuation... I think now what I write I know how to, to order the paragraphs... I just did how Dean Meyers [the author] organize them..." (Samway, 2006, p. 122).

Many different strategies are possible that give students a meaningful reason to revisit the story. The above are just some examples.

15

Linking the Story to Subject Matter

> *"Let the jury consider the verdict,"* the King said,
> *for about the twentieth time that day.*
> —Lewis Carroll, *Alice's Adventures in Wonderland* (1865/1974, p. 117)

Mathematics

In the following vignette Zinnia's first graders engage in a math activity based on *The Doorbell Rang*. Zinnia's lesson sequence is modeled after suggestions in *Math and Literature K–3* by Burns (1992). She has prepared laminated cardboard "cookies" and has invited two volunteers to act out the roles of Sam and Victoria:

T: [reads] *I've made some cookies for tea. Share them between yourselves. I made plenty.* [Points to the plate of "cookies" on her desk.] How many cookies did I make?

Ss: Plenty!

T: How many? [lifting cookies up, one by one] One . . .

Ss: Two! Three! Four! Five! Six! Seven! Eight! Nine! Ten! Eleven! Twelve!

T: Good! Twelve cookies. Now, how many cookies will each of you get?

S1: I know! [begins to divide the cookies] One for me, one for you|

S2: one for you, one for me, one for you [Children take turns until the cookies are divided.]

S1: Miss, six.

T: Uhuh, so you have six cookies. What about you?

S2: Me, I have six.

T: Good, each one got six cookies. Twelve cookies divided between two children gave each six. Twelve divided by two equals 6. [writes $12 \div 2 = 6$ on the board]. OK. [Reads] "*No one makes cookies like Grandma,*" *said Ma as the doorbell rang. It was Tom and Hannah from next door. "Come in," said Ma. "You can share the cookies."*

T: OK. Rabieh and Helen, come here. You can be Tom and Hannah. Now, how many cookies will each one get?

S3: One for me [takes a cookie].

S4: One for me [takes a cookie].

S3: One for him [gives Rabieh a cookie].

S4: One for her [gives Helen a cookie].

Children continue until cookies are divided. Zinnia continues through the story, inviting more children to come up. At each division, she states the mathematical sentence and records the numbers on the board. Although children will not be introduced formally to division until grade two, the activity provides good preparation in a highly meaningful, real-life context. Afterward, children were given an opportunity to act out the story a number of times, as the teacher re-read it.

In her fourth-grade math class, Lily uses Geriger's *Three Hat Day* to engage her students in some problem solving. Like Zinnia's previous lesson, Lily's lesson idea comes also from Burns' (1992) *Math and Literature K–3*.

In small groups, children write story problems for their peers to solve. Here is one example:

> R. R. Pottle had lots of shoes. She had pink slippers, yellow Crocks, red party shoes, and brown ski-boots. When she was feeling sad, she always put two different shoes in her two feet. Once, she was feeling really, really sad. So she said to herself, "I will be sad for a very long time." How many days can she be sad if she wants to wear a different combinashion of shoes each day?

Much of the language is borrowed from the original, but the footwear was generated by the children, as was the question.

Science

In his third-grade class, Rowan reads *The Slow Little Snail* (Ghosn, 1999), a story featuring a little snail who decides to go for a morning "walk." On its way, it encounters six different creatures and invites each one to join in. All refuse, saying the snail is too slow. Finally, another little snail comes along and the two continue their journey together. Rowan reads the story a number of times over a week, and, because of children's interest, engages the class in a study of snails, although invertebrates are not part of his third grade science curriculum.

T: What can you tell me about snails? What do you know about snails?
S1: Teacher, teacher! Snails very ((delicious)).
T: Uhuh, you like to eat snails?
S1: Yes, teacher.
S2: My ((grandmother)) she eat snails!
T: OK. So we know we can eat snails, what else do you know?
S3: They ((slimy)) and soft.
T: OK, they they are a little bit slimy, they leave some slime behind them [writes "slimy" and "soft" on the board]. What else?
S1: They have [gestures with his hands] like a house.
T: Yes, they have a shell. Is the shell hard or soft?
S1: Hard, teacher.
T: OK, so snails have a hard shell [writes "hard shell"]. OK, what else? Yes, Hani?
S4: Teacher, look ((what are these))? [points to the snail's tentacles in cover illustration of the book]
T: Very good, Hani. Snails have these tentacles, tentacles. How many tentacles does it have? Tareq.
S5: Four?
T: Four tentacles or feelers [writes "4 tentacles"]. Right. Yes, Ali?
S6: Teacher, where are the eyes?
T: Good question, Ali. Where are its eyes? The snail has eyespots here at the end of the long tentacles. Here, but we can't see them here [writes "eyespots"].

Rowan brought in some snails as well as some empty snail shells for children to observe. He placed the snails in an empty aquarium with some soil and rocks at the bottom and covered it with a wire mesh. Children observed the snails daily.

The snails' movement generated curiosity, because in the story the snail was going for a "walk." One boy asks, "It don't have feet so how it walk?" Rowan invited children to look up information about snails on the Internet, and they discovered that words "creep" and "crawl" are used for snails, and they also discovered that the slime helps snails move. Children examined the empty shells and drew pictures of them during their art period. After collective editing and revising, the class generated the following text:

> We have some snails. The snails are slimy. They have soft bodies. They have hard shells and four tentacles. Two tentacles have eyespots and two not have any eyespots. Their bodies have some brown and some black. Their shells have different colors.

For more on snail science, see Scribner-MacLean and Greenwood's (1998) article, which Rowan identified as his reference when planning the unit.

Eric Carle's *The Very Hungry Caterpillar* is used by many Lebanese kindergarten teachers as part of the unit on the life cycle of butterflies and moths. I worked with Daisy when she used the story in her kindergarten class (Ghosn, 1997). Silk production was an important industry in Lebanon between 1870 and 1910, and continued in small scale until the 1980s. Some people still grow silkworms. One of the teachers in the school happened to be a grower and gave Daisy three silkworm cocoons. Daisy set up a box for the cocoons in the science corner, and the class spent much of their free time observing the cocoons, from which silk moths eventually emerged. The moths were then carefully taken out and released to a mulberry tree.[1] Units on life cycle of fish and frogs can be structured around Leo Lionni's *Fish is a Fish*.

If Dahlia's time and resources would permit for a follow-up on the *Stone Soup*, she could bring in a selection of local vegetables and invite children to examine them for color, shape, texture, and smell. Then, with the vegetables on the table for inspection, children could be encouraged to think of different ways to classify the vegetables. Matching picture cards would enable concrete manipulation and sorting. Children should understand that things can be grouped in many different ways; the important thing is that the groupings have some relationship with each other. For example, vegetables could be grouped by their color, size, the part of the plant that is eaten, how they are eaten (e.g., raw, cooked, either), number of syllables in the name, and so on. The teacher should avoid the temptation of telling children how they should sort the items and allow for children's creativity. After sharing their reasoning for their decisions, children can paste the picture cards on poster boards and label their categories.

Social Studies

Violet wants to raise her sixth graders' awareness about social and racial discrimination and has her students read *The Dragonfly Surprise* (Ghosn, 1999), where a dark-skinned Mallika, daughter of a Sri Lankan domestic worker, is shunned by her teacher and classmates. Only one girl befriends her, and, using deception, tries to help her win an art contest.

> **T:** What do you think about [the teacher's] behavior?
> **S1:** It was very wrong, Miss, because ((God created us all equal)).
> **S2:** Yes, she was mean. I think the principal must ((fire her))!
> **T:** So you think she should be fired from her job?
> **Ss:** Yes!
> **S3:** She, Miss, she should learn about ((the human rights)).
> **T:** Uhuh, you think that she doesn't know about the Declaration of Human Rights?
> **S3:** Miss, I think she knows, I mean she is a teacher ((she would have learned about it at the university)).
> **T:** OK. Yes, it was really wrong to discriminate against Mallika because of her skin color and her mom's work. OK. Let's talk about Heba [the friend]. What do you think about her?
> **S5:** I think that Heba is a very good friend.
> **Ss:** Yes!!
> **T:** But she took [the dragonfly] without permission and lied about it. What about that?
> **S4:** Yes, Miss, but she did it to help Mallika ((we should always help our friends)).
> **S6:** I agree with Lamiss, because Heba was helping her friend and nobody else loved her.
> **T:** OK, but is it right to lie to help your friends?
> **S2:** It's not so right, but sometimes you ((are obliged to)).

A lengthy exchange ensued, at the end of which opinions of the class were divided. In another class, the same story also generated mixed emotions. This letter to Heba was written by the same fifth-grade student who wrote the newspaper report about the story, cited in Chapter 13:

> Dear Heba,
>
> I'm sad and happy from you. Sad because you took the Dragonfly from Mallika without her permission, but happy, because you let Mallika to have the dragon fly in the contest.
>
> Good bye
>
> Your friend, H. Z. (age 11)

Creating New Stories

Stories (and poems) give children a base for their own explorations of language and its possibilities. One way of helping even very beginning learners to produce their own versions of stories is to use a class-dictated version, such as Rowan's students wrote about *Harry the Dirty Dog*, for instance. Children can begin to compose their own personal versions of the story by adding and changing some elements. The more beginners the learners are, the closer they will adhere to the original text in their own writing. If learners are too young to write, the teacher can print and copy children's dictation for them to illustrate, as Daisy did with her kindergarten students. Writing generated by students will provide the teacher with instructional material for further language teaching.

If you recall from the plot profile episode, Zinnia read *The Three Bears* to her first graders. As children re-told the story, the teacher wrote the text on large flip chart papers. Galdone's (1972) story version, which Zinnia read, features Little Wee Bear, the Middle-Sized Bear, and the Great Big Bear. During their re-telling of the story, children opted for more simple names—Father Bear, Mother Bear and Little Bear—which they had encountered in kindergarten. In the process, parts of the story had to be re-read to check details, and the class ended up re-reading the dictated sentences several times until everyone was satisfied. Children then copied the class story in their copybooks.

The following day, children read their story version chorally a few times. Then Zinnia suggested that they write their own Goldilocks story. The suggestion had the children puzzled at first, but when she asked, "What if Goldilocks lived in Lebanon?" one of the children quickly volunteered (in Arabic) that there are no bears in Lebanon. Another child then suggested that in Lebanon, Goldilocks might run into a family of foxes. The teacher validated the response by saying, "Yes, we do have foxes in Lebanon," and wrote "fox" on the board. Hyena and wolf were identified as additional possibilities and listed on the board. When one child suggested a family of rabbits, the class quickly dismissed the notion, because "rabbits will not be scary." The teacher then moved to question the bears' food; what other food could have been in the bowls? Children quickly offered suggestions, and during the lengthy and animated discussion, corn flakes and local foods from lentil soup to rice pudding were mentioned, and the teacher wrote the English words for them on the board.

She then invited the children to write their own stories, reminding them that they could refer to the flipchart story they had dictated earlier, and also to the words listed on the board. Children began eagerly to work on their own individual stories. Some children changed only the animals, with more than one child writing about Goldilocks and three foxes. Some others changed only the food, while some changed both the animals and the food:

> Once upon a time there were three foxes. They were Little Fox, Mother Fox, and Father Fox. One day they went for a walk.... Goldilocks tasted the rice pudding of Father Fox. But it was too hot....

One little boy's story featured some original elements, as well as invented spellings:

> Onsapona time there were three gorillas. They were Baby Gorilla, Mother Gorilla, and Father Gorilla.... Goldilocks tasted the pizza of Father Gorilla. But it was too hot....

Stories with simple plot lines and repetitive refrains serve as good templates for beginning learners' story construction, while classic folktales, trickster tales and *pourqoui* stories provide models for older learners. When copying stories they have read, children explore the language of the story and begin to develop an understanding of what language means. To quote the nine-year-old English language learner, Heddie, again: "Writing stories *is* learning. It's really helpful because you can use your imagination. The more you write, the more you learn how to write" (Maguire & Graves, 2001, p. 561).

Copying target language texts is important for young learners whose native language employs an alphabetic system and/or text directionality different from English. Copying while creating their own story versions is much more meaningful than simply copying texts for the sake of copying. In the process, the class-generated versions are read many times, and, because the changes in students' own stories reflect their own interlanguage, they can read their own stories with understanding and can read them to others. Writing helps children to explore the concepts, find connections between the story world and real life, and articulate their thoughts. The opportunity to share one's own writing with others, wheather classmates or family, is an empowering experience for a young second language learner.

EXPLORING IT

1. What do you think about the different approaches used by the teachers in chapters 12 to 15? Which one's approach appealed to you most? Which approach or approaches might be best aligned with your or your school's philosophy of teaching?
2. If you have not yet used storybooks in your classroom, would you be willing to try some in your classroom? If you have already experimented with storybooks, did you find any new ideas you would like to try out?

Note

1. Butterfly and moth larvae kits can be ordered at http://educationalscience.com

PART IV

Closing Summations

In the previous chapters, a case has been laid in defense of story-based language instruction. The case was supported by both theory and evidence, with the evidence provided emanating from numerous research studies of the past 30 years, as well as from actual classrooms. Chapter 16 summarizes the evidence in favor of story-based second language instruction. Chapter 17 presents the criteria for selecting books for the classroom and lists also select titles with their key language features.

16

Summary in Defense of Authentic Children's Literature in Primary School ELT

"We can talk," said the Tiger-lily: "when there's anybody worth talking to."
—Lewis Carroll, *Through the Looking Glass*, 1865/1974, p. 143

Language, Content and Approach

The rapid spread of English language teaching in primary school classrooms around the globe has resulted in a flood of young learner courses on the market. Internationally marketed "global coursebooks," however, are often far removed from the life experiences and world of young language learners. In addition to being culturally distant, these courses present simplified and unnatural language not characteristic of English language in actual daily use. An examination of current young learner courses reveals little evidence about complex word knowledge as being the goal. In many cases, exposure to a given word is limited to one lesson unit, which may not give individual learners sufficient opportunities to use the word. Often, the new words do not have the necessary contextual saliency that would enable them to be learned from limited exposure.

Authentic literature, in contrast, offers a wide range of texts appropriate for young learner classes. The motivational appeal of a good story is well established, and the rich natural, often repetitious, language characterizing children's literature, picture books in particular, facilitates language learning. Vocabulary has contextualized saliency, enabling learning of words even from few encounters. Culturally situated stories lend themselves to culture learning when used appropriately.

The critical difference between the cultural content in coursebooks and the culture-specific content of storybooks is the approach(es) available to the teacher. The typical global coursebook presents learners with communicative situations, where learners must use the new language to communicate about often unfamiliar concepts and content. Stories, however, provide a context within which learners can remain in their own character and talk about and explore the new concepts or ideas. Qualitatively very different discourse is observed when teachers and children work with stories than what is associated with activities and texts in the typical coursebook.

Value and Motivational Power of Stories

Young learner materials ought to take into account the needs of the developing child and go beyond addressing their linguistic development to contributing also to their psycho-social development. Current young learner courses reflect little concern for the holistic development of young learners they are meant to instruct. Contrary to the watered-down, often trivial content of the global coursbook, children's literature features universal themes that are of concern to children everywhere: need for love and acceptance; need to belong; need for achievement; courage; fears, and so on. Children's authors understand the life experience of the developing child and her understanding of the world; hence, authentic children's literature contributes to children's holistic development.

Because children are avid consumers of stories, whether as listeners or readers, children's literature provides a highly motivating instructional medium for language teaching. Learning is an affective process rather than merely a cognitive one, and children's literature by its nature generates emotions, thus contributing to motivation and learning.

Research Evidence

Discourse Evidence

Research in ESL and EFL classrooms show that discourse in literature-based classrooms differs from that associated with traditional language classes, with meaningful dialogue being central around literature. Teachers use more repetition and paraphrasing of student output, and ask more clarifying questions than their colleagues in typical communicative classes. Students have plenty of opportunities to use the new language in meaningful and cognitively more complex ways when they talk about stories and engage in reader response activities. Talking about story content is characterized by negotiated exchanges, which result in connected, interactive discourse that carries over several turns.

Consistently, when asked, children prefer story reading and story work to the traditional language teaching activities, and identify the opportunity to interact and share ideas with others as one of the most enjoyable features of the literature-based approach.

Skills Evidence

Research since the 1970s points to the positive influence storybooks have on the development of all language skills. Book flood studies carried out by Warwick Elley and his colleagues in the South Pacific, Singapore, Sri Lanka, and South Africa have involved thousands of children and show that exposure to storybooks develops not only children's oral language and vocabulary, but also enhances their grammar awareness and reading and writing skills. Several smaller scale studies in the United States, the United Kingdom, India, Poland, the Netherlands, and Lebanon have confirmed these findings.

Potential for English-Medium Instruction

The less than satisfactory achievement of scores of language learners in English-speaking countries, the spread of English to ever younger age groups and the increasing popularity of English-medium instruction in many countries necessitate examination of whether, and to what extent, the current young learner materials help learners develop their cognitive academic language skills. Typically, primary school ELT materials focus on aural/oral language development, with little, if any, attention to the development of literacy. Explicit instruction in reading and writing is mostly absent. In contrast, good children's stories have the potential to develop children's cognitive academic language proficiency conceptualized by Jim Cummins (1984). Carefully selected stories further have the potential to contribute to children's subject matter learning and concept development. Promising research findings are emerging, which suggest literature has a place also in the subject matter classes, particularly in mathematics, sciences and social studies classes.

Characteristics of Literature-Based Approaches

Focus on Literacy

Central to the literature-based approach is the role of reading; beginning learners engage in dialogic or shared reading with the teacher, whereas more advanced learners read on their own. While story-telling has long been popular with language teachers, reading has typically not been introduced to beginners. This may well be fine where English is taught one or two hours per week as enrichment. Yet, it is clear from the available research evidence and the classroom examples presented that young learners are quite capable of tackling reading and writing early, provided given the right stimulus and the right support without pressure. Delay in exposure to print is especially of concern in settings where, sooner or later, children must be able to learn academic subject matter in English.

Role of the Mother Tongue

Finally, the transcripts presented in this volume draw attention to a factor that helps explain children's high motivational level. In the classes visited, teachers were speakers of the children's mother tongue, and were, therefore, able to validate children's L1 contributions. Being able to use their mother tongue when discussing stories is both empowering and motivating, as it enables children's active participation in the classroom discourse, regardless of their second language development. Students feel successful when their contributions are validated by the teacher, and the sense of success is essential in maintaining motivation. Allowing children to use their L1 when necessary also lowers their level of anxiety, or the "affective filter," which determines how much input can filter in. In addition, children's L1 comments are a valuable instructional resource for the teacher, who can recast them in English, thus introducing new language that is personally meaningful to the children since it expresses their own ideas.

First-language allowance, I believe, is one of the keys to successful story-based approach. García and Codina (1994), for example, write that young learners may have difficulty attending to teacher's oral reading of books when no first language support is provided. How children respond to teacher's oral reading of storybooks depends also on *how* the reading is conducted and how well it matches with what children bring to the situation from their own socio-cultural background. Thornburg (1993) found that young second language learners did not respond well to story reading when teachers used cognitive approaches, such as prediction questions and questions about story grammar, but their participation (i.e., motivation) improved when they were invited to relate the story content to their personal experience. Another reason for children not responding well in Thornburg's study might have been the inability to use their first language, which may have enabled them to respond in their mother tongue to the cognitively more demanding questions.

It may well be that teachers' lack of knowledge of children's mother tongue is one reason for story-based instruction not having found a permanent place in ESL programs in core-English countries despite the research-proven success of the approach elsewhere. Teachers not skilled in children's L1 will not be able to entertain children's L1 contributions and thus cannot provide the crucial validation of the ideas children try to express. Being unable to participate—and thus not receive reinforcement for participation—distances children from the lesson and lowers their motivation, ultimately hindering their learning.

The interactive social context created around shared reading of storybooks and the ability to use one's own language when necessary are very much aligned with the Vygotskian socio-cultural learning theory, in which dialogic instruction plays a key role. Through the dialogue about stories with the teacher and their classmates, children can develop their higher mental processes. The social interaction allows children to gain also new information and creates a level of linguistic interaction that adds a verbal level to their understanding (Echevarria & Graves, 1998). Such dialogic approach is difficult to accomplish successfully with young learners who are not able to draw on their L1 when participating in classroom discourse. Thus, story-based instruction's motivational power is perhaps best realized in classes where teachers have at least basic knowledge of children's mother tongue.

The following five quality teaching principles, derived from Kreidler (1990, pp. xvii–xviii), which also foster peace-building skills, are a valuable guideline:

1. Teacher listens to the children and demonstrates genuine interest in their opinions.

2. Teacher creates a caring classroom environment where children learn caring, cooperation, empathy, and tolerance through daily, personal experience.
3. Teacher's attitudes, values, and behaviors model those expected from the children.
4. Teacher helps develop children's discussion skills by making sure that one person speaks at a time and that everyone's contribution is respected and by encouraging children to express what they think. When children hear the opinions of others, their thinking skills are sharpened. Rules help the discussions stay under control and safe for all. Children may need to be explicitly taught respectful and considerate ways of disagreeing and presenting differing opinions: "I liked when you said that... but I think..."; "I think what you said about... was really interesting."; "I have something else to add."; "I think differently about this character."; "I agree with Zeina that..."; "I disagree with Hani, because..."
5. Teacher helps children learn to live with ambiguity. Not every question has a clear, yes-no answer; some problems are not easy to solve; there are many viewpoints to issues.

Negotiation of meaning is associated with successful second language learning; therefore, children will benefit from learning to ask clarifying questions: "What did you mean when you said...?; "I'm not sure I understand what (x) means." The ability to ask questions is particularly important for children who need to access academic subject matter content in the new language.

It is important that children learn to justify their opinions and support their arguments with evidence while also considering opposing viewpoints. They must begin to develop an understanding that people often have different beliefs about things, that there are many viewpoints to most issues, and that their own opinion is only as good as the reasoning given to support it. There is nothing wrong about conflicting views. What is important, however, is how one reacts to and expresses disagreement. It is the discussion following the reading that may actually be more valuable than the reading itself, as it is during the discussions that children will develop their thinking process, explore their values and viewpoints, and open their minds to different perspectives expressed by others.

THINK ABOUT IT

1. In some schools, there is a policy that English language learners must use only English in their communication efforts. What is your view on this and why?
2. What is the key difference between teachers using only English and requiring children to use only English?

17

Selecting Books for Language Teaching

> "... and what is the use of a book," thought Alice, "without pictures or conversation?"
> —Lewis Carroll, *Alice's Adventures in Wonderland* (1872/1974, p. 9)

Literary and Aesthetic Merit

When selecting literature for young learner classes, we ought to keep in mind that, for scores of children, particularly in disadvantaged regions, the only exposure to books may be in school, whether they be textbooks or supplementary materials. Thus, the books children encounter in school ought to be of the highest quality, and include literature of the kind defined in Chapter one. We should read the texts carefully and then ask ourselves: Did I enjoy it? What insight, if any, did I gain from it? Did it leave me with any questions? Grocery stores and discount bookshops offer a multitude of inexpensive and colorful storybooks that, while providing a moment of entertainment, lack any aesthetic or literary merit. While they serve a purpose in a doctor's waiting room or at an airport departure lounge, I would not include such books in the classroom library. High quality children's literature in English is available in low-cost paperback editions from many publishers, and used copies of some of the best children's books can be bought on the Internet literally with pennies.

Enduring Value

Next, we need to evaluate the literary and artistic standard of the work. What aspect of human condition does it address? How likely is it that this story will remain of interest and enjoyment to children and why? Some of the best works of English language children's literature have endured for decades, continuing to be entertained by generations of children. Good examples are Marjorie Flack's *The Story of Ping* (1933), Munro Leaf's *The Story of Ferdinand* (1936), Esphyr Slobodkina's *Caps for Sale* (1940), Robert McCloskey's *Make Way for Ducklings* (1941), and Eleanor Este's *The Hundred Dresses* (1944), which continue to go for reprints because of the high demand. All happen to be also very appropriate in a primary school language class. The works of Theodore Geisel (aka Dr. Seuss), Judith Viorst, Maurice Sendak, Eric Carle, and Leo Lionni will also undoubtedly be enjoyed by children for many years to come and are good material for language teaching.

Developmental Appropriateness

The third question is about the developmental levels. How appropriate is the story—in its theme/s and plot development—to the target audience? For example, Arnold Lobel in his *Frog and Toad* series and Elsie Minarik in her *Little Bear* books reflect their in-depth understanding of young children and their needs. Parent–child relationships, budding friendships, and concerns about competencies are important for the youngest learners. Slightly older learners will benefit from stories where characters must learn to deal with conflicts, overcome obstacles, and maintain relationships. Judith Viorst's *Alexander* books, Betsy Byar's *The Summer of the Swans,* and Katherine Paterson's *The Great Gilly Hopkins* are just a few examples.

Themes

Children the world over can identify with stories that address universal themes, such as fear, hope, courage, love, belonging, and the need to achieve. *Harry and the Terrible Whatzit* (Gackenbach, 1977) and *There's a Nightmare in My Cupboard* (Mayer, 1983) are both humorous but insightful stories about overcoming one's fears. The theme is also central in *The Owl Who Was Afraid of the Dark* (Tomlinson, 1973), while courage and perseverance are portrayed in the classic *Call it Courage* (Sperry, 1963) and in *Day of the Blizzard* (Moskin, 1997). Universal themes are highly generative, allowing for a variety of spin-off activities, an important consideration in language teaching. Many folktales also feature themes of universal concern.

Care should be exercised, however, with folktales, so as not to select stories that depict outdated or derogatory images of other cultures.

Plot

For beginning learners, the plot should be clear and uncomplicated, but with some rising action and a simple, yet satisfying conclusion. Avoid stories with melodramatic conclusions, flashbacks, complex characters and concepts that are beyond the learners' age and developmental level. High quality children's stories allow for a wide variety of interpretations at different levels and are thus potentially enjoyable to various age groups. Excellent examples of this are *The Story of Ferdinand* by Munro Leaf (1987) and *The Giving Tree* by Shel Silverstein (1963), mentioned in earlier chapters.

Illustrations

Illustrations should be aesthetically pleasing and support and clarify the text, not deviate from it. For example, if the text describes a brown-eyed child with curly hair, the illustrations must match that description, or if the text talks about five ducklings, the illustrations must confirm that number. Illustrations should also be synchronized with the story line, and, ideally allow for discussion within which key vocabulary can be exploited.

Language

Then, there is the language of the story and its potential to offer something for a young second language learner. Are the phrases well turned? How much enjoyable repetition of words and/or phrases is there? Will the language be immediately useful for the young learners? A good children's story does not rely on words drawn from graded vocabulary lists or on stilted, grammatically distorted discourse.

The language in picturebooks should be rich and expressive, but with some amusing repetition that allows for reader/listener predictions and confirmations. Ideally, grammatical structures and useful formulaic expressions will be repeated and made clear in the story context. Look also for vocabulary that provides synonyms and alternative expressions. Some of the best examples of picturebooks that are perfect for language learning include Eric Carle's classic *The Very Hungry Caterpillar* and *Caps for Sale* by Slobodkina, mentioned a number of times already. Table 17.1 lists select titles with their respective language teaching values.

TABLE 17.1. Repetitious Language in Select Storybooks

Author & Title	Examples of Repetitive Language (Number of Repetitions)	
Carle, E. *Have You Seen my Cat?*	My (19) Have you seen? (9) This is not (8)	Have you seen my cat? This is not my cat (emphasis in the original).
Carle, E. *The Grouchy Ladybug*	If you insist (12) not big enough (12) said (42) flew off (14) flew on (2) at (time) o'clock (12)	At six o'clock it met a yellow jacket. "Hey you," said the grouchy ladybug. "Want to fight?" "If you insist," said the yellow jacket... "Oh, you're not big enough," said the grouchy ladybug and flew off.
Carle, E. *The Very Hungry Caterpillar*	On Monday, Tuesday... (6) ate (7) through (7) was (7) still hungry (5) wasn't (2)	On Monday he ate through one apple. But he was still hungry
Galdone, P. *Goldilocks and the Three Bears*	This ____ is (9) too hot/cold/soft/hard (4)	This chair is too soft. This chair is too hard. This chair is just right.

(continued)

TABLE 17.1 Repetitious Language in Select Storybooks (continued)

Author & Title	Examples of Repetitive Language (Number of Repetitions)	
Hoberman, M. A. & Wescott, N. B. *The Lady with the Alligator Purse*	called (3) in (4) out (3) came (3) went (3) said (6)	Miss Lucy called the doctor. Miss Lucy called the Nurse. Miss Lucy called the lady with the alligator purse.
Hutchins, P. *Good-night Owl!*	tried to (11) other regular past tense verbs with –ed (20)	Owl tried to sleep. The bees buzzed, buzz, buss, and Owl tried to sleep.
Little Red Hen	Who will help me ___ (5) said (20) asked (5) I will (7)	"Who will help me plant this wheat?" "Not I," said the cat.
Martin, B. *Brown Bear, Brown Bear, What Do You See?*	What do you see? (7) I see ___ looking at me (7)	Brown Bear, Brown Bear, what do you see? I see a yellow duck looking at me.

School Subject Focus

Mathematics Focus

In order to select appropriate stories for the classroom, teachers need to know what to look for. Hunsader's (2004) 12-item rubric facilitates evaluation of the mathematical and literary quality of trade books. Her criteria (six for math and six for literary merit), scored at a five-point scale, are summarized in Table 17.2. For language teachers, I would add to the list accurate mathematical language; vocabulary likely to be useful in the math class; and phrases likely to be of use to children in their personal communication about mathematics.

Hunsader rates a number of children's books featuring some mathematics content or concepts, identifying many titles of both literary and mathematical value. The following are just a few examples, some of them already mentioned in Chapter four. *How Big is a Foot?* (Myller, 1991) stresses the importance of standard units of measure. *Anno's Mysterious Multiplying Jar* (Anno & Anno, 1983) presents the concept of factorials in an enjoyable way, and the book includes a detailed explanation of the concept at the end. *Anno's Magic Seeds* (Anno, 1995) and *The King's Chessboard* (Birch, 1988) illustrate the speed of exponential growth. *The Doorbell Rang* (Hutchins, 1986) and *The Remainder of One* (Pinczes, 1995) deal with the concept of

TABLE 17.2 Mathematical and Literary Standards

Mathematical Standard	Literary Standards
1. Mathematical content must be accurate and correct.	1. Good, strong plot development and well developed characters (if any).
2. Mathematics content is presented clearly and effectively.	2. Vivid and interesting style likely to engage children.
3. The mathematics content is intellectually and developmentally appropriate for the target group.	3. Text-relevant, appealing illustrations age-appropriate for the target group.
4. The math imbedded in the text invites the reader to "do the math."	4. Age appropriate readability level.
5. The mathematics and story line complement each other.	5. Plot, style and illustrations complement each other to create an enjoyable product.
6. Resources needed to realize the benefits of the mathematics in the story are readily available.	6. Respects the reader by presenting positive cultural and ethical values.

Source: Hunsader, P. (Apr 2004). Mathematics trade books: Establishing their value and assessing their quality. *The Reading Teacher,* 57(7), p. 620. Used with permission.

division, while *Two of Everything* (Hong, 1993) is about doubling. *Spaghetti and Meatballs for All* (Burns, 1997) is a delightful introduction to perimeter and area. Teachers can consult the NCTM journal, *Teaching Children Mathematics*, for more titles (http://www.nctm.org).

Science Focus

The use of science-oriented literature is not straightforward. If and when science oriented trade books are used, the teacher must be careful both in selecting books and in choosing the pedagogical approach, as "certain types of pedagogical approaches or styles may inhibit or support such discipline-appropriate thinking" (Langer, Confer, & Sawyer, 1993, p. 38). For example, the methods readers employ when approaching texts differ depending on their perceived purpose for the reading. Louise Rosenblatt, a renowned scholar and theorist, has identified two approaches to reading. "Efferent reading" is reading for information, and is typically employed in content area reading, while "aesthetic reading" involves readers' "experiencing, thinking, and feeling during reading" (Rosenblatt, 1991, p. 444), often also including examination of the writer's craft in conjuring up particular responses. Because children are accustomed to factual questions in their science classes, as well as in many other classes, including apparently also language arts classes, they may read a science-related story solely for its factual content. Aesthetic reading, however, is more likely to help children grasp the bigger picture (Royce & Wiley, 1996). In other words, through aesthetic reading children will be able to identify links between concepts as well as their connection to their real world experiences.

Mayer (1995) further cautions that, because children bring into the reading situation their own background experiences, including their biases and limited understanding of the world, literature may interfere with their understanding of science concepts if the text and/or illustrations are misinterpreted by children. Therefore, teacher guidance is important in facilitating comprehension.

When selecting books with science content, the following guidelines should be kept in mind. First, the science concepts presented must be accurate. There is no excuse for presenting young learners with conceptually inaccurate information simply because "we are just teaching language, not science, and having some fun," as one teacher said when justifying why she used a six-legged representation of a spider in her kindergarten ELT class. While most of Eric Carle's books, such as *The Very Hungry Caterpillar*, for example, represent the best in children's literature and introduce many science concepts quite accurately, Trundle and Troland (2005) point out that Carle's *Papa, Please Get the Moon for Me* (Carle, 1996) misrepresents the lunar phases. Second, if the story is fictional, facts should be clearly discernible from fiction (Mayer, 1995). For a second language class, the language of the story needs to be considered as well, and while the language needs to be simple, it must also be accurate. Butzow and Butzow (2000) further stress that the concepts must be compatible with the child's developmental stages.

The following titles are all appropriate for young learners. *The Tiny Seed* (Carle, 1987), *The Carrot Seed* (Krauss, 1989), are about seeds growing. *The Very Hungry Caterpillar* (Carle, 1987), *Fish is Fish* (Lionni, 1995), and Andersen's classic *The Ugly Duckling* describe animal life cycles. *The Very Busy Spider* (Carle, 1984), *The Very Quiet Cricket* (Carle, 1990), and *Stellaluna* (Cannon, 1993) introduce specific animal characteristics, while also providing empathetic introductions to creatures not so common in children's stories, particularly if the teacher encourages aesthetic reading. Although too difficult for young second language learners to read on their own, *Stellaluna* is a heart-warming read-aloud story about a little bat's friendship with some birds. *The Great Kapok Tree* (Cherry, 1990) describes the wonders of the rain forest, highlighting the interdependence of living things, and *Who Sank the Boat?* (Allen, 1982) will nicely accompany an introduction to buoyancy.

NSTA publishes an annual list of outstanding science trade books for children, accessible through the association's website (http://www.nsta.org). The association's journal, *Science and Children*, runs a monthly column on teaching through tradebooks, and many of the ideas presented in the journal are adaptable to second language classes. NSTA publishes also an annual list of *Outstanding Science Trade Books for Children*.

Social Studies Focus

When selecting books with social studies content, it is useful to keep in mind the themes of the local social studies curriculum. For example, in the United States, the National Council for the Social Studies (NCSS) curriculum standards include the following ten thematic strands:

1. culture
2. time, continuity, and change
3. people, places, and, environments
4. individual development and identity
5. individuals, groups, and institutions
6. power, authority, and governance
7. production, distribution, and consumption

8. science, technology, and society
9. global connections
10. civic ideals and practice

Since curricular standards vary from country to country, language teachers will find it useful to consult social studies teachers in their school when selecting titles that appropriately contribute to the specific standards in their own context. The NCSS website (http://www.ncss.org) provides annotated lists of the *Notable Social Studies Trade Books for Young People*. While the most recent year's list is accessible only to members, the previous ones can be accessed by anyone. The following are some of the titles with social studies themes.

A rich array of multicultural literature is available in English, with many titles also suitable for young English language learners. *The Day of Ahmad's Secret* by Florence Parry Heide (1990) is a heartwarming account of a young working boy's day in Cairo, Egypt, with illustrations depicting authentic scenes from the streets of the Egyptian capital. Diane Turnage Burgoyne's (1982) *Amina and Muhammad's Special Visitor* tells of the daily life of an urban family in the Kingdom of Saudi Arabia and includes notes on the text that further illuminate the life and traditions in the Kingdom. *The Swirling Hijaab* (Na'imh bint Robert, 2002), a dual Arabic–English book, also features a young Muslim girl, while in *Make a Wish, Molly* (Cohen, 1994) the main character is a young Jewish girl, and *Just Plain Fancy* (Polacco, 1990) is set in an Amish community.

The Ballad of Mulan (Song Nan Zhang, 1998), an easy-to-read retelling of an ancient Chinese popular song, possibly based on true events, shows that women, given the opportunity, are as capable as men. The book includes a historical note as well a map of China tracing Mulan's route. *Phoenician Friends* (Ghosn, 2011) is set in ancient Phoenicia, and *Voyage to the Pharos* (Gauch, 2009) tells a young Greek boy's trip to the ancient lighthouse in Alexandria. *Follow the Drinking Gourd* (Winter, 1988), *Sweet Clara and the Freedom Quilt* (Hopkinson, 1995), and *Jumping the Broom* (Wright, 1994) are set in the U.S. slavery era. *Watch the Stars Come Out* (Levinson, 1985) and *Molly's Pilgrim* (Cohen, 1983) describe the immigrant experience in the 1800s and 1900s, while *Sarah, Plain and Tall* (MacLachlan, 1996) is a touching story about a family living in the prairie.

Sadako and the Thousand Paper Cranes (Coerr, 1977) is a heart-moving story about the devastating consequences of the Hiroshima atomic bomb. *Sweet Dried Apples* (Breckler, 1996), set in Vietnam, and *Sami and the Time of the Troubles* (Perry Heide, 1992), taking place in Beirut, Lebanon, movingly portray children's first-hand experiences with war. *The Librarian of Basra*

(Winter, 2005) tells the true story of the chief librarian of Basra's central Library in Iraq, who keeps moving books to safety as the war rages around her.

All the above titles will complement units in social studies, even where social studies classes are taught in children's mother tongue. The selection gets richer and richer as children advance to middle and secondary school.

References

Adair-Hauck, B., & Donato, R. (1994). Foreign language explanations within the zone of proximal development. *The Canadian Modern Language Review, 50*(3), 532–544.

Adair-Hauck, B., & Donato, R. (2002). The PACE model: A story-based approach to meaning and form for standards-based language learning. *The French Review, 76*(2), 265–276.

Adoniou, M. (2001). Who decides what young EFL learners learn? *English as a Foreign Language Newsletter, 21*(1), 7.

Al-Shaboul, Y. M., Asassfeh, S. M., Al-Tamimi, Y. A., & Alshboul, S. Sh. (2010). Curriculum development in Jordan: Continuous improvement toward excellence. In J. D. Kirylo & A. K. Nauman (Eds.), *Curriculum development. Perspectives from around the world* (pp. 170–181). Chicago: Association for Childhood Education International.

Alshamrani, H. M. (2003). *The attitudes and beliefs of ESL students about extensive reading of authentic texts.* Unpublished doctoral dissertation, Indiana University of Pennsylvania. UMI #AAT 3080428.

Ameis, J. A. (2002). Stories invite children to solve mathematical problems. *Teaching Children Mathematics* 8.5:260+ *Expanded Academic ASAP.* Web. 18 Feb.2012.

Anderson, J. R. (1995). *Learning and memory: An integrated approach.* New York: Wiley.

Appleyard, J. (1990). *Becoming a reader: The experience of fiction from childhood to adulthood.* Cambridge University Press.

Apuleius, L. (1951). *The transformations of Apuleius, otherwise known as the Golden Ass* (R. Graves, trans.). New York, NY: Farrar, Strauss and Giroux.

Aranha, M. (1985). Sustained silent reading goes east. *Reading Teacher 39*(2), 214–217.

Ariaz, S. K. (2010). *Vocabulary acquisition of bilingual students through the implementation of dialogic shared storybook reading techniques.* M.S. Thesis, The University of Texas at El Paso. MAI 48/06, Dec 2010.

Arndt, V. (1987). Six writers in search of texts: A protocol-based study of L1 and L2 writing. *ELT Journal, 41,* 257–267.

Artelt, C. (2005). Cross-cultural approaches to measuring motivation. *Educational Assessment, 10*(3), 231–255.

Austin, M., & Morrison, C. (1963). *The first R.* New York: Macmillan.

Bacha, N., Ghosn, I.-K., & McBeath, N. (2008). The textbook, the teacher and the learner: A Middle East perspective. In B. Tomlinson (Ed.), *English language learning materials: A critical review* (pp. 281–299). London: Continuum.

Barkley, R. A. (1996). Critical issues in research on attention. In G. R. Lyon & N. A. Krasnegor (Eds.), *Attention, memory and executive function* (pp. 45–56). Baltimore, MD: Brookes Publishing Co.

Beard, L. A. (2003, September). *The effects of integrating mathematics and children's literature instruction on mathematics achievement and math anxiety by gender.* Doctoral dissertation, University of Southern Mississippi, DAI-A 64/03.

Bearne, E. (1996). Mind the gap. In M. Styles, E. Bearne, & V. Watson (Eds.), *Voices off* (pp. 310–329). London: Cassell.

Beck, I., & McKeown, M. (1991). Conditions of vocabulary acquisition. In R. Barr, M. L. Kamil, P. Mosenthal, & P. D. Pearson (Eds.), *Handbook of reading research* (Vol. II, pp. 789–814). New York: Longman.

Belsky, S. (2006). *The effects of using children's literature with adolescents in the English as a foreign language classroom.* Doctoral dissertation, University of North Texas. DAI-A 68/02, August 2007.

Bennett, K. J., Brown, S. K., Boyle, M., Racine, Y., & Offord, D. (2003). Does low reading achievement at school entry cause conduct problems? *Social Science and Medicine, 56,* 2443–2448.

Berova, N., & Dachkova, L. (2003). Foreign language teaching to children in Bulgaria. In M. Nikolov & H. Curtain (Eds.), *An early start: Young learners and modern languages in Europe and beyond* (pp. 101–116). Graz, Austria: Council of Europe, Centre for Modern Languages. Online at http://archive.ecml.at/documents/earlystart.pdf

Bettelheim, B. (1989). *The uses of enchantment. The meaning and importance of fairy tales.* New York: Vintage Books.

Blau, E. K. (1981). The effect of syntax on readability for ESL students in Puerto Rico. *TESOL Quarterly, 16*(4) 517–528.

Blaxton, T. A. (1989). Investigating dissociations among memory measures: Support for a transfer-appropriate processing framework. *Journal of Experimental Psychology: Learning, Memory and Cognition, 15*(4), 657–668.

Bloom, B. S. (1956). *Taxonomy of educational objectives: Handbook I. The cognitive domain.* New York: David McKay.

Botelho, M. J., & Rudman, M. (2009). *Critical multicultural analysis of children's literature: Mirrors, windows and doors.* New York: Routledge.

Brock, C. A. (1984). The effects of referential questions on ESL classroom discourse. *TESOL Quarterly, 20*(1), 47–59.
Brown, C. L. (2007). Strategies for making social studies texts more comprehensible for English-language learners. *The Social Studies, 98*(5), 185–188.
Brown, G., & Wragg, E. C. (1993). *Questioning.* London: Routledge.
Brumfit, C., Moon, J., & Tongue, R. (1995). *Teaching English to children. From practice to principle.* Harlow, Essex: Addison-Wesley Longman.
Bruner, J. (1986) *Actual minds, possible worlds.* Cambridge, MA: Harvard University Press.
Bruner, J. (1987). Life as narrative. *Social Research, 54,* 11–32.
Bullock Report, The (1975). *A language for life.* Report of the Committee of Enquiry appointed by the Secretary of State for Education and Science under the Chairmanship of Sir Alan Bullock. London: Her Majesty's Stationary Office.
Burns, M. (1992). *Math and literature (K–3). Book one.* Sausalito, CA: Math Solutions Publications.
Bus, A. G., deJong, M. T., & Verhallen, M. J. A. J., (2006). The promise of multimedia stories for kindergarten children at risk. *Journal of Educational Psychology, 98*(2), 410–419.
Butler, Y. (2004, Summer). What level of English proficiency do elementary school teachers need to attain to teach EFL? Case studies from Korea, Taiwan, and Japan. *TESOL Quarterly, 38*(2), 245–278.
Butzow, C., & Butzow, J. (2000). *Science through children's literature. An Integrated approach.* (2nd ed.). Englewood, CO: Teacher Ideas Press.
Cameron, L. (1994). Organizing the world: Children's concepts and categories, and implications for the teaching of English. *ELT Journal, 48,* 28–39.
Cameron, L. (2001). *Teaching languages to young learners.* Cambridge: Cambridge University Press.
Carger, C. L. (1993, November). Louie comes to life: Pretend reading with second language emergent readers. *Language Arts, 70,* 542–547.
Carlson, K. (2005). Reading science. *Science Scope, 28*(6), 40–41.
Carter, R., & McRae, J. (2002). Reading language: A fifth skill. *IATEFL Issues, 165,* 10.
Casey, B., Erkut, S., Ceder, I., & Mercer Young, J. (2008). Use of storytelling context to improve girls' and boys' geometry skills in kindergarten. *Journal of Applied Behavioral Psychology, 29,* 29–48.
Celce-Murcia, M. (1991). *Language teaching approaches: An overview.* New York: Newbury House.
Chaaya, D., & Ghosn, I.-K. (2010). Supporting young second language learners' reading through guided reading and strategy instruction in a second grade classroom in Lebanon. *Educationa Research and Reviews, 5*(6), 329–337. Online http://www.academicjojurnals.org/ERR2

Chaaya, D. (2006). *How young English language learners experience reading instruction in a mixed reading ability classroom: Implementing the guided reading approach.* Unpublished M.A. thesis, Lebanese American University, Beirut.

Chambers, A. (1985). The child's changing story. *Signal, 40,* 36–52.

Chastain, K. (1988). *Developing second-language skills: Theory and practice* (3rd ed.), San Diego, CA: Harcourt Brace Jovanovich.

Chaudron, C. (1988). *Second language classrooms.* Cambridge: Cambridge University Press.

Chen-Y.- L. (2004). Storyreading in an EFL primary classroom: An analysis of teacher–student interaction. University of Newcastle upon Tyne *ARECLS E-Journal, 1*(3). Retrieved from http://www.ecls.ncl.ac.uk/publish/Volume1/Jenny/Jenny.htm

Chen-Y.- L., & Seedhouse, P. (2010). Classroom interactions in story-based lessons with young learners. *Asian EFL Journal 12*(2), 288–312. [Online] http://www.asian-efl-journal.com/PDF/June-2010.pdf

Chomsky, N. (1986). *Knowledge of language: Its nature, origin, and use.* New York: Praeger.

Christian, D., Pufahl, I., & Rhodes, N. (2005). Fostering foreign language proficiency: What the U.S. can learn from other countries. *Phi Delta Kappan, X,* 226–228.

Ciampa, K. (2010). *The impact of a digital children's literature program on primary students' reading motivation.* M.Ed. thesis, Brock University, St. Catharines, Ontario. Retrieved from http://dr.library.brocku.ca/handle/10464/3037.

Clay, M. (1991). *Becoming literate: The construction of inner control.* Portsmouth, NH: Heinemann.

Clay, M. (2002). *An observation survey of early literacy achievement.* (2nd ed.) Auckland, New Zealand: Heinemann.

Coady, J. (1997). L2 vocabulary acquisition: A synthesis of the research. In J. Coady & T. Huckin (Eds.), *Second language vocabulary acquisition.* Cambridge: Cambridge   University Press.

Coady, J., Magoto, J., Hubbard, P., Graney, J., & Mokhtari, K. (1993). High frequency vocabulary and reading proficiency in ESL readers. In T. Huckin, M. Haynes, & J. Coady (Eds.), *Second language reading and vocabulary learning* (pp. 217–228). Norwood, NJ: Ablex Publishing.

Colby, A., & Kohlbrg, L. (1987). The measurement of moral judgment (Vol.1). *Theoretical foundations and research validation.* Cambridge: Cambridge University Press.

Collier, V. (1995). *Acquiring a second language for school. Directions in language & education.* National Clearinghouse for Bilingual Education [online] http://www.ncbe.gwu.edu/ncbpubs/ Directions.04.htm

Collins, M. F. (2005, October–December). ESL preschoolers' English vocabulary acquisition from storybook reading (English as a second language). *Reading Research Quarterly, 40*(4), 406–410.

Collison, O. (1974). Concept formation in a second language: A study of Ghanaian school children. *Harvard Education Review, 44*(3), 441–457.

Corbin, D. (1990). *Using literature to teach historical concepts in fifth-grade social studies.* Doctoral dissertation, The University of Iowa, DAI-A 51/12, p. 4082, June 1991.

Cordova, D. I., & Lepper, M. R. (1996). Intrinsic motivation and the process of learning: Beneficial effects of contextualization, personalization and choice. *Journal of Educational Psychology, 88,* 715–730.

Crookes, G. (2003). *A practicum in TESOL. Professional development through teaching practice.* Cambridge: Cambridge University Press.

Cruz, CA: National Center for Research on Cultural Diversity and Second Language [online] http://www.ncbe.gwu.edu/miscpubs/ncrcdsll/rr15.htm

Crystal, D. (1987). *Child language, learning and linguistics: An overview for teaching and therapeutic professions.* London: Edward Arnold.

Cummins, J. (1984). Wanted: A theoretical framework for relating language Proficiency to academic achievement among bilingual students. In C. Rivera (Ed.), *Language proficiency and academic achievement* (pp. 2–17). Clevedon, Avon: Multilingual Matters.

Daily, L., & Sharko, S. (2010). *Motivating students to write through the use of children's literature.* M.A. thesis. Saint Xavier University, Chicago. ERIC Document Reproduction Service No. ED509396.

Dann, K. (2007, September–October). Nothing like the real thing! *IATEFL Voices 198,* p. 6.

Darn, S. (2007). Content and language integrated learning. BBC, British Council Teaching English, Retrieved on October 25, 2007, from http://www.teachingenglish.org.uk

de'Ath, P. (2001). The Niue literacy experiment. *International Review of Education, 46*(3/4),137–146.

DeFord, D. (1981). Literacy: Reading, writing and other essentials. *Language Arts, 58,* 652–658.

Dégh, L. (1994 July). The approach to worldview in folk narrative study. *Western Folklore, 53,* 243–252.

DeKeyser, R. (2000). The robustness of critical period effects in second language acquisition. *Studies in Second Language Acquisition, 22,* 499–533.

Delgado-Gaitán, C. (1989). Classroom literacy activity for Spanish-speaking students. *Linguistics and Education, 1,* 285–297.

Demircioğlu, I. (2008). Using historical stories to teach tolerance: The experience of Turkish 8th-grade students. *The Social Studies, 93*(3), 105–110.

DeSpain, C., & Heflin, D. (1997, October). *Science enhancement through the use of children's literature hands-on instruction.* Masters thesis,Texas Woman's University. Dissertation MAI 35/05, 1130.

Devine, J. (1988). Language competence and L2 reading proficiency. In P. L. Carrell, J. Devine, & D. E. Esky (Eds.), *Interactive approaches to second language reading* (pp. 260–277). Cambridge: Cambridge University Press.

Diamond, M. C. (1988). *Enriching heredity: The impact of the environment on the anatomy of the brain.* New York: Free Press.

Dickinson, D. K., & McCabe, A. (1991). A social interactional account of language and literacy development. In J. Kavanough (Ed.), *The language continuum* (pp. 1–40). Parkton, MD: York Press.

Dolitsky, M. (2006). The French communicative connection. In M. L. McCloskey, J. Orr, & M. Dolitsky, M. (Eds.), *Teaching English as a foreign language in primary school* (pp. 177–190). Alexandria, VA: TESOL.

Dörnyei, Z. (2001). *Motivational strategies in the language classroom.* Cambridge: Cambridge University Press.

Dressel, J. H. (1990). The effects of listening and discussing different qualities of children's literature on the narrative writing of 5th graders. *Research in Teaching of English, 24,* 397–414.

Droop, M., & Verhoeven, L. (1998). Background knowledge, linguistic complexity, and second language reading comprehension. *Journal of Literacy Research, 30*(2), 253–271.

Dulay, H., & Burt, M. (1973). Should we teach children syntax? *Language Learning, 23*(2), 245–258.

Dulay, H., & Burt, M. (1977). Some remarks on creativity in language acquisition. In W. Richie, (Ed.), *Second language acquisition research: Issues and implications* (pp. 65–89). New York: Academic Press.

Eade, J. (1997). Using a core text with bilingual children. *English in Education, 31*(3), 32–39.

Eagan, K. (1979). *Educational development.* Oxford: Oxford University Press.

Echevarria, J., & Graves, M. (1998). *Sheltered content instruction: Teaching English language learners with diverse abilities.* Needham Heights, MA: Allyn & Bacon.

Edelenbos, P., & Suhre, C. J. (1996). English in Dutch primary schools. In P. Edelenbos & J. Johnstone (Eds.), *Researching language at primary school. Some European perspectives* (pp. 47–58). Stirling: Scottish CILT.

Edelsky, C. (1982). Writing in a bilingual program: The relation of L1 and L2 texts. *TESOL Quarterly, 16*(2), 211–28.

Egan, K. (1979). *Educational development.* Oxford: Oxford University Press.

Eisele, B., Yang Eisele, C., York Hanlon, R., & Hanlon, S. (2004). *Hip hip hooray!* White Plains, NY: Pearson Education.

Elley, W. (1989). Vocabulary acquisition from listening stories. *Reading Research Quarterly, 24,* 174–87.

Elley, W. B. (1991, September). Acquiring literacy in second language: The effects of book-based programs. *Language Learning, 41*(3), 375–411.

Elley, W. (1997). *In praise of incidental learning: Lessons from some empirical findings on language acquisition.* Retrieved from http://cela.albany.edu/iisamples/issamples/oop/cfullhit.htw

Elley, W. B. (2000). The potential of book floods for raising literacy levels. *International Review of Education, 46*(3/4), 233–255.

Elley, W. B., & Mangubhai, F. (1983, Fall). The impact of reading on second language learning. *Reading Research Quarterly, 14*(1), 53–67.

Elley, W., Cutting, B., Mangubhai, F., & Hugo, C. (1996). *Lifting literacy levels with story books: Evidence from the South Pacific, Singapore, Sri Lanka and South Africa.* Paper presented at the World Conference on Literacy, Philadelphia.

Ellis, N. (1994). *Implicit and explicit learning of language.* London: Academic Press.

Ellis, N. C. (2003). Constructions, chunking, and connectionism: The emergence of second language structure. In D. J. Doughty & M. H. Long (Eds.), *The handbook of second language acquisition* (pp. 63–103). Oxford: Oxford University Press.

Ellis, R. (1985). *Understanding second language acquisition.* Oxford: Oxford University Press.

Elman, J. L., Bates, E. A., Johnson, M. H., Karmiloff-Smith, A., Parisi, D., & Plunkett, K. (1996). *Rethinking innateness: A connectionist perspective on development.* Cambridge, MA: MIT Press.

Enever, J. (2011). *ELLiE. Early language learning in Europe.* London: British Council.

Eurydice Network. (2008). *Eurydice: Key data on teaching languages at schools in Europe—2008 edition.* Brussels: Commission of the European Communities. Online at: eacea.ec.europa.eu/education/Eurydice/documents/key_data_series/095EN.pdf

Escott, C. (1995). Bridging the gap: Making links between children's reading and writing. In E. Bearne (Ed.), *Greater expectations. Children reading writing* (pp.18–24). London: Cassell.

Faklova, Z. (2003). Baseline study on ELT to young learners in the Czech Republic. In M. Nikolov & H. Curtain (Eds.), *An early start: Young learners and modern languages in Europe and beyond* (pp. 79–91). Graz, Austria: Council of Europe, Centre for Modern Languages. Online at http://archive.ecml.at/documents/earlystart.pdf

Fazio, B., Naremore, R., & Connell, P. (1996). Tracking children from poverty at risk for specific language impairment: a 3-year longitudinal study. *Journal of Speech and Hearing Research, 39*(3), 611–624.

Feagans, L. (1982). The development and importance of narrative for school adaptation. In L. Feagans & D. C. Farran (Eds.), *The language of children reared in poverty* (pp. 95–116). New York: Academic Press.

Flores Jiménez, E. P. (2006). Pass it on: English in the primary schools in Coahuíla, Mexico. In M. L. McCloskey, J. Orr, & M. Dolitsky (Eds.), *Teaching English as a foreign language in primary school* (pp. 41–58). Alexandria, VA: TESOL.

Fountas, I. C., & Pinnell, G. S. (1996). *Guided reading. Good first teaching for all children.* Portsmouth, NH: Heinemann.

Fox, G. (1998). Using corpus data in the classroom. In Tomlinson, B. (Ed.), *Materials development in language teaching* (pp. 25–43). Cambridge: Cambridge University Press.

Fox, M. (n.d.). *So you want to write a picturebook.* Retrieved from http://www.memfox.com

Freeman, G., & Taylor, V. (Eds.), (2006). *Integrating science and literacy instruction: A framework for bridging the gap.* Lanham, MD: Rowman & Littlefield Publishing Group.

Friedman, E. (1997). What is the math moral of the story? *Childhood Education, 74*(1), 33–35.

Gadbonton, E., & Segalowitz, N. (2005). Rethinking communicative language teaching: A focus on access to fluency. *Canadian Modern Language Review, 61*(3), 325–353.

Galda, L., & Cullinan, B. E. (1991). Literature for literacy: What research says about the benefits of using trade books in the classroom. In J. Flood, J. M. Jensen, D. Lapp, & J. R. Squire. (Eds.), *Handbook of research on teaching language arts* (529–535). New York: Macmillan.

García, G. (1991). Factors influencing the English reading test performance of Spanish speaking Hispanic children. *Reading Research Quarterly, 26*(4), 371–392.

García, G. E., & Codina, H. (1994). *Bilingual preschool children's classroom literacy experiences: 'Once upon a time' and its alternatives.* ERIC Document Reproduction Service No. ED 381770.

Gass, S. (1997). *Input, interaction, and the second language learner.* Mahwah, NJ: Lawrence Erlbaum Associates.

Gass, S., & Varonis, E. M. (1985). Task variation and nonnative-nonnative negotiation of meaning. In S. Gass & C. G. Madden (Eds.), *Input and second language acquisition* (pp. 149–161). Rowley, MA: Newbury House.

Genesee, F. (1994). Introduction. In F. Genesee (Ed.), *Educating second language children. The whole child, the whole curriculum, the whole community* (pp. 1–12). Cambridge University Press.

Genesee, F. (2000). *Brain research: Implications for second language learning.* Digest, EDO-FL-00-12 December. Retrieved from http://www.gse.berkeley.edu/research/crede/products/print/erics/0012-genesee-brain.pdf

Ghosn, I. K. (1997). ESL with children's literature. The way whole language worked in one Kindergarten class. *English teaching FORUM 35*(3), 14–19/29. Available online at http://exchanges.state.gov/forum/vols/vol39/no1/p10.htm

Ghosn, I.-K. (1999). *Caring kids: Social responsibility through literature.* Beirut: dar El-Ilm Lilmalayin.

Ghosn, I.-K. (2001a). [Emotional intelligence] http://exchanges.state.gov/englishteaching.forum/archives/docs/01-39-1-c.pdf

Ghosn (2001b). *Teachers and students interacting around the textbook: An exploratory study of children developing academic second language literacy in primary school English language classes in Lebanon.* Ph.D. Dissertation, University of Leicester School of Education (DAI-A 63/04, p. 1232, Oct. 2002).

Ghosn, I. K. (2003a). Talking like texts or talking about texts: How some primary school coursebook tasks are realized in the classroom. In B. Tomlinson (Ed.), *Developing materials for language teaching* (pp. 291–305). London: Continuum.

Ghosn, I. (2003b). *Story-Based Instruction for academic L2 literacy for young learners.* Paper presented at the 37th International IATEFL Conference, Brighton, U.K.

Ghosn, I.-K. (2003c). Socially responsible language teaching using literature. *The Language Teacher, 27*(3), 15–20.

Ghosn, I.-K. (2004). Story as culturally appropriate content and social context for young English language learners: A look at Lebanese primary school classes. *Language, Culture and Curriculum, 17*(2), 109–126.

Ghosn, I.-K. (2005). *Story-based instruction for language and academic literacy.* Workshop handouts. Lebanese American University Teacher Training Institute, March 4, 2005. [online http://www.caringkidsbooks.com]

Ghosn, I.-K. (2006 April). *Young learners developing foreign language literacy.* Paper presented at the 40th International IATEFL Conference, Harrogate, U.K.

Ghosn, I.-K. (2007). Output like input: Influence of children's literature on young L2 learners' written expression. In B. Tomlinson (Ed), *Language acquisition and development. Studies of learners of first and other languages* (pp. 171–186). London: Continuum.

Ghosn, I.-K. (2010). Five-year outcomes from children's literature-based programs vs. programs using a skills-based ESL course: The Matthew and Peter Effects at work? In B. Tomlinson & H. Masuhara (Eds.), *Research on the effects of materials development for language teaching* (pp. 22–36). London: Continuum International Publishing.

Ghosn, I.-K. (2012). Literate language features in the narratives of Lebanese fifth-graders learning English as a first foreign language. Manuscript submitted for publication.

Ghosn, I.-K. (2013). Language learning for young learners. In B. Tomlinson (Ed.). *Applied linguistics applied.* London: Bloomsbury.

Gibbons, P. (1995) *Learning to learn in a second language.* London: Primary English Teaching Association.

Gilbert, I. (2002). *Essential motivation in the classroom.* London: Routledge.

Gimenez, T. (2009). English at primary school level in Brazil: Challenges and perspectives. In J. Enever, J. Moon, & U. Raman (Eds.), *Young learner English language policy and implementation: International perspectives* (pp. 53–60). Reading, U.K.: Garnet Education and IATEFL.

Goforth, F. (1998). *Literature & the learner.* Belmont, CA: Wadsworth Publishing Company.

Golden, D. (1994). Building a better brain. *Life,* July, 63–70.

Goleman, D. (1995). *Emotional intelligence.* New York: Bantam Books.

Gordon, T. (2007). *Teaching young children a second language.* Westport, CT: Praeger.

Grabe, W. (1991). Current developments in second language reading research. *TESOL Quarterly, 25,* 375–406.

Graesser, A. C., Hauft-Smith K., Cohen, A. D., & Pyles, L. D. (1980). Advanced outlines, familiarity, text genre, and retention of prose. *Journal of Experimental Education, 48,* 209–220.

Graves, D. (1983). *Writing: Teachers and children at work.* Portsmouth, NH: Heinemann.

Gregory, E. (1996). *Making sense of a new world: Learning to read in a second language.* London: Paul Chapman Publications.

Guan-Lea L., & Myers, D. A. (2010). Curriculum development in Korea: English language instruction. In J. D. Kirylo & A. K. Nauman (Eds.), *Curriculum development. Perspectives from around the world* (pp. 194–207). Chicago: Association for Childhood Education International.

Guzzetti, B., Kowalinski, B., & McGowan (1992). Using a literature-based approach to teaching social studies. *Journal of Reading, 10*(36:2), 114–121.

Hadjikyriacou, S., Englezaki, A., Ioannou-Georgiou, S., & Pavlou, P. (n.d.). *Pilot curriculum, English as a foreign language in Cyprus primary schools (years 1–6).* Cyprus Ministry of Education and Culture. Retrieved from http://www.moec.gov/cy/dde/programs/oloimero/pdf/curriculum_english.pdf

Halliday, M. (1975). *Learning how to mean: Explorations in the functions of language.* London: Edward Arnold.

Hamayan, E., & Perlman, R. (1990). *Helping language minority students after they exit from Bilingual/ESL programs.* Washington, DC: National Clearinghouse for Bilingual Education.

Harcourt Science level 3 (2002). Orlando, FL: Harcourt School Publishers.

Hasbrouck, J. E., & Tindal, G. (2005). Oral reading fluency norms: A valuable assessment tool for reading teachers. *The Reading Teacher, 59*(7), 636–644.

Hatch, E. (1978). Discourse analysis and second language acquisition. In E. Hatch (Ed.), *Second language acquisition: A book of readings* (pp. 401–435). Rowley, MA: Newbury House.

Hayes, D. (2006). Developing teachers in the developing world of Sri Lanka. In M. L. McCloskey, J. Orr, & M. Dolitsky (Eds.), *Teaching English as a foreign language in primary school* (pp. 141–156). Alexandria, VA: TESOL.

Hazenburg, S., & Hulstijn, J. H. (1996). Defining a minimal receptive second-language vocabulary for non-native university students: An empirical investigation. *Applied Linguistics, 17,* 145–163.

Hemphill, L., Picardi, N., & Tager-Flusberg, H. (1991). Narrative as an index of communicative competence in mildly retarded children. *Applied Psycholinguistics, 12,* 263–279.

Hermes, L. (2009, Spring). Literature and the teaching of literature in teacher education. *IATEFL Young Learners and Teenagers, 1*(9), 26–28.

Herrera, M., & Pinkley, D. (2005). *Packpack 3.* White Plains, NY: Pearson Education.

Hidi, S. (1990, Winter). Interest and its contribution as mental resource for learning. *Review of Educational Research, 60*(4), 549–571.

Hidi, S., & Harackiewicz, J. (2000). Motivating the academically unmotivated: A critical issue for the 21st century. *Review of Educational Research, 70*(2), 151–180.

Hilke, E. V. (1999). Children's literature and the K–4 social studies standards. *Fastback 453.* Bloomington, IN: Phi Delta Kappa.

Hill, D., & Reid Thoma, M. (1988). Graded readers: A survey review (Part I). *ELT Journal 42*, 44–52.

Hoffman, M. (1984). Interaction effect and cognition in empathy. In C. E. Izard, J. Kagan, & R. Zajonc (Eds.), *Emotions, cognition and behavior* (pp.103–131). Cambridge: Cambridge University Press.

Holdaway, D. (1979). *The foundations of literacy*. Sydney, Australia: Ashton Scholastic.

Holdaway, D. (2001). Shared book experience: Teaching reading using favorite books. *Theory into Practice, 21*, 293–300.

Holt, R. (2005). *Blue skies 4*. Harlow, Essex: Pearson Education.

Hong, H. (1996). Effects of mathematics learning through children's literature on math achievement and dispositional outcomes. *Early Childhood Research Quarterly, 11*, 477–494.

Howe, K. (1990). *Children's literature and effects on cognitive and noncognitive behaviors in elementary social studies*. Doctoral dissertation, University of Minnesota. Dissertation Abstracts International, 51/12A, 4044.

Huck, C. S., Hepler, S., Hickman, J., & Kiefer, B. Z. (2001). *Children's literature in the elementary school* (7th ed.). New York: McGraw-Hill Higher Education.

Hudelson, S. (1983). *Janice: Becoming a writer of English*. Paper presented at the 17th Annual Meeting of the Teachers of English to Speakers of Other Languages. Toronto, Canada.

Hudelson, S. (1989). *Write on. Children writing in ESL*. Center for Applied Linguistics and Prentice Hall Regents.

Hudelson, S. (1984). Kan yu ret an rayt ingles: Children become literate in English as a Second Language. *TESOL Quarterly, 18*(2), 221–238.

Huie, K., & Yahya, N. (2003). Learning to write in the primary grades: Experiences of English language learners and mainstream students. *TESOL Journal, 12*(1), 25–31.

Hunsader, P. (2004, April). Mathematics tradebooks: Establishing their value and assessing their quality. *The Reading Teacher, 57*(7), 618–630.

Ioannou-Georgiou, S. (n/d). *Foreign language learning in primary schools in Cyprus*. Retrieved October 12, 2010, from University of Warwick, Modern Languages in Primary School Web site: http://www/warwick.ac.uk/CELTE/MLPS.Research/casestudies/cyprus.htm

Jalongo, M. (2007). Beyond benchmarks and scores: Reasserting the role of motivation and interest in children's academic achievement. An ACEI Position Paper. *Childhood Education, International Focus Issue*, 395–407.

Jantscher, E., & Landsiedler, I. (2003). Austrian primary schools: An overview. In M. Nikolov & H. Curtain (Eds.), *An early start: Young learners and modern languages in Europe and beyond* (pp. 13–28). Graz, Austria: Council of Europe, Centre for Modern Languages. Online at http://archive.ecml.at/documents/earlystart.pdf

Jarvis, J., & Robinson, M. (1997). Analyzing educational discourse: An exploratory study of teacher response and support to pupils' learning. *Applied Linguistics, 18*(2), 212–228.

Jenner, D. (2002, November). Experiencing and understanding mathematics in the midst of a story. *Teaching Children Mathematics, 9*(3), 167.

Jennings, C. M., Jennings, J. E., Richey, J., & Dixon-Krauss, L. (1992). Increasing interest and achievement in mathematics through children's literature. *Early Childhood Research Quarterly, 7*, 263–276.

Jensen, E. (1998). *Teaching with the brain in mind.* Alexandria, VA: Association for Supervision and Curriculum Development.

Jiménez, R. T., García, G. E., & Pearson, P. D. (1995). Three children, two languages, and strategic reading: Case studies in bilingual/monolingual reading. *American Educational Research Journal, 32*, 31–61.

Johnson, T. D., & Louis, D. R. (1987). *Literacy through literature.* Portsmouth, NH: Heinemann.

Johnson, J. S., & Newport, E. L. (1989). Critical period effects in second language learning: The influence of maturational state on the acquisition of English as a second language. *Cognitive psychology, 21*, 60–99. Read more: http://www.oxbridgewriters.com/essays/linguistic/language-learning-critical-period-vs-adulthood.php#ixzz25aTJhIvD

Kamii, C. (1991). What is Constructivism? In C. Kamii, M. Manning, & G. Manning (Eds), *Early literacy: A constructivist foundation for whole language* (pp. 17–29). Washington, DC: National Education Association.

Kincade, K. M., & Pruitt, N. E. (1996). Using multicultural literature as an ally to elementary social studies text. *Reading Research and Instruction, 36*(1), 18–32.

Kirgöz, Y. (2006). Teaching EFL at the primary level in Turkey. In M. L. McCloskey, J. Orr, & M. Dolitsky (Eds.), *Teaching English as a foreign language in primary school* (pp. 85–100). Alexandria, VA: TESOL.

Koskinen, P. S., Blum, T. H., Bisson, S. A., Phillips, S. M., Creamer, T. C., & Baker, T. K. (1999). Shared reading, books, and audiotapes: Supporting diverse students in school and at home. *Reading Teacher, 52*(5), 430–444.

Kotulak, R. (1996). *Inside the Brain.* Kansas City, MO: Andrews & McMeel.

Kourtis-Kazoullis, V., & Skourtou, E. (2004). The Internet and English language learning. Opening up spaces for constructivist & transformative pedagogy. In J. Cummins & C. Davison (Eds.), *International handbook of English language teaching* (2nd ed., pp. 761–775). Amsterdam: Kluwer Academic Publishers.

Krashen, S. (1981). *Second language acquisition and second language learning.* Oxford: Pergamon Press.

Krashen, S. (1982). *Principles and practice in second language acquisition.* Oxford: Pergamon Press.

Krashen, S. (1989). We acquire vocabulary and spelling by reading: Additional evidence for the input hypothesis. *Modern Language Journal, 78*, 450–464.

Krashen, S. (2003). *Explorations in language acquisition and use.* Portsmouth, NH: Heinemann.

Kretzschmar, M. J. (2011, October). *The emphasis of formal grammar teaching in second language programs: The natural approach through children's literature.* MA thesis, University of Wyoming. MAI 49/05.

Kreidler, W. J. (1990). *Elementary perspectives: Teaching concepts of peace and conflict.* Cambridge, MA: Educators for Social Responsibility.

Kubota, M. (1989). *Question-answering behavior in ESL and EFL classrooms.* Masters Research Paper, Georgetown University. ERCI Document Reproduction Service No. ED313913.

Kuruppu, L. (2001). The 'books in schools' project in Sri Lanka. *International Journal of Educational Research, 35,* 181–191.

Kubanek-German, A. (2003). Early language programs in Germany. In In M. Nikolov & H. Curtain (Eds.), *An early start: Young learners and modern languages in Europe and beyond* (pp. 59–70). Graz, Austria: Council of Europe, Centre for Modern Languages. Online at http://archive.ecml.at/documents/earlystart.pdf

Lambert, J. G. (1991). *The effects of oral story sharing on vocabulary acquisition in English as a second language.* Unpublished manuscript, University of Southern California, Los Angeles.

Lamme, L., & Ledbetter, L. (1990). Libraries: The heart of whole language. *Language Arts, 67*(3), 735–741.

Langer, J. A., Confer, C., & Sawyer, M. (1993/1938). *Teaching disciplinary thinking in academic coursework.* Albany, NY: National Research Center on Literature Teaching and Learning. ERIC Document Reproduction Service No. ED 354 518.

Larsen-Freeman, D., & M. Long (1991). *An introduction to second language acquisition research.* London: Longman.

Laufer, B. (2005). Instructed second language vocabulary learning: The fault in the 'Default Hypothesis'. In A. Housen & M. Pierrard (Eds.), *Investigations in instructed second language acquisition* (pp. 311–332). New York: Mouton de Gruyter.

Laufer, B., & Nation, P. (1999). A vocabulary size test of controlled productive ability. *Language Testing, 16*(1), 33–51.

Lauritzen, C., & Jaeger, M. (1992). *The power of story in science learning.* Paper presented at the Annual NCTE Convention, Louisville, KY (ERIC ED 358469).

LeDoux, J. (Dec 1993). Emotional memory systems in the brain. *Behavioral Brain Research, 58*(1/2), 69–79.

Lee, W. K. (2009). Primary English language teaching in Korea. Bold risks on the national foundation. In J. Enever, J. Moon, & U. Raman (Eds.), *Young learner English language policy and implementation: International perspectives* (pp. 95–102). Reading, U.K.: Garnet Education/IATEFL.

Leitze, A. R. (1997). Connecting process problem solving to children's literature. *Teaching Children Mathematics, 3*(7), 398(9).

Lemke, J. L. (1990). *Talking science: Language, learning and values.* New York: Ablex.

Leung, C. (1996). Context, content and language. In T. Cline & N. Frederickson (Eds.), *Curriculum related assessment, Cummins and bilingual children* (pp. 26–40). Clevedon, Avon: Multilingual Matters.

Lewis, B., Long, R., & Mackay, M. (1993, April). Fostering communication in mathematics using children's literature. *Arithmetic Teacher, 40,* 470–473.

Lewis, C. S. (1963). On three ways of writing for children. *The Horn Book Magazine, 39*(5), 460.
Lightbown, P. M., & Spada, N. (2006). *How languages are learned* (3rd ed.). Oxford: Oxford University Press.
Livo, N., & Riertz, S. (1986). *Storytelling: Process and practice.* Littleton, CO: Libraries Unlimited.
Lo, Y-H. G. (2006). Leading the way in the new millennium: An integrated multiage EFL program in Taiwan. In M. L. McCloskey, J. Orr, & M. Dolitsky, M. (Eds.), *Teaching English as a foreign language in primary school* (pp. 25–40). Alexandria, VA: TESOL.
Long, M. (1981). Input, interactions and second language acquisition. *Annals of the New York Academy of Sciences 379,* 259–278. doi:10.1111/j.1749–6632.1981.tb42014x
Long, M. H., & Sato, C. J. (1983). Classroom foreigner talk discourse: forms and functions of teachers' questions. In H. W. Seliger & M. H. Long (Eds.), *Classroom-oriented research in second language acquisition* (pp. 268–285). Rowley, MA: Newbury House.
Lopriore, L. (2006). The long and winding road: A profile of Italian primary EFL teachers. In M. L. McCloskey, J. Orr, & M. Dolitsky (Eds.), *Teaching English as a foreign language in primary school* (pp. 59–84). Alexandria, VA: TESOL.
Lugossy, R. (2006). Browsing and borrowing your way to motivation through picture books. In J. Enever & G. Schmid-Schönbein (Eds.), *Picture books and young learners of English* (pp. 23–34). München: Münchener Arbeiten zur Fremdsprachen-Forschung.
Luoto, T., & Luoto, S. (2001). Satu ja tarina elää päiväkodissa [Fairytale and story live in the daycare center]. In N. Suojala & M. Karjalainen (Eds.), *Avaa lastenkirja.* [Open a children's book] (pp. 184–200). Helsinki: Lasten Keskus.
Lustig, M. W., & Koester, J. (2006). *Intercultural competence. Interpersonal communication across cultures.* (5th ed.), Boston, MA: Allyn and Bacon.
Lyster R., & Ranta, L. (1997). Corrective feedback and learner uptake: Negotiation of form in communicative classrooms. *Studies in Second Language Acquisition, 19,* 37–66.
MacGowan-Gilhooly, A. (1996). Fluency first: Reversing the traditional ESL sequence. In B. Leeds (Ed.), *Writing in a second language* (pp. 48–59). London: Longman.
Machura, L. (1995). Using literature in language teaching. In C. Brumfit, J. Moon, & R. Tongue (Eds.), *Teaching English to children* (pp. 67–80). Harlow, Essex: Addison-Wesley Longman.
MacIntyre, A. (1981). *After virtue: A study in moral theory* (2nd ed.). Notre Dame, IN: University of Notre Dame Press.
Madrazo, G. M. (1997, March). Using trade books to teach and learn science. *Science and Children, 34*(6), 20–21.
Maersk Nielsen, P. (2003). English in Argentina: A sociolinguistic profile. *World Englishes, 22*(2), 199–209.

Maguire, M., & Graves, B. (2001). Speaking personalities in primary school children's L2 writing. *TESOL Quarterly, 35*, 561–593.

Mangubhai, F. (2001). Book floods and comprehensible input floods: providing ideal conditions for second language acquisition. *International Journal of Educational Research, 35*, 147–156.

Mangubhai, F., & Elley, W. (1982). The role of reading in promoting ESL. *Language Learning and Communication, 1*(2), 121–232.

Marinova-Todd, S. (2003). Know your grammar: What the knowledge of syntax and morphology in an L2 reveals about the critical period for second/foreign language acquisition. In M. García Mayo de Pilar & M. L. García Lecumberri (Eds.), *Age and acquisition of English as a foreign language* (pp. 59–73). Clevedon: Multilingual Matters.

Markwardt, F. C. (1998). *Peabody individual achievement test—Revised.* (Normative Update). Circle Pines, MN: American Guidance Service.

Marsh, D. (2005, April 8). Adding language without taking away. *The Guardian Weekly*, 3.

Martinie, S., & Bay-Williams, J. (2003, November). Using literature to engage students in proportional reasoning. *Mathematics Teaching in the Middle School, 9*(3), 142.

Mayer, D. A. (1995). How can we best use literature in teaching? *Science and Children, 32*, 16–44.

Mayer, R. E. (1996). Learning strategies for making sense out of expository text: The SOI model for guiding three cognitive processes in knowledge construction. *Educational Psychology Review, 8*, 357–371.

Mayer, J., Caruso, D., & Salovey, P. (1999). Emotional intelligence meets standards for a traditional intelligence. *Intelligence, 27*, 267–298.

McCarty, D. M. (2007). Using multicultural National Council of Social Studies 'Notable Books' in the elementary classroom. *The Social Studies, 98*(2), 49–53.

McCauley, J. K., & McCauley, D. S. (1992). Using choral reading to promote language learning for ESL students. *The Reading Teachers, 45*(7), 526–533.

McCloskey, M. L., Levine New, L., Thornton, B., & El Naggar, Z. (2006). In M. L. McCloskey, J. Orr, & M. Dolitsky (Eds.), *Teaching English as a foreign language in primary school* (pp. 157–176). Alexandria, VA: TESOL.

McConaghy (1990). *Children learning through literature.* Portsmouth: Heinemann.

McKinney, C. W., & Jones, H. J. (1992, January). *Effects of children's book and a traditional textbook on fifth grade students' achievement and attitudes toward social studies.* Paper presented at the meeting of the Southwest Educational Research Association, Houston, TX.

McLaughlan, B. (1987). Reading in a second language. Studies with adult and child learners. In S. R. Goodman & T. Traube (Eds.), *Becoming literate in English as a second language* (pp. 57–70). Norwood, NJ: Ablex.

Mechling, K. R., & Oliver, D. L. (1983). *Science teaches basic skills* (Vol. 1). Washington, DC: National Science Teachers' Association.

Meek, M. (1995). The critical challenge of the world in books for children. *Children's Literature in Education, 26*(1), 5–22.

Merriam-Webster's Collegiate Dictionary (1994) (10th ed.). Springfield, MA: Merriam-Webster Inc.

Mihaljevic Djigunovic, J. (1993). Investigation of attitudes and motivation in early foreign language learning. In M. Vilke & I. Vrhovac (Eds.), *Children and foreign languages* (pp. 45–71). Zagreb: Faculty of Philosophy, University of Zagreb.

Mikkelsen, N. (1984). Literature and the storymaking powers of children. *Children's Literature Association Quarterly, 9*, 9–14.

Ministry of Education and Higher Education [MEHE] (2006). *Preliminary statistics for school year 2005–2006*. Beirut: Office of Educational Research Statistics Department, NCERD.

Mishra, A. (2003). Age and school related differences in recall of verbal items in a story context. *Social Science International, 19*, 12–18.

Mohanraj, J. (2006). Flavoring the salt: Teaching English in primary schools in India. In M. L. McCloskey, J. Orr, & M. Dolitsky (Eds.), *Teaching English as a foreign language in primary school* (pp. 101–110). Alexandria, VA: TESOL.

Moon, J. (2005). *Children learning English*. Oxford: Macmillan.

Morgan, A. S. (2007, September). *Alternative methodologies for teaching mathematics to elementary students. A pilot study using children's literature.* Doctoral dissertation, The American University, DAI-A 68/03.

Morgan, P., & Meier, C. (2008). Dialogic reading's potential to improve children's emergent literacy skills and behavior. *Preventing School Failure, 52*(4), 11–16.

Nagy, W., Diakidoy, I., & Anderson, R. C. (1993). The acquisition of morphology: Learning the contribution of suffixes to the meaning of derivatives. *Journal of Reading Behavior, 25*, 155–170.

Nagy, W. E., García, G. E., Durgunoğlu, A., & Hancin-Bhatt, B. (1993). Spanish–English bilingual children's use and recognition of cognates in English reading. *Journal of Reading Behavior, 25*(3), 241–259.

Nagy, W., & Herman, P. (1987). Breadth and depth of vocabulary knowledge: Implications for acquisition and instruction. In M. McKeown & M. Curtis (Eds.), *The nature of vocabulary acquisition* (pp. 19–35). Hillsdale, NJ: Erlbaum.

Nagy, W., Herman, P., & Anderson, R. (1985). Learning words from context. *Reading Research Quarterly, 20*, 233–253.

Nagy, W. E., & Scott, J. A. (2000). Vocabulary processes. In M. L. Kamil, P. B. Mosenthal, P. D. Pearson, & R. Barr (Eds.), *Handbook of reading research* (Vol. III, pp. 269–284). Mahwah, NJ: Lawrence Earlbaum Associates, Inc.

Nation, I. S. P. (1990). *Teaching and learning vocabulary*. New York: Newbury House.

Nation, I. S. P. (2001). *Learning vocabulary in another language*. Cambridge: Cambridge University Press.

Nation, P., & Wang, K. (1999). Graded readers and vocabulary. *Reading in a Foreign Language, 12*, 355–379.

Nation, P., & Warig, R. (1997). Vocabulary size, text coverage, and word lists. In N. Schmitt & M. McCarthy (Eds.), *Vocabulary: Description, acquisition, and pedagogy* (pp. 6–19). Cambridge: Cambridge University Press.

National Council for the Social Studies [NCSS]. *Notable children's books.* http://www.socialstudies.org/resources.notable

National Council of Teachers of Mathematics [NCTM] (2000). *Principles and standards for school mathematics.* Reston, VA: Author.

National Institute of Child Health and Human Development Early Child Care Research Network (2005). Pathways to reading: The role of oral language in the transition to reading. *Developmental Psychology, 41,* 428–442.

National Science Teachers' Association [NSTA]. http://www.nsta.org

Ng, S. M. (1994). Improving English language learning in the upper primary levels in Brunei Darussalam. In M. L. Tickoo (ED.), *Research in reading and writing: A Southeast Asian collection* (pp. 41–54). Singapore: SEAMEO Regional Language Center.

Ng, S. M., & Preston W. (1993). Teaching English in primary school in Brunei Darussalam. In K. D. Samway & D. McKeon (Eds.), *Common threads of practice. Teaching English to children around the world* (pp. 47–56). Alexandria, VA: TESOL.

Ng, S. M., & Sullivan, C. (2001). The Singapore reading and English acquisition program. *International Journal of Educational Research, 35*(2), 157–167.

Nikolov, M. (1999). 'Why do you learn English?' 'Because the teacher is short.' A study of Hungarian children's foreign language learning motivation. *Language Teaching Research, 3*(1), 33–56.

Nikolov, M. (2003). Teaching foreign languages to young learners in Hungary. In M. Nikolov & H. Curtain (Eds.), *An early start: Young learners and modern languages in Europe and beyond* (pp. 29–40). Graz, Austria: Council of Europe, Centre for Modern Languages. Online at http://archive.ecml.at/documents/earlystart.pdf

Nikolov, M., & Curtain, H. (Eds.), (2003). *An early start: Young learners and modern languages in Europe and beyond.* Graz, Austria: Council of Europe, Centre for Modern Languages. Online at http://archive.ecml.at/documents/earlystart.pdf

Nummela Caine, R., & Caine, G. (1990). Understanding a brain-based approach to learning and teaching. *Educational Leadership, 48*(2), 66–70.

O'Neill, D. K., Pearce, M. J., & Pick, J. L. (2004). Preschool children's narratives and performance on the Peabody Individualized Achievement Test—Revised: Evidence of a relation between early narrative and later mathematical ability. *First Language, 24*(2), 149–183.

Oh, S.-Y. (2001). Two types of input modification and EFL reading comprehension: Simplification versus elaboration. *TESOL Quarterly, 35*(1), 69–96.

Ohlstain, E., Shohamy, E., Kemp, J., & Chatow, R. (1990). Factors predicting success in EFL among culturally different learners. *Language Learning, 40,* 23–44.

Okhee, L., & Fradd, S. (1996). The interplay among languages, science knowledge and cognitive strategy use with linguistically diverse students. *NYSABE Journal, 11*, 26–45.

Order, T. (2003). Early language teaching in Estonia. In M. Nikolov & H. Curtain (Eds.), *An early start: Young learners and modern languages in Europe and beyond* (pp. 147–150). Graz, Austria: Council of Europe, Centre for Modern Languages. Online at http://archive.ecml.at/documents/earlystart.pdf

Orlich, D. C., Harder, R. J., Callahan, R. C., Kauchak, D. P., & Gibson, H. W. (1994). *Teaching strategies. A guide to better instruction.* Lexington, MA: D. C. Heath and Co.

Ormrod, J. E. (2013). *Human learning* (6th ed.). Upper Saddle River, NJ: Pearson Prentice Hall.

Ovando, C. J., & Collier, V. P. (1985). *Bilingual and ESL classrooms: Teaching in multicultural contexts.* New York: McGraw–Hill.

Padrón, Y. (1992). The effect of strategy instruction on bilingual students' cognitive strategy use in reading. *Bilingual Research Journal, 16*, 35–52.

Padrón, Y. (1994). Comparing reading instruction in Hispanic/limited English-proficient schools and other inner-city schools. *Bilingual Research Journal, 18*, 49–66.

Padrón, Y., Knight, S. L., & Waxman, H. C. (1986). Analyzing bilingual and monolingual students' perceptions of their reading strategies. *The Reading Teacher, 39*(5), 430–433.

Paran, A., & Watts, E. (2003). *Storytelling in ELT.* Whitstable, Kent: IATEFL.

Pesola, C. A. (1991). Culture in the elementary school foreign language classroom. *Foreign Language Annals, 24*(4), 331–346.

Pettig, K. L. (2002, October). *The influence of children's literature on instructional practices for mathematics.* Doctoral Dissertation, University of Rochester, DAI-A 63/64, 1249.

Pinilla-Padilla, C. (2006). Multilingualism in the educational system in Valencia, Spain. In M. L. McCloskey, J. Orr, & M. Dolitsky (Eds.), *Teaching English as a foreign language in primary school* (pp. 9–24). Alexandria, VA: TESOL.

Pinsent, P. (1997). *Children's literature and the politics of equality.* London: David Fulton.

Pinter, A. (2006). *Teaching young language learners.* Oxford: Oxford University Press.

Plato (1992). *Republic.* (G. M. A. Grube, Trans., C. D. C. Reeve, Rev.). Indianapolis, IN: Hacket Publishing Company, Inc. (Original work published ca. 377).

Pufahl, I., Rhodes, N., & Christian, D. (2000). *Foreign language teaching: What the United States can learn from other countries.* Washington, DC: Center for Applied Linguistics.

Qing, Bi. (1993). Teaching English to children in China. In K. D. Samway, D. McKeon, & R. Tongue (Eds.), *Teaching English to children* (pp. 93–98). Alexandria, VA: ASCD.

Raimes, A. (1987). Language proficiency, writing ability, and composing strategies. *Language Learning, 37*, 439–468.

Ralea, C-M. (2003). Foreign language teaching to young learners in Romania. In M. Nikolov & H. Curtain (Eds.), *An early start: Young learners and modern languages in Europe and beyond* (pp. 93–99). Graz, Austria: Council of Europe, Centre for Modern Languages. Online at http://archive.ecml.at/documents/earlystart.pdf

Ramirez, J. D., Yuen, S. D., Ramey, D. R., & Pasta, D. J. (1991). *Executive summary. Final report: Longitudinal study of structured English immersion strategy, early-exit and late-exit transitional bilingual education programs for language-minority children* (Vols. I and II) San Mateo, CA: Aguirre International.

Raphael, T., & Hu, K. A. (1998). *Literature-based instruction: reshaping the curriculum.* Norwood, MA: Christopher Gordon Publisher.

Rathmell, E. (1994). Planning for instruction involves focusing on children's thinking. *Arithmetic Teacher, 41*(6), 290(2) [online] http://infotrac.london.galegroup.com.

Realbook News. Selecting real picture books—a skilled task? http://www.realbooks.co.uk/articles/ selecting.htm

Renandeyas, W., Rajan, B., & Jacobs, G. (1999). Extensive reading with adult learners of English as a second language. *RELC Journal, 30,* 39–66.

Rest, J., Thoma, S., & Edwards, L. (1997). Designing and validating a measure of moral judgment. *Journal of Educational Psychology, 89,* 5–28.

Reynolds, S. V. (1995). *Effects of using children's books and a traditional textbook on student achievement and higher level thinking skills.* Doctoral dissertation. Oklahoma State University. UMI 9608935.

Richard-Amato, P. A. (1988). Making it happen. *Interaction in the second language classroom.* New York & London: Longman.

Richards, J. (1976). The role of vocabulary teaching. *TESOL Quarterly, 10*(1), 77–89.

Richards, J., & Lockhart, C. (1994). *Reflective teaching in second language classrooms.* Cambridge: Cambridge University Press.

Richgels, D., Tomlinson, C., & Tunnell, M. (1993). Comparison of elementary students' history textbooks and tradebooks. *Journal of Educational Research, 86,* 161–171.

Rigg, P. (1981). Beginning to read in English the LEA way. In Reading English as a second language: moving from theory. In C. W. Twyford, W. Diehl, & K. Feathers (Eds.), *Monographs in Teaching and Learning, 4*(81–90). Bloomington, IN: Indiana University.

Roberts, T., & Neal, H. (2004). Relationships among preschool English language learners' oral proficiency in English, instructional experiences and literacy development. *Contemporary Educational Psychology, 29,* 283–311.

Roberts, T. (2008). Home storybook reading in primary or second language: Evidence of equal effectiveness for second language vocabulary acquisition. *Reading Research Quarterly, 43*(2), 103–130.

Robinson, P. (1996). Learning simple and complex second language rules under implicit, incidental, enhanced and instructed conditions. *Studies in Second Language Acquisition, 18,* 27–27.

Robinson, P. (1997). Generalizability and automaticity of second language learning under implicit, incidental, enhanced and instructed conditions. *Studies in Second Language Acquisition, 19*, 223–247.

Rosenblatt, L. M. (1991). Literature—S.O.S.! *Language Arts, 68*, 444–448.

Ross, E. P. (1994). Using children's literature across the curriculum. *Fastback 373*. Bloomington, IN: Phi Delta Kappa.

Royce, C. A. (2002). *The effects of the use of children's literature as an instructional approach on the science knowledge achievement and attitudes of third grade students*. Doctoral dissertation, Temple University, Philadelphia, PA.

Royce, C., & Wiley, D. (1996). Children's literature and the teaching of science: Possibilities and cautions. *The Clearing House, 70*(1), 18–20.

Rulon K., & McCreary (1986). Negotiation of content: Teacher-fronted and small-group interaction. In R. Day (Ed.), *Talking to learn: Conversation in second language acquisition* (pp. 182–199). Rowley, MA: Newbury House.

Sadowska-Martyka, A. (2006). Read, read, read. In J. Enever & G. Schmid-Schönbein (Eds.), *Picture books and young learners of English* (pp. 131–135). München: Münchener Arbeiten zur Fremdsprachen-Forschung.

Samway, K. D. & Taylor, D. (1993). The collected letters of two collaborative researchers. In S. J. Hudelson & J. Wells Lindfors (Eds), *Delicate balances: Collaborative research in language education* (pp. 67–92). Urbana, IL: National Council of Teachers of English.

Samway, K. D. (1987). Formal evaluation of children's writing: An incomplete story. *Language Arts, 64*(3), 289–98.

Samway, K. D. (2006). *When English language learners write. Connecting research to practice, K–8*. Portsmouth, NH: Heinemann.

Saragi, T., Nation, I. S. P., & Meister, G. F. (1978). Vocabulary learning and reading. *System 6*(2), 72–78.

Savage, J. F. (1998). *Teaching reading & writing. Combining skills, strategies & literature* (2nd ed.). Boston, MA: McGraw-Hill.

Schiefele, U. (1991). Interest, learning and motivation. *Educational Psychologist, 26*(3/4), 299–323.

Schmidt, R. (2010). Attention, awareness, and individual differences in language learning. In W. M. Chan, S. Chi, K. N. Cin, J. Istanto, M. Nagani, J. W. Sew, T. Suthiawan, & D. Walker. *Proceedings of CLaSIC 2010, Singapore, December 2–4* (pp. 721–737). Singapore: national University of Singapore, Center for Language Studies. Retrieved from http://nflrc.hawaii.edu/PDFs/SCHMIDT%20Attention,%20awareness,%20and%20individual%20differences.pdf

Schmitt, N. (2000). *Vocabulary in language teaching*. Cambridge: Cambridge University Press.

Schollar, E. (2001). A review of two evaluations of the application of the READ primary schools program in the Eastern Cape Province of South Africa. *International Journal of Educational Research, 35*, 205–216.

Scott, J., & Nagy, W. E. (2004). Developing word consciousness. In J. F. Bauman & E. J. Kame'enui (Eds.), *Vocabulary instruction: research to practice* (pp. 201–217). New York: Guildford Press.

Scribner-MacLean, M., & Greenwood, A. (1998, May). Invertebrate inquiry. *Science and Children*, 18–21.

Sebesta, S. L., Monson, D. L., & Senn, H. Doces (1995, March). A hierarchy to assess reader response. *Journal of Reading*, 444–450.

Selecting REALpictureBooks—a skilled task? Realbook News. http://www.realbooks.co.uk/articles/ selecting.htm

Sheehan, E., Lennon, R., & McDevitt, T. (1989). Reactions to AIDS and other illnesses: Reported interaction in the workplace. *The Journal of Psychology, 123*, 525–536.

Sheffield, S. (1995). *Math and literature (K–3). Book Two.* Sausalito, CA: Math Solutions Publications.

Sinclair, J. McH., & Coulthard, R. M. (1975). *Towards an analysis of discourse. The English used by teachers and pupils.* Oxford: Oxford University Press.

Singh, G. (2001). Literacy impact studies in Solomon Islands and Vanuatu. *International Journal of Educational Research, 35*, 227–236.

Sinh, H. V. (2006). Is grade 3 too early to teach EFL in Vietnam? In M. L. McCloskey, J. Orr, & M. Dolitsky, M. (Eds.), *Teaching English as a foreign language in primary school* (pp. 111–122). Alexandria, VA: TESOL.

Sirotnik, K. A. (1983, February). What you see is what you get—Consistency, persistency, and mediocrity in classroom. *Harvard Educational Review, 53*(1), 16–31.

Skinner, B. F. (1957). *Verbal behavior.* New York: Appleton-Century-Crofts.

Smallwood, B. Ansin (1991). *The literature connection. A read-aloud guide for multicultural classrooms.* Reading, MA: Addison-Wesley.

Solomon, J., & Rhodes, N. C. (1995). *Conceptualizing academic language.* Santa Cruz, CA: National Center for Research on Cultural Diversity and Second Language [online] http://www.ncbe.gwu.edu/miscpubs/ncrcdsll/rr15.htm

Sprenger, M. (1999). *Learning & memory. The brain in action.* Alexandria, VA: Association for Supervision and Curriculum Development.

Stauffer, R. G. (1969). *Directing reading maturity as a cognitive process.* New York: Harper & Row.

Stokic, L., & Mihalevic Djigunovic, J. (2003). Early foreign language education in Croatia. In M. Nikolov & H. Curtain (Eds.), *An early start: Young learners and modern languages in Europe and beyond* (pp. 41–49). Graz, Austria: Council of Europe, Centre for Modern Languages. Online at http://archive.ecml.at/documents/earlystart.pdf

Suits, B. (2003). Guided reading and second-language learners. *Multicultural Education, 11*(2), 27–34.

Sullivan, P. R. (1994). *Children's literature as a tool for teaching second language to adolescents.* Unpublished doctoral thesis, Claremont Graduate School and San Diego State University.

Sutherland, Z. (1997). *Children and books* (9th ed.). New York: Longman.
Swain, M., & Lapkin, S. (1995). Problems in output and the cognitive processes they generate: A step towards second language learning. *Applied Linguistics, 16*(3), 371–391.
Swann Report, The. (1985). *Education for all.* Report of the Committee of Enquiry into the Education of Children from Ethnic Minority Groups. London: Her Majesty's Stationary Office.
Swift, G. (1993). *Effects of a children's book and a traditional textbook on third-grade students' achievement and attitude toward social studies.* Doctoral dissertation, Oklahoma State University. DAI-A 54/05, p. 1752 No 1993.
Sylwester, R. (1995*). A celebration of neurons: An educator's guide to human brain.* Alexandria, VA: Association for Supervision and Curriculum Development.
Taguchi, E., Takayasu-Maass, M., & Gorsuch, G. J. (2004). Developing reading fluency in EFL: How assisted repeated reading and extensive reading affect fluency development. *Reading in a Foreign Language, 16*(2), 70–96.
Tarone, E. (1974). *A discussion of the Dulay and Burt studies.* Working Papers on Bilingualism, No. 4. Ontario Institute for Studies in Education, Bilingual Education-Project, Toronto. ERIC Document No. ED 123876.
Tate, G. M. (1967). *Teaching structure: A teachers handbook.* Wellington: A. H. & A. W. Reed.
Taylor, E. (2000). *Using folktales.* Cambridge University Press.
Thomas, W. P., & Collier, V. (1997). *School effectiveness for language minority students.* Washington, DC: National Clearinghouse for Bilingual Education.
Thompson, D. L., & Lehr, S. S. (2008). Challenges to children's literature: Deskilling, censoring, and obsolescence. *Language Arts, 85*(3), 246–248.
Thornburg, D. (1993). Intergenerational literacy learning with bilingual families: A context for the analysis of social mediation on thought. *Journal of Reading Behavior, 25*(3), 321–352.
Tinker Sachs, G., & Mahon, T. (2006). Enabling effective practices in the teaching and learning English in Hong Kong. In M. L. McCloskey, J. Orr, & M. Dolitsky (Eds.), *Teaching English as a foreign language in primary school* (pp. 201–222). Alexandria, VA: TESOL.
Tomlinson, B. (2003). Humanizing the coursebook. In B. Tomlinson (Ed), *Developing materials for language teaching* (pp. 162–173). London: Continuum.
Tongue, R. (Ed.). *Teaching English to young children. From practice to principle.* (pp. 67–80). Harlow, Essex: Longman.
Trundle, K. C., & Troland, T. H. (2005, October). The moon in children's literature. *Science and Children, 43*(2), 40–43.
Tsui, A. B. M (1995). *Introducing classroom interaction.* London: Penguin.
Tsui, A. (2005 April). *Language and identity.* Plenary paper presented at the 39th International Annual IATEFL Conference, Cardiff, Wales.
Tunnell, M. O., & Jacobs, J. S. (1989). Using 'real' books: Research findings on Literature based reading instruction. *The Reading Teacher, 42*(7), 470–477.

Uhl Chamot, A., & O'Malley, J. M. (1986). *A Cognitive academic language learning approach: An ESL content-based curriculum.* Washington, DC: National Clearinghouse for Bilingual Educations.

Uhl Chamot, A., & O'Malley, J. M. (1994). *The CALLA handbook.* Reading, MA: Addison-Wesley Publishing Company.

Ullman, M. (2001a). The neurocognitive perspectives on language: The declarative/procedural model. *Nature Reviews Neuroscience, 2,* 717–726.

Ullman, M. (2001b). The neural basis of lexicon and grammar in first and second language: The declarative/procedural model. *Bilingualism: Language and Cognition, 4*(1), 105–122.

Underwood, B., & Briggs, S. (1980). *The influence of perspective-taking and aggressiveness on attitudes toward Iran,* Unpublished manuscript.

Vacca, R. T., & Vacca, J. L. (1999). *Content area reading: Literacy and learning across the curriculum* (6th ed.). United States: Addison-Wesley Educational Publishers.

Vale, D., & Feunteun, A. (1995). *Teaching children English.* Cambridge: Cambridge University Press.

Van Allen, R., & Allen C. (1967). *Language experiences in reading.* Chicago, IL: Encyclopedia Britannica Press.

Vandergrift, K. (1990). Children's literature. Theory, research and teaching. Englewood, CO: Libraries Unlimited, Inc.

Verhallen, M. J. A. J., & Bus, A. G. (2010, February). Low-income immigrant pupils learning vocabulary through digital picture storybooks. *Journal of Educational Psychology, 102*(1), 54–61. doi: 10.1037/a0017133.

Villano, T. A. (2005). Should social studies textbooks become history? A look at alternative methods to activate schema in the intermediate classroom. *Reading Teacher, 59*(2), 122–130.

Voss, J. F., & Schauble, L. (1992). Is interest educationally interesting? An interest-related model of learning. In K. A. Renninger, S. Hidi, & A. Krapp (Eds.), *The role of interest in learning and development* (pp. 101–120). Hillsdale, NJ: Erlbaum.

Wai-King Tsang (1996). Comparing the effects of reading and writing on writing performance. *Applied Linguistics, 17*(2), 210–233.

Walling, B. (1994). *Effects of using children's historical fiction and nonfiction on student achievement and attitudes toward American Indians and social studies.* Unpublished doctoral dissertation, Oklahoma State University.

Weinberg, S. (1996, March). Going beyond ten black dots. *Teaching Children Mathematics, 2*(7), 432.

Welchman-Tischler, R. (1992). *How to use children's literature to teach mathematics.* Reston, VA: National Council of Teachers of Mathematics.

Wells, G. (1986) *Meaning makers. Children learning language and using language to learn.* Portsmouth, NH: Heinemann.

Wenli Tsou. (2005). The effects of cultural instruction on foreign language learning. *RELC Journal, 36*(1), 39–57.

Whitin, D., & Gary, C. (1994). *Promoting mathematical explorations through children's literature. Arithmetic Teacher, 41* (7), 394(6).
Wijesinha, R. (2007, Spring). Accessing literacy in Sri Lankan primary classes. *IATEFL Young Learners*, 14–16.
Wolfe, P. (2001). *Brain matters. Translating research into classroom practice.* Alexandria, VA: Association for Supervision and Curriculum Development.
Wright, A. (1995). *Storytelling with children.* Oxford University Press.
Yang, A. (2001). Reading and the non-academic learner: A mystery solved. *System* 29, 451–466.
Yano, Y., Long, M., & Ross, S. (1994). The effects of simplified and elaborated texts on foreign language reading comprehension. *Language Learning, 44*(2), 189–219.
Zamel, V. (1992). Writing one's way into reading. *TESOL Quarterly, 26,* 463–485.
Zehang C. (2006). *Classroom interaction in Chinese primary* classrooms—*three case studies.* Paper presented at the 40th International IATEFL Conference, Harrogate, UK.
Zimmerman, C. Boyd (2009). *Word knowledge. A vocabulary teacher's handbook.* Oxford: Oxford University Press.

Children's Books Cited

Addison-Wesley Publishing. (1987). *The rabbit and the turnip.*
Allen, P. (1982). *Who sank the boat?* Penguin Putnam Books for Young Readers.
Andersen, H. C. (1983/1889). *The ugly duckling.* Chancellor Press.
Anno, M., & Anno, M. (1983). *Anno's mysterious multiplying jar.* Penguin Putnam.
Anno, M. (1995). *Anno's magic seeds.* Penguin Putnam Books for Young Readers.
Birch, D. (1988). *The king's chessboard.* Puffin Books.
Bradman, T., & Chamberlain, M. (1989). *Look out he's behind you.* Putnam.
Breckler, R. (1996). *Sweet dried apples.* Houghton Mifflin.
Briggs, R. (1970). *Jim and the beanstalk.* Putnam & Grosset Group.
Burns, M. (1997). *Spaghetti and meatballs for all.* Scholastic Press.
Butterworth, B. (1994). *Story without end.* Longman Group Ltd.
Butterworth, N. (1989). *One snowy night.* Harper-Collins.
Cannon, J. (1993). *Stellaluna.* Harcourt Brace & Company.
Carle, E. (1987). *The very hungry caterpillar.* Philomel Books.
Carle, E. (1996). *Papa, please get the moon for me.* Hamish Hamilton Ltd.
Carle, E. (1984). *The very busy spider.* Philomel Books.
Carle, E. (1987). *The tiny seed.* Aladdin Paperbacks.
Carle, E. (1987). *The very hungry caterpillar.* Philomel Books.
Carle, E. (1990). *The very quiet cricket.* Philomel Books.
Carroll, L. (1974/1865). *Alice's adventures in wonderland and through the looking glass.* London: Bodley Head Ltd.
Cherry, L. (1990). *The great kapok tree.* Gulliver Books.
Climo, S. (1989). *The Egyptian Cinderella.* Harper-Collins.

Climo, S. (1999). *The Persian Cinderella.* Harper Trophy.
Coerr, E. (1977). *Sadako and the thousand paper cranes.* A Dell Yearling Book.
Cohen, B. (1994/1983). *Make a wish Molly.* Yearling Books.
Cohen, B. (1995). *Molly's pilgrim.* Bantam Doubleday Dell.
Crews, D. (1995/1968). *Ten black dots.* Harper-Collins.
Dahl, R. (1988/1964). *Charlie and the chocolate factory.* Penguin.
Estes, E. (1973/1944). *Hundred dresses.* Scholastic.
Flack, M. (1970/1933). *The story of Ping.* Scholastic.
Gackenbach, D. (1977). *Harry and the terrible Whatzit.* Scholastic.
Galdone, P. (1972). *The three bears.* Scholastic.
Gauch, S. (2009). *Voyage to the Pharos.* Viking.
Geriger, L. (1985). *Three hat day.* Harper & Row.
Ghosn, I. (1999). *Children who hugged the mountain.* Dar El-Ilm Lilmalayin.
Ghosn, I. (1999). *Mr. G. Reed makes a deal.* Dar El-Ilm Lilmalayin.
Ghosn, I. (1999). *Slow little snail.* Dar El-Ilm Lilmalayin.
Ghosn, I. (1999). *The dragonfly surprise.* Dar El-Ilm Lilmalayin.
Ghosn, I.-K. (2011). *Phoenician friends.* Dar El-Ilm Lilmalayin.
Hickox, R. (1998). *The golden sandal.* Holiday House.
Hong, L. (1993). *Two of everything.* Albert Whitman & Co.
Hopkinson, D. (1995). *Sweet Clara and the freedom quilt.* A Knoph.
Hunt, R. (1988/1986). *Pirate adventure.* Oxford University Press.
Hutchins, P. (1986). *The doorbell rang.* Scholastic.
Jewell, N. (1978). *Bus ride.* Harper & Row.
Keats, E. J. (1975). *Louie.* Greenville Books.
Krauss, R. (1989/1945). *The carrot seed.* Harper-Collins.
Krull, K. (1996). *Wilma unlimited: How Wilma became the world's fastest woman.* Harcourt Brace & Co.
Leaf, M. (1987/1936). *The story of Ferdinand.* Puffin Books.
Levinson, R. (1985). *Watch the stars come out.* Puffin Unicorn Books.
Lionni, L. (1995/1970). *Fish is a fish.* Scholastic.
Lobel, A. (1980/1976). *Frog and toad all year.* World's Work Ltd.
Lobel, A. (1980/1971). *Frog and toad together.* World's Work Ltd.
MacLachlan, P. (1996). *Sarah, plain and tall.* Scholastic.
Mathis, S. Bell. (1975). *The hundred penny box.* Scholastic.
Mayer, M. (1974). *Frog goes to dinner.* Dial Press.
Orwell, G. (1946). *Animal farm.* Signet Classic.
Mayer, M. (1983). *There's a nightmare in my cupboard.* Pocket Bears.
McCloskey, R. (1969/1941). *Make way for ducklings.* Scholastic.
Mehta, L. (1985). *The enchanted anklet.* Lilmur Publishing.
Milne, A. A. (1928). *The house at Pooh corner.* Dutton.
Milne, A. A. (1926). *Winnie-the-Pooh.* Dutton.
Minarik, E. (1980/1968). *A kiss for Little Bear.* World's Work Ltd.

Minarik, E. (1979/1957). *Little Bear*. World's Work Ltd.
Moskin, M. (1997/1978). *Day of the blizzard*. Scholastic.
Myller, R. (1991/1962). *How big is a foot?* A Dell Young Yearling.
Na'ihm bint R. (2002). *The swirling hijab*. Mantra.
Parkes, B. (2001). *Royal dinner*. Kingscourt/McGraw-Hill.
Parry Heide, F. (1990). *The day of Ahmad's secret*. Mulberry Books.
Paterson, K. (1978). *The great Gilly Hopkins*. Crowell.
Paton Walsh, J. (1982). *The green book*. Farrar, Straus and Giroux.
Perry Heide, F. (1992). *Sami and the time of the troubles*. Clarion Books.
Perry Heide, F. (1990). *The day of Ahmad's secret*. Mulberry Books.
Pinczes, E. J. (1995). *A remainder of one*. Houghton Mifflin.
Polacco, P. (1990). *Just plain fancy*. Dragonfly Books.
Poole, J. (1997). *Jack and the beanstalk*. Macdonald Young Books.
Rowling, J. K. (1998). *Harry Potter and the sorcerer's stone*. Scholastic.
Roy, R. (1987). *Three ducks went wondering*. Clarion Books.
San Souci, R. D. (1990). *The talking eggs*. Scholastic.
Silverstein, S. (1963). *The giving tree*. Harper & Row.
Slobodkina, E. (1987/1940). *Caps for sale*. Harper Trophy.
Smucker, B. (1995). *Selina and the bear paw quilt*. Stoddart.
Song Nan Zhang. (1998). *The ballad of Mulan*. Pan Asian Publications.
Sperry, A. (1963/1940). *Call it courage*. Scholastic.
Steig, W. (1969). *Sylvester and the magic pebble*. Aladdin.
Steptoe, J. (1987). *Mufaro's beautiful daughters*, Lothrop, Lee & Shepard Books.
Stone Soup. A classic folktale.
Tolkien, J. R. R. (1938). *The hobbit*. Houghton.
Tomlinson, J. (1973/1963). *The owl who was afraid of the dark*. Puffin Books.
Turnage Burgoyne, D. (1982). *Amina and Muhammad's special visitor*. Middle East Gateway Series.
Viorst, J. (1972). *Alexander and the terrible, horrible, no good, very bad day*. Atheneum.
Viorst, J. (1978). *Alexander who used to be rich last Sunday*. Atheneum.
Viorst, J. (1995). *Alexander who's not (Do you hear me? I mean it!) going to move*. Aladdin Paperbacks.
Williams, M. (1985). *The velveteen rabbit*. New York: Dragonfly Books.
Winter, J. (1988). *Follow the drinking gourd*. Alfred A. Knoph.
Winter, J. (2005). *The librarian of Basra*. Harcourt.
Wright, C. (1994). *Jumping the broom*. Holiday House.
Zion, G. (2002/1956). *Harry the dirty dog*. Harper-Collins.

Subject Index

A

academic achievement
    language proficiency, xxviii
    motivation, 44
    narrative ability and, 34, 111
academic language competence, 74, 174
academic language functions
    general, 34
    literature and, 35
    mathematics, 34
    science, 38
affect and learning, 46, 49
affective filter, 43
    input and, 11, 43, 174
anxiety
    affective filter and, 11, 43
    choral reading and, 148–149
    existential, 9
    learning environment and, 43,
Argentina, xxvi
Austria, xxiv
awareness
    grammatical, 37
    emotions of 41
    of self, 6–7
    of the world, 7

B

background knowledge, 24
Bahrain, xxv
Belgium, xxiv
big books, 19, 59,
book flood, 55, 77–79
brain research, 14, 47–48
Brazil, xxvi
Bulgaria, xxvii

C

children's literature
    academic language functions and, 35
    as catharsis, 8
    as instructional material, 10–11
    culture learning and, 41
    definitions, 4
    language of, 17–20
    moral reasoning and, 8
    psycho-social development and, 7
    significance of, 6–10
    violence in, 9
China, xxv
classroom episodes, 26, 27, 30,
classroom interactions, 59

coursebook dialogues and, 63–65
negotiated, 59–60
stories and, 60–63
student initiations, 63
student responses, 66–68
teacher feedback and, 69–70
teacher initiations, 60
teacher questions and, 65
teacher talk, 60–61
turn-taking, 63
CLIL, xxvi
cognitive academic language proficiency (CALP), 33
communicative approach
cultural expectations and, 29
role expectations and, 28,
coursebook, communicative
content, 23
discourse and
language of, 13, 15–17
shared reality (assumed), 24–25
criteria for selecting books
aesthetic and literary merit, 179–180
art work, 181
developmental level, 180
language, 181
plot, 181
school subjects, 184–188
themes, 180
Croatia, xxiv
cultural awareness, xvii, 41
cultural beliefs and interactions, 29
culture learning, 31–32
Cyprus, xxv

D

dialogue practice, 63–64
discourse
academic, 34
communicative language tasks and, 63
story-based instruction and, 61
unfamiliar topics and, 25–28
diversity, tolerance for, appreciation of, xvii, 41

E

Egypt, xxv, xxvii
elaboration and comprehension, 17–18
EMI (*see* English medium instruction), xxvi,
emotional intelligence, areas of
empathy, 10
emotional facilitation of thought, 10
emotional management, 10
emotional perception, 9
understanding of emotions, 7, 8
emotions and learning, 46
empathy (*see also* emotional intelligence)
lack of story, 10
tolerance and, 10
English medium instruction (EMI)
demand of, xxvi
English language teaching
curricula, xvii
Estonia, xxiv, xxvii
experience
emotional, 10, 32
personal, 70
repeated, 10
vicarious, 7, 9, 10
with literature, 11

F

fantasy
imagination and, 8
aggression and, 8
Fiafia, 79
fiction (*see* stories/storybooks)

G

Germany, xxiv
grammar
errors, 93
explicit instruction, 93
implicit learning, 94
memory and, 48
PACE model, 98

Universal, 94
  young learners and, 94–95
Greece, xxv

H

hidden curriculum, xvii
homo narrans, 4
Hong Kong, xxiii, 58, 66, 96
Hungary, xxv, xxvii, 43, 56, 59

I

imagination, 8
input, 94
  affective filter and, 11
  exposure to, 14
  frequency of
instructional materials
  as models for writing, 101–103
  learner interest and, 70–71
  significance of, 10
  learning environment and, 1
interest
  individual, 43
  situational, 43
  text characteristics and, 44
Israel, xxv
Italy, xxiv, xxvii

J

Japan, xxvi, 17
Jordan, xxv

K

Korea, xxv, 17
Kuwait, xxvii

L

language
  coursebook, of, 15–17
  exposure to, 14, 94
  formulaic chunks of, 28, 40, 47, 50, 66

real life, 16
  repetitious, 20, 44, 49, 50, 136, 167
language experience approach (LEA), 149–152
language minority students, xxvii
language teaching texts
  content of, 14
  humanizing value of, xvii
  learner interests and, 45
  significance of, 10
  social intent of, xvii
Lebanon, xviii, xxv, xxvii, 31, 56, 60, 75, 80, 91, 97, 104, 123, 132, 164
learning brain
  structured, graded syllabus and, 14
learning environment, 10
Luxemburg, xxiv

M

Malaysia, xxvii
materials development, xxviii
math morals, 36–37
mathematics
  children's literature and, 34–38
  communication and, 36
  concept development, 110
  learning of and language, 34
  literature and attitude toward, 114
  problem solving and literature, 37, 112
memory 47
  automatic, 48
  emotional, 49
  episodic, 48
  language learning and, 47–49
  long term, connectionist view of, 50
  procedural, 48
  retrieval of information, 49–50
  semantic, 47
  types of, 47–49
Mexico, xxvi
mother tongue use, 30, 57, 127, 134, 149, 154, 174–175
motivation, 31, 43
  academic achievement, 43

218 ▪ Subject Index

intrinsic interest and, 43
learner engagement and, 6
role of mother tongue in, 70, 127, 174–175
situational interest and, 43
stories and, 55–59
teacher feedback and, 70
Morocco, xxv

N

narrative, 4
  children's discourse and, 15
  link to school subjects, 34
negotiation, 59
  of content, 60
  of form, 60
  of meaning, 60, 176
negotiation strategies, 59
  clarification requests, 60
  comprehension checks, 60
  confirmation checks, 60
neural activity
  formation of synapses, 13
  interconnectedness of neurons, 13
neuroscience research, 11

O

Oman, xxv
output, 14, 59–60, 66, 69, 71

P

parallel distributed processing, 50
past tense verbs
  absence of, 15
  importance of, 15
  in daily discourse, 15
  natural discourse and, 16
perspective taking, 40, 41, 111, 106, 143
positionality, xvi,
primary school ELT, spread of, xxiii–xxvi
pseudo-communication, 28

R

READ, 77–78
Read, read, read, 78
reader responses
  aesthetic, 139–144
  efferent, 139
  written, 76, 142–143
reading
  aloud, xvi
  background knowledge, 73
  choral, 148–149
  dialogic, 133–136
  extensive, 75–76, 98
  fluency, 77, 81, 149
  instructional approach in ELT, 73–74
  learner perceptions of, 74–75
  oral, purposes for, 144–145
  round robin, 138, 144
  shared, 79
  silent, 144
  story-based instruction and, 75
  strategy instruction, 80–83
REAP, 77, 79, 96,
rehearsal, 49
RELA, 79, 80
repetitive refrains, 5, 19–20,
role-play, 30,
role taking ability, 10
Romania, xxiv

S

scaffolding, 61
school subjects and literature
  mathematics, 34–38, 109–113
  science, 38–39, 113–114
  social studies, 40–42, 114–117
science
  discourse of, 38
  literature and attitude toward, 114
  language of, 38
  literacy and, 38,
  trade books

second/foreign language instruction
    social intent of, xvii
simplified texts
    classics, 6
    comprehension and, 17
    graded readers, 19, 21, 59
    language learning, 17
    unnatural language, 16
social interaction around stories, 175
social studies
    literature and attitude toward, 115–116
    textbooks, 40
    trade books and, 40
        faith traditions, 41
        multicultural literature and, 41
Solomon Islands, 103
Spain, xxiv, xxvi
Sri Lanka xxiii, 77, 102
stories
    affective filter and, 36
    appeal of, 11
    awareness of language and, 18
    classroom interactions and, 60–63
    contextualized verbs in, 19
    curriculum concepts and, 33
    human need for, 11
    in young learner coursebooks, 15–16
story narratives
    verb acquisition and, 15
story tradition, 3
story-based instruction, xv, xvi, xviii [16]
    approach, 174–176
    culture learning, 41
    discourse, 61
    potential in curriculum, 34
storybooks
    classroom interactions and, 29
    content, 29
    digital, 90–91
    emotional experience and, 46
    language, 17, 19
    motivation and, 11, 29
    mathematics attitude, 112–113
    mathematics communication and, 34

mathematics anxiety, 112
science and, 38
simplified, 6
social studies and, 40,
storytelling, xvi
Sweden, xxiv
syntactic features
    emergence of, 13
    emergence vs. exposure, 14
    in young learner syllabus, 13
    past tense verbs, 15
Syria, xxv

T

Taiwan xxvi, 31
Tate Readers, 80
teacher feedback
    instructional texts and, 69
    learner initiations and, 69
    motivation and, 59, 69
    positive, 69
    rejecting, 69
    scaffolding,
    validation of learner output, 69–70
teacher qualifications, xxvii
teacher questions, 65–69
    classifying, 66
    classroom discourse and, 65
    closed, 65–69
    convergent vs. divergent, 65
    learner output and, 67–69
    open-ended, 65, 68
teaching principles, 175–176
text characteristics and interest, 43
Thailand, xxvi
tolerance, 10, 41, 116
trade books
    mathematics and, 35–37
    science and, 38
    social studies and, 40
transcription conventions, xx
Turkey, xxv, 59, 116

V

Vanuatu, 103
Vietnam, xxvi
vocabulary
    challenge of, 86
    explicit instruction of, 89
    extensive reading and, 88
    incidental learning of, 88, 89, 90, 91
    intentional learning of, 88
    learning, 88
    learning and encounters with, 88
    learning and stories, 89
    memory and, 49
    reading problems and, 85

W

word consciousness, 87
word families, 86
word knowledge, 86
    complex, 87
    conceptual, 86
    grammatical, 87
    morphological, 86
    phonological, 87
    pragmatic, 87
    semantic, 87
writing
    copying, 167
    definition, 99
    in story-based programs, 102
    learning, 99
    texts as models for, 101–102
    young learner coursebooks in, 99–100, 101
    teaching, 99, 102
    young L2 learner and,

Author Index

A

Adair-Hauck, B., 94, 95, 98
Adoniou, M., 45
Allen C., 149
Al-Shaboul, Y. M., xxv
Alshamrani, H. M., 75
Alshboul, Y. M., xxv
Al-Tamimi, Y. A., xxv
Ameis, J. A., 112
Anderson, J. R., 49
Anderson, R. C., 87, 89
Appleyard, J., 7
Apuleius, L., 3
Aranha, M., 75
Ariaz, S. K., 91
Arndt, V., 101
Artelt, C., 44
Asassfeh, xxv
Austin, M., 138, 144

B

Bacha, N., xxv
Baker, T. K., 79
Barkley, R. A., 49
Bates, E. A., 14
Bay-Williams, J., 112
Beard, L. A., 111
Bearne, E., 40
Beck, I., 88
Belsky, S., 55, 56
Bennett, K. J., 85
Berova, N., xxiv
Bettelheim, B., 7, 9, 10
Bisson, S.A., 79
Blau, E. K., 17
Blaxton, T. A., 49
Bloom, B. S., 69
Blum, T.H., 79
Botelho, M. J., 7
Boyle, M., 85
Brigg, S., 10
Brock, C. A., 66
Brown, G., 40
Brown, S. K., 85
Brumfit, C., xvi
Bruner, J., 34
Bullock Report, The, xxviii
Burns, M., 38, 161, 162
Burt, M., 43, 94
Bus, A. G., 96

Butler, Y., xxvi
Butzow, C., 18, 39, 113, 186
Butzow, J., 18, 39, 113, 186

C

Caine, G., 47
Callahan, R. C., 65
Cameron, L., xxviii, 28, 86
Carger, C. L., 90
Carlson, K., 38
Carter, R., 18
Caruso, D., 9
Casey, B., 110, 112
Ceder, I., 110, 112
Celce-Murcia, M., 94
Chaaya, D., 80, 81, 82
Chambers, A., 4, 18
Chastain, K., 21
Chatow, R., 43
Chaudron, C., 60
Chen-Ying Li 55, 57, 62
Chomsky, N., 94
Christian, D., xxv
Clay, M., 82, 107
Coady, J., 85, 88
Codina, H., 174
Cohen, A.D., 34
Colby, A., 8, 9
Collier, V. P., xxviii, 33, 149
Collins, M. Fuller 89
Collison, O., 38
Confer, C., 185
Connell, P., 34
Corbin, D., 115
Cordova, D. I., 110
Creamer, T.C. 79
Crookes, G., xvi
Crystal, D., 15, 16
Cullinan, B. E., 11
Cummins, J. 33
Curtain, H., xxvii
Cutting, B., 77

D

Dachkova, L., xxiv
Dann, K., 59
Darn, S., xxvi
de'Ath, P., 79
DeFord, D., 74, 101
Dégh, L., 4
deJong, M. T., 96
DeKeyser, R., 93, 94
Delgado-Gaitán, C., 74
Demircioğlu, I., 116
DeSpain, C. D., 113
Devine, J., 74
Diakidoy, I., 87
Diamond, M. C., 47
Dickinson, D. K., 34
Dixon-Krauss, L., 109
Dolitsky, M., xxvii
Donato, R., 94, 95, 98
Dörnyei, Z., 51
Dressel, J. H. 101
Droop, M., 24
Dulay, H., 43, 94
Durgunoğlu, A., 74

E

Eade, J. 75
Echevarria, J., 175
Edelsky, C. 101
Edwards, L., 9
Egan, K., 34
Eisele, B., 15
El Naggar, Z., xxv
Elley, W., 76, 77, 88, 90, 91, 95
Ellis, N., 50, 88, 93
Ellis, R., 60
Elman, J. L., 14
Enever, J., xxix
Erkut, S., 110, 112
Escott, C., 15
Eurydice Network xxiv, xxix

F

Faklova, Z., xxv
Fazio, B., 34
Feagans, L., 34
Feunteun, A., xvi
Flores Jiménez, E. P., xxvi
Fountas, I. C., 80
Fox, G., 16
Fox, M., 23
Fradd, S., 38
Freeman, G., 36
Friedman, E., 36

G

Gadbonton, E., 50
Galda, L., 11
García, G., 24, 74, 86, 174
Gary, C., 36, 38
Gass, S., 59, 60
Genesee, F., xxviii, 14
Ghosn, I. K., xxv, 10, 29, 30, 39, 45, 55–56, 60, 61, 71, 76, 91, 96–97, 103–104, 158
Gibbons, P., 34
Gibson, H. W., 65
Gilbert, I., 46, 70
Gimenez, T., xxvi
Goforth, F., 5, 8, 40, 41, 135
Goleman, D., 9, 10, 49
Gordon, T., 88
Gorsuch, G. J., 75
Grabe, W., 85
Graesser, A. C., 34
Graney, J., 85
Graves, B., 101, 167
Graves, D., 100
Graves, M. 175
Greenwood, A., 164
Gregory, E., xxvii
Guan-Lea Lee, xxv
Guzzetti, B., 115

H

Hadjikyriacou, S., xxv
Hamayan, E., xxviii
Hancin-Bhatt, B., 74
Hanlon, S., 15
Harackiewicz, J., 44
Harder, R. J., 65
Hasbrouck, J.E., 149
Hatch, E., 28, 65
Hauft-Smith K., 34
Hayes, D., xxiv
Hazenburg, S., 86
Heflin, D., 113
Hemphill, L., 34
Hepler, S., 42
Herman, P., 89
Hermes, L., 4
Herrera, M., 24
Hickman, J., 42
Hidi, S., 44, 45
Hilke, E. V., 40
Hill, D., 17
Hoffman, M., 10
Holdaway, D., 76
Holt, R., 25
Hong, H., 113
Howe, K., 40, 115
Hu, K. A., 40
Hubbard, P., 85
Huck, C. S., 42
Hudelson, S., 99, 101, 104
Hugo, C., 77
Huie, K., 102
Hulstijn, J.H., 86
Hunsader, P., 184

I

Ioannou-Georgiou, S., xxv

J

Jacobs, G., 75
Jacobs, J. S. 78
Jaeger, M., 114

Jalongo, M., 44
Jantscher, E., xxiv
Jarvis, J., 69
Jenner, D., 112
Jennings, C. M., 109
Jennings, J. E., 109
Jensen, E., 46
Jiménez, R. T., 74
Johnson, J. S., 94
Johnson, M. H., 14
Johnson, T.D., 155, 156

K

Kamii, C., 100
Karmiloff-Smith, A., 14
Kauchak, D. P., 65
Kemp, J., 43
Kiefer, B. Z., 42
Kincade, K. M., 44
Kirgöz, Y., xxv
Knight, S. L., 74
Koester, J., 29
Kohlbrg, L., 8, 9
Koskinen, P. S., 79
Kotulak, R., 47
Kourtis-Kazoullis, V., xxv
Kowalinski, B.115
Krashen, S., 11, 43, 59, 91, 94, 149
Kreidler, W. J., 175
Kretzschmar, M. J., 98
Kubanek-German, A., xxiv
Kubota, M., 66, 139
Kuruppu, L., 77, 102, 103

L

Lambert, J. G., 90
Lamme, L., 40
Landsiedler, I., xxiv
Langer, J.A., 185
Lapkin, S., 59
Larsen-Freeman, D., 13
Laufer, B., 88, 106
Lauritzen, C., 114
Ledbetter, L., 40

LeDoux, J. 46
Lee, W. K., xxv
Lehr, S. S., 40
Leitze, A. R., 37
Lemke, J. L., 38
Lennon, R., 10
Lepper, M. R., 110
Leung, C., 28
Lewis, B., 36
Lewis, C.S., 5
Lightbown, P., 15, 60, 65
Livo, N., 4
Lo, Y-H. G., xxvi
Lockhart, C., 29
Long, M., 13, 17, 60, 65
Long, R., 36
Lopriore, L., xxiv
Louis, D. R., 155, 156
Lugossy, R., 44, 59
Luoto, S., 7
Luoto, T., 7
Lustig, M. W., 29
Lyster R., 60, 134

M

MacGowan-Gilhooly, A. 101
Machura, L., 39, 55
MacIntyre, A., 4
Mackay, M., 36
Madrazo, G. M., 39
Maersk Nielsen, P., xxvi
Magoto, J., 85
Maguire, M., 101, 167
Mahon, T. xii, 55
Mangubhai, F., 76, 77, 90, 95, 103, 104
Marinova-Todd, S., 94
Marsh, D., xxvii
Martinie, S., 112
Mayer, D. A., 185, 186
Mayer, J., 9
Mayer, R. E., 49
McCabe, A., 34
McCarty, D. M., 40
McCauley, D. S., 149
McCauley, J. K., 149

McCloskey, M. L., xxv
McConaghy, J., 140
McCreary, J. 60
McDevitt, T., 10
McGowan, T. N., 115
McKeown, M., 88
McKinney, C. W., 115
McNeil, xxv
McRae, J., 18
Meara, P., 86
Mechling, K. R., 113
Meek, M., 15, 19
Meier, C., 85
Meister, G. F., 89
Mihaljevic Djigunovic, J. xxix, 43
Mikkelsen, N., 101
Mishra, A., 34
Mohanraj, J., xxiii
Mokhtari, K., 85
Monson, D. L., 140, 141, 143
Moon, J., xxix, 64
Morgan, A. S., 110
Morgan, P., 85
Morrison, C., 134, 144

N

Nagy, W. E., 74, 86, 89
Naremore, R., 34
Nation, I. S. P., 85, 86, 87, 88, 89, 106
National Council for the Social Studies 40
National Council of Teachers of Mathematics 34, 37
National Science Teachers' Association 38
Neal, H., 89
New Levin, L ., xxv
Newport, E. L., 94
Ng, S. M., 59, 77, 79, 96, 102
Nikolov, M., xxv, 43
Nummela Caine, R., 47

O

O'Malley, J. M., 34, 38, 39

O'Neill, D. K., 111
Offord, D., 85
Oh, Sun-Young 17
Ohlstain, E., 43
Okhee, L., 38
Oliver, D. L., 113
Order, T., xxv
Orlich, D. C., 65
Ormrod, J. E., 50, 93
Ovando, C. J., 149

P

Padrón, Y., 74, 83
Paran, A., xvi
Parisi, D., 14
Pasta, D. J., 74
Pearce, M.J., 111
Pearson, P. D., 74
Perlman, R., xxviii
Pesola, C. A., 31
Pettig, K. L., 113
Phillips, S.M., 79
Picardi, N., 34
Pick, J.L., 111
Pinilla-Padilla, C., xxiv
Pinkley, D., 24
Pinnell, G. S., 80
Pinsent, P., 10
Pinter, A., xvi
Plato 4
Plunkett, K., 14, 50
Preston W. 59
Pruitt, N. E., 41
Pufahl, I. xxv
Pyles, L.D., 34

Q

Qing, Bi., xxvi

R

Racine, Y., 85
Raimes, A., 101
Rajan, B., 75
Ralea, C-M., xxiv

Ramey, D. R., 74
Ramirez, J.D., 74
Ranta, L., 60, 134
Raphael, T., 40
Rathmell, E., 37
Reid Thoma, M., 17
Renandeyas, W., 75
Rest, J., 9, 17
Reynolds, S. V., 115, 116
Rhodes, N. C., xxv, 34
Richard-Amato, P. A., 149
Richards, J., 29
Richey, J., 109
Richgels, D., 40
Riertz, S., 4
Rigg, P., 101
Roberts, T., 89
Robinson, M., 69
Robinson, P., 93
Rosenblatt, L. M., 139, 185
Ross, E. P., 40
Ross, S., 17
Royce, C. A., 39, 114, 185
Rudman, M., 7
Rulon K., 60

S

Sadowska-Martyka, A., 78
Salovey, P., 9
Samway, K. Davies 99, 101, 102, 104, 159
Saragi, T., 89
Sato, C. J., 65
Savage, J. F., 144, 145
Sawyer, M., 184
Schauble, L., 49
Schiefele, U., 44
Schmidt, R., 93, 94
Schmitt, N., 86
Schollar, E., 77, 78
Scott, J. A., 86, 87
Scribner-MacLean, M., 164
Sebesta, S. L., 140, 141, 143
Seedhouse, P., 55, 62
Segalowitz, N., 50

Senn, H. Doces 140, 141, 143
Sheehan, E., 10
Sheffield, S., 38
Shohamy, E., 43
Singh, G., 80, 102
Sinh, H.V., xxv
Sirotnik, K. A., 65
Skinner, B. F., 59
Skourtou, E. xxv
Smallwood, B. Ansin, xvi
Solomon, J., 34
Spada, N., 15, 60, 65
Sprenger, M., 47, 48, 49, 50, 51
Stauffer, R. G., 136
Stokic, L., xxiv
Suits, B., 82
Sullivan, C., 77, 79, 96
Sutherland, Z., 5
Swain, M., 59
Swann Report, The, xxviii
Swift, G., 115
Sylwester, R., 46

T

Tager-Flusberg, H., 34
Taguchi, E., 75
Takayasu-Maass, M., 75
Tarone, E., 95
Tate, G. M., 79, 80
Taylor, D., 101, 104
Taylor, E., 104
Taylor, V., 38
Thoma, S., 9
Thomas, W. P., xxviii
Thompson, D. L., 40
Thornburg, D. 175
Thornton, B., xxv
Tindal, G., 149
Tinker Sachs, G., xiii, 58
Tomlinson, B., xvii
Tomlinson, C., 40
Tongue, R., xvi
Troland, T. H., 185
Trundle, K. C., 185

Tsui, A. B. M xxvii, 60, 61
Tunnell, M. O., 40, 78

U

Uhl Chamot, A., 34, 38, 39
Ullman, M., 47, 48, 95
Underwood, B., 10

V

Vacca, J. L., 40
Vacca, R. T., 40
Vale, D., xvi
Van Allen, R., 149
Vandergrift, K., 7
Varonis, E.M., 60
Verhallen, M. J. A. J., 90, 91, 96
Verhoeven, L., 24
Villano, T. A., 40
Voss, J. F., 49

W

Wai-King Tsang, 96
Walling, B. H., 115
Wang, K., 88
Warig, R., 86, 88

Watts, E., xvi
Waxman, H. C., 74
Weinberg, S., 111
Welchman-Tischler, R., 35, 38
Wells, G., 6
Wenli Tsou, 31
Whitin, D., 36, 37
Wijesinha, R., xxiv
Wiley, D., 39, 185
Wolfe, P., 144
Wragg, E. C., 69
Wright, A., xvi

Y

Yahya, N., 102
Yang, A., 75
Yang Eisele, C., 15
Yano, Y., 17
York Hanlon, R., 15
Young J. M., 110, 112
Yuen, S. D., 74

Z

Zamel, V., 100, 101
Zehang Chen., xxv
Zimmerman, C. Boyd, 88

Children's Book Index

Alexander and the Terrible, Horrible, No Good, Very Bad Day, 10, 30, 31, 69, 124, 141, 159
Alexander Who's Not (Do you hear me? I mean it!) Going to Move, 19, 31, 70
Alice's Adventures in Wonderland, 36
Amina and Muhammad's Special Visitor, 187
Anno's Magic Seeds, 36, 184
Anno's Mysterious Multiplying Jar, 184
The Ballad of Mulan, 187
The Black Stallion, 67
Bus Ride, 140
Brown Bear, Brown Bear, What Do You See?, 183
Call it Courage, 180
Caps for Sale, 20, 44, 180, 181
The Carrot Seed, 186
Charlie and the Chocolate Factory, 59
Children Who Hugged the Mountain, 106, 143, 155
Cinderella, 152
The Day of Ahmad's Secret, 141, 187
Day of the Blizzard, 139, 180
The Doorbell Rang, 19, 36, 124, 134, 161, 184
The Dragonfly Surprise, 142, 165
The Egyptian Cinderella, 152
The Enchanted Anklet, 152
Fish is a Fish, 186
Follow the Drinking Gourd, 187

Storybridge to Second Language Literacy, pages 229–232
Copyright © 2013 by Information Age Publishing
All rights of reproduction in any form reserved.

Frog and Toad, 180
Frog Goes to Dinner, 111
The Giving Tree, 143, 181
The Golden Sandal, 152
Goldilocks and the Three Bears, 156, 182
Goodnight Owl, 183
The Great Gilly Hopkins, 180
The Great Kapok Tree, 114, 186
The Green Book, 114
The Grouchy Ladybug, 182
Harry and the Terrible Whatzit, 180
Harry Potter and the Sorcerer's Stone, 8
Harry the Dirty Dog, 152, 166
Have You Seen My Cat?, 182
The Hobbit, 8
How Big is a Foot?, 184
Hundred Dresses, 8, 46, 144, 180
The Hundred Penny Box, 8, 138, 140, 142
Jim and the Beanstalk, 113
Jumping the Broom, 187
Just Plain Fancy, 187
The King's Chessboard, 36, 184
The Lady with the Alligator Purse, 183
The Librarian of Basra, 187
Little Bear, 180
The Little Red Riding Hood, 158
Look Out He's Behind You, 75
Louie, 90
Make a Wish Molly, 187
Make Way for Ducklings, 180
Molly's Pilgrim, 187
Mr. G. Reed Makes a Deal, 142
Mufaro's Beautiful Daughters, 141, 155
One Snowy Night, 18
The Owl Who Was Afraid of the Dark, 180
Papa, Please Get the Moon for Me, 186
The Persian Cinderella, 152
Phoenician Friends, 187
Pirate Adventure, 58, 59
The Rabbit and the Turnip, 5, 19, 135
A Remainder of One, 36, 184
The Royal Dinner, 55

Sadako and the Thousand Paper Cranes, 187
Sami and the Time of the Troubles, 187
Sarah, Plain and Tall, 187
Selina and the Bear Paw Quilt, 112
Slow Little Snail, 163
Spaghetti and Meatballs for All, 185
Stellaluna, 186
Stone Soup, 131, 150, 164
The Story of Ferdinand, 180, 181
The Story of Ping, 180
Story without End, 151
The Summer of the Swans, 180
Sweet Clara and the Freedom Quilt, 187
Sweet Dried Apples, 187
The Swirling Hijab, 187
Sylvester and the Magic Pebble, 9, 46
The Talking Eggs, 141
Ten Black Dots, 111
There's a Nightmare in My Cupboard, 180
The Three Bears, 166
Three Ducks Went Wondering, 90
Three Hat Day, 162
The Tiny Seed, 186
Two of Everything, 185
The Ugly Duckling, 46, 130, 186
The Velveteen Rabbit, 18
The Very Busy Spider, 186
The Very Hungry Caterpillar, 15, 39, 55, 57, 164, 181, 182, 185, 186
The Very Quiet Cricket, 186
Voyage to the Pharos, 187
Watch the Stars Come Out, 187
We're Going on a Bear Hunt, 62
Who Sank the Boat?, 39, 186
Wilma Unlimited: How Wilma Became the World's Fastest Woman, 113
Winnie-the-Pooh, 8

CPSIA information can be obtained at www.ICGtesting.com
Printed in the USA
LVOW01s1339020814

397212LV00001B/14/P